The Boy Beneath My Skin

A Black Trans Man Living in the South

The Boy Beneath My Skin

A Black Trans Man Living in the South

by
Charley Burton

Published by
Transgender Publishing

an imprint of
Castle Carrington Publishing Group
Victoria, BC
Canada

2022

The Boy Beneath My Skin
A Black Trans Man Living in the South

First published in paperback in 2022

Cover Design: Margot Wilson
All photographs (except where otherwise noted): from the author's private collection

ISBN: 978-1-990096-69-3 (paperback)
ISBN: 978-1-990096-70-9 (Kindle electronic book)
ISBN: 978-1-990096-71-6 (Smashwords electronic book)

Published in Canada by
TransGender Publishing
www.transgenderpublishing.ca

an imprint of
Castle Carrington Publishing Group
Victoria BC
Canada
www.castlecarringtonpublishing.ca

TRANSGENDER
PUBLISHING

CASTLE
CARRINGTON
PUBLISHING GROUP

This is a journey for me to heal myself. A journey to recall these past hurts. I am searching, searching for an understanding of love versus hate. This is my journey. This is my path to heal.

Charley Burton, 2021

And then it happens…

One day you wake up and you're in this place.

You're in this place where everything feels right.

Your heart is calm.
Your soul is lit.
Your thoughts are positive.
Your vision is clear.

You're at peace, at peace with where you've been, at peace with what you've been through, and at peace with where you're headed.

The Minds Journal

Contents

Acknowledgements

Foreword

We do not regret the past nor wish to shut the door on it.
Alcoholics Anonymous

We will love you, until you can love yourself.
Alcoholics Anonymous

I first came to know Charley Burton when he submitted a piece, "Trans Elder in the South" for *TRANScestors: Navigating LGBTQ+ Aging, Illness, and End of Life Decisions, Volume I: Generations of Hope*,[1] which I edited with Jude Patton. I was struck by Charley's perceptive, honest, and forthright writing style and the depth of understanding he portrayed in his story, not only of his own experience but that of others too.

Our paths crossed again the following year at the Moving Trans History Forward conference, which was hosted virtually (because of COVID 19) by the Chair in Transgender Studies at the University of Victoria in the spring of 2021.[2] Charley was a speaker on a panel about "Mentoring in the Trans Masculine Community," with Jamison Green, Jude Patton, and Zander Keig. I was struck by how kind, authentic, articulate, and engaged Charley was, and I sent him a private message asking if he would be interested in collaborating on writing his life story. He immediately responded by saying, "Yes." Subsequently, Charley and I agreed to meet weekly to discuss what that collaboration would look like. I have now enjoyed over a year of engaging conversations with him, and I say with great joy that our collaboration has evolved into an enduring friendship.

It was not long before I discovered that Charley is a prolific writer, journaler, and blogger, all of which have become integral parts of his life story. Beyond this, Charley is the former National Program Director for Black Transmen Inc., the first national organization solely for Black transmen.[3] He also founded Diversity in Recovery, a recovery group for the LGBTQ/BIPOC community and their allies in Charlottesville,

---

[1] "Trans Elder in the South," TRANScestors: Navigating LGBTQ+ Aging Illness, and End of Life Decisions, Volume I: Generations of Hope, 2020, pp. 38-42, TransGender Publishing, https://transgenderpublishing.ca/life-trips/.

[2] https://www.uvic.ca/mthf2021/.

[3] https://blacktransmen.org/.

Virginia.[4] He is a board member of PFLAG of the Blue Ridge, Charlottesville Pride, and former Chair of the University of Virginia Trans Advisory Board. In 2021, Charley received the OUTstanding Virginians 2021 Award from Equality Virginia[5] and the Community Root Award from Richmond Virginia Black Pride RVA.[6] In 2022, Charley began a Morehouse College degree, and, in March of this year, he was nominated as Morehouse Man of the Week.

Twelve-step program speakers describe their experiences in recovery using the following questions: What was it like? What happened? and What is it like now? This format underpins the telling of Charley's life story. Book 1, "My Early Life: Under the Influence," was originally written when Charley was self-admittedly "still drinking and drugging." It is a heartfelt rendering of how his early life experiences led him into drugs and alcohol. In Book 2, "Visiting the Dark Side: Writings to Myself, a Therapeutic Journal," Charley engages with recovery and seeks therapeutic support. Book 3, "Finding My Way in a New Life," is an edited version of a blog that Charley wrote, documenting his transition from female to male. Book 4, "What Happened," comprises the transcript from an interview I undertook with

---

[4] https://www.diversityinrecovery.com/board.
[5] https://equalityvirginia.org/events/outstanding-virginians-2021/.
[6]
https://www.facebook.com/blackpriderva/photos/pcb.874175463197344/874174853197405/.

Charley's long-time partner, a romantic relationship that ended in violence but happily transformed into a lifelong friendship. Book 5, "What It's Like Now," reflects on how Charley's life has changed, magnified, and succeeded in recent years since his recovery.

A survivor of abuse, addiction, gender dysphoria, anomie, and loneliness, Charley's story speaks to the indomitable spirit that characterizes the core of his being. Moreover, it provides inspiration, direction, and hope for others who find themselves (or their loved ones) in similar circumstances. Charley tells his story with wit, insight, candor, and unfathomable courage. His strength, kindness, compassion, and humanity, flow freely across the pages and engage the reader in one man's story that is, in many ways, the story of us all.

Margot Wilson, PhD
Editor and Owner
TransGender Publishing
Victoria, BC, Canada
www.transgenderpublishing.ca

Preface

The Black Boy Underneath This Skin[7]

The mind is like a parachute, it works better when it's open.
Alcoholics Anonymous

I look at my arms and look past the brown, smooth skin. I look past the tiny hairs popping through. Underneath this boyish-looking skin was a Black girl for almost 50 years. For most of those 50 years I heard words like "nigger," "bull dyke," "she/he," "freak." I let them all soak in under this skin and believed them. I adopted other words: "mental case," "drunk," "druggie," and "unfortunate." These too pierced my skin along with my thoughts.

I was born and raised in North Garden, Virginia. "Town," as we called it, was Charlottesville. Growing up, I was just always used to being the only one at places. The black one, that is. That's just the way "Town" was. I never felt like I fit in at most places. Years later, I would discover drugs and alcohol allowed me to fit in better or at least so I thought. The most I ever felt like I fit was with other boys. Not for the physical or sexual need but because I felt like I understood their

---

[7] Originally published in *Lunar Phoenix: An Anthology of Black Voices*, Taneasha White, Lashelle Johnson, and Lana C. Marilyn (eds.), Quail Bell Magazine, pp. 86-89, in press 2021.

language. I always wanted the bike with the bar across, not the sissy-looking bike with the slanted bar. I didn't want to play house or dolls. I wanted to be outside, dirty, with my shirt off, playing basketball.

I thought that one day, magically, I would be the boy, marry the girl, and all would be fine. But my brown skin told me differently. It told me that it was a girl's skin, and there was nothing I could do about it. But deep down, past the layers of my brown skin, I was the happiest with the baseball cap and dirty Keds sneakers on.

As I grew, so did other parts. I began to look like a girl. I was expected to know how to do girl things. Be in the house, wear dresses. Act like a girl. But my brown skin underneath was telling me differently. As I grew, I couldn't hide anymore. The baseball cap and dirty white sneakers couldn't camouflage who I was born as.

As like most Black people in North Garden, VA and the town of Charlottesville, the Black church was the main hub of our lives. I listened to the "burn in hell" sermons. That those people were evil. I sat on the pew in our country church and my skin would be on fire. I wanted to rip it off and stand up and show everyone. Look, my skin is different but please love me anyway! But I just sat there and suffered in silence. Knowing that if I pulled the skin back and opened my mouth, I would be rejected, prayed for, and told I needed Jesus.

I got older, and I announced I was gay. I was not shunned by my family, but I'm not sure how much they understood that there was more. How could I tell them there was more when I didn't even know myself? So, there I was, not sure who to love or how to even love with this newfound discovery. Not even comfortable with this discovery. In town, there weren't too many like me, or I couldn't find them, Black women loving Black women who looked like me. I wore men's clothes, and I liked hanging around guys. That was the best description of telling people who I was.

That's when those dreaded words came back. "Bull dyke," "freak." They stung the skin even more this time because I believed those words. I didn't have any other words to describe me, so I just accepted and adopted them into my own.

I got into my first real relationship with someone. My world was opened up to different cultures. I finally met black women who looked like me. Those women in town just were not to be found. I was going to a church for gay people. butch people, femme people, transmen and transwomen. Black, White, and being themselves. They were even praying to a God that I was told, all my life, would not accept me, not love me, not welcome me.

My first time seeing a Black transman, my skin burned. I hid it a little harder. I could not accept that it was me. I was in fear. My skin was screaming to come out. It was as if my skin was coming to life. But I was doing all I could do to deaden it. I heard them using their pronouns, and I wanted that too. I hated the pronoun "she." Most of the time, people didn't know what I was. I wanted a pronoun. I wanted to match the skin underneath.

At the end of each weekend, I would drive back to town. For each mile, as I got closer to Charlottesville, my skin would die a little. The proud brown skin, 100 miles before, was leaving. It would have to wait and be awakened on the next trip.

As I got more comfortable wanting to look at this beautiful brown skin, I became more aware of what was underneath. There was something different. I was now clean and sober and more in touch with myself. That piece that had been missing was now screaming out to me. "Pull it back! Look at it!" I was in fear. I couldn't be one of them. Who would love me?

Out of that relationship now, I would lie in bed and want to take a razor blade and rip at my skin. I was depressed. I didn't want to be exposed as something different again. I didn't want to hear hateful words about me. I didn't want to be kicked out of the Black community for saying the one word my skin was trying to help me accept, "I am a transman."

I battled for months, what seemed like years. I went to therapy. I struggled. One day, on that couch, in front of this young white woman, I pulled the skin back and opened my voice. "I think I am trans." The one thing I feel that I battled for years has finally been spoken. I remember telling her there was nothing I could do about it. My family won't understand, the community will hate me. I was searching for everything to pull that layer of my beautiful brown skin over again. As I had done for so many years.

That was 11 years ago. I am now a proud Black transman of my community. I look back at those nights alone, wanting to end my life instead of embracing what was under my skin. Afraid my own culture and family would disown me. Yes, some of that has happened. My family is more loving and accepting of me than ever. I have made some wonderful friends. There are churches where I know I am not welcome.

That is their fear of their own skin, not mine. I am a beautiful, black, trans brother. I am respected in my trans community, and, recently, I am opening my voice up more in my community. I mentor young trans guys in both recovery and everyday walks of life.

I know that, today, I am hated and feared by white women. I see the stares. I see their fear. I am a target for many hate-filled white men. I am their worst enemy. I know if they knew all the boxes I checked, I would be hated even more or even killed. You see, at first, they see Black man, then, if I allow them to, they see Black transman.

I owe my confidence in being who I am to Carter Brown and Black Transmen Inc. I am one of the founding board members. Carter has stuck with me for 11 years. He helped show me that "One is Not Born A Man: He Becomes One."

Today, I hold down a job. I have a roof over my head. I sit on several boards and have a voice as a Black transman. I mentor. I am so much more.

My skin is now exposed. It is raw and, in these days of unrest, it bleeds. It bleeds of sweat and fear. It bleeds tears of how I am looked at, how I am hated. Slowly, I allow it to heal every day. As it heals, it creates its own protection for me. I slowly, day by day, become more comfortable in the skin that I am in. That voice that was smothered, it speaks. I have a voice that people want to hear.

There are times in the still quiet of the night that I rub my beautiful brown skin. It feels smooth and there is a comfort when I touch it. It is a blend of the girl I was and the man I have become. I smile as I touch my skin because I never thought, those many years ago, that I am finally the Black man who was hiding underneath that skin.

Book I

What Was It Like?
(Under the Influence)

It's Ok to look at the past—just don't stare.
Alcoholics Anonymous

Chapter 1

"Him"

But for the grace of God.
Alcoholics Anonymous

I don't know when it began. I just remember not being there one day when "he" touches me. I remember floating away, just floating off in space. "His" touch hurts. If this is loving me, what does hate feel like? I am five and all I want is to fish and ride my bike. "He" tells me that "he" will take my bike away if I do not do what I am told to do.

"Take the panties off and just let me rub you there."

That is all "he" says that "he" wants to do, but I know what rubbing is supposed to feel like and this is not rubbing. This is the first time I float away. Superman is over in the corner telling me to be quiet. The fish in the creek are telling me to just stay still. They are all talking at the same time. Who am I supposed to listen to? So many voices, so much noise.

Every morning, I lie in my bed and listen, waiting to hear "his" sound. I listen to the kitchen sounds of my mother and father, going over the course of their day. How I wish I could just jump out of the bed and tell them to please take me with them. Please. Do not leave me with "him." I do not want the rubbing to continue. Each time, the rubbing hurts more. All I can do is float away and listen to the fish and to Superman, just letting them talk to each other. But who am I supposed to listen to? Superman is supposed to be my savior, the fish are supposed to be my friends.

One day, I will run away from "him." One day, I am going to be strong and just run. Take my trusty Collie with me and just run. But where will I go? I am fast: he is old and cannot run fast. But I have to plot out the course of where I can run. I have to find a path. I have to get away. But where? The world is so big, and I am afraid, scared to run, scared to stay. What am I to do? Even Superman doesn't have an answer.

I know that if I stay, the rubbing will hurt more. I can sense it in "his" eyes. I can feel it in my soul. This is going to hurt more. "He" wants more. "He" says that all little girls have to feel this. "He" says that all little girls want to feel this. Why do I not want to feel this? Why do I not want "his" love? Is it love? Is the rubbing love?

My closet is my friend. I hide there and talk to "the people"—my friends. They entertain my thoughts. They keep me warm when the cold waves come over my body. Oh, those cold waves sometimes feel just like "his" skin against me. How can I make the waves stop? I guess that I just have to endure the pain. But why am I taking on this task at such an early age?

***

This morning, "he" does not take me to the creek. The one safe place I have is my bedroom. Why is "he" coming into my room? "Stay very still and maybe "he" will go away," the voices are screaming in my head. Or is it me?

"Shut up," is all I keep hearing.

Is it me or is it my neighborhood of friends? I tend to think of them as "the neighborhood." I know of seven at this time. Each one serves a purpose for me. Strength, endurance, laughter. Each one of them serves me when I cannot serve myself. Each of the seven is my friend even though, many times, I cannot take my pain and they take it for me. They are the source of my strength. I remember talking to them in the closet, and they are telling me how I can turn into them whenever I want. How I can just move from neighbor to neighbor. I am so little, so fragile. I do not know who to believe. But I feel that I can believe them. I want to feel that I can trust all seven of them. But then, I think that I should be able to trust "him" too. All I ever wanted to do was to go fishing. I want to be the little tomboy I believe myself to be. I am confused about being a girl. But "he" keeps telling me that "he" needs to do these things so that I will know that I am a girl.

This morning, in my room, I can feel "his" breath. I can feel the covers being pulled back.

"Not here!" they scream. "We all have to run. Not here! This is our safe place. This is our neighborhood."

All I know is that seven people are telling me to run. Seven people are telling me to step inside them and let one of them take over. I do not know what that means, but I am willing to trust them at that very moment. I am willing to become one of them. I have fought it for too long. Even at this young age, I know that this is different. I know that if

I let one of them step in, there is going to be a change in me that will be there for a very long time. I will be even more different than I am now.

I can feel "his" hand and I know it is time to make a decision. "He" has "his" brown bottle in hand and asks if I want an eye opener. One of my people loves drinking that nasty stuff. As my hand shakes, I take the bottle and taste the nasty smelling liquid. It burns, but it gives me courage. I step away and let the little boy step in. He is fast, and he has a lot of courage. As the covers are pulled back, the little boy kicks "him" where it hurts, and he, the six others, and I run. As we run, the little boy says that as long as it is not in our room, we can let "him" do what "he" needs to do. If we don't, we might die.

"He" always tells me that if I do not do what "he" wants that God is going to kill me. I do not want to die. I want to learn how to ride my bike. I have a lot of things I want to do before I die. I would miss my dog, my family, and the sunshine. How I love the sunshine!

I know him only as one of the little boys. He screams out to me in the bed, "I am a little boy, and I am strong. Let me do this. You can't do this. You are too young, not strong enough. I can be strong for you."

As we run out of the house, I know "he" is angry and will be after me soon.

I know that when I am at the creek and "he" is touching me, I hear voices, and I see Superman in the corner of my mind. But I think that maybe it is just pretend. I never understood that they were actually here to take care of me. They are not all in my mind. They are all a part of the life I need to live at this time. Am I different? Am I crazy? Will "he" kill me?

At this moment, someone screams out.

"I am a little girl. Let me take "his" touches. I can stand them. "He" just wants to be loved. Let "him" love me the only way "he" knows how."

She takes over and the little boy steps away, and "he" catches the little girl.

And so, it is the little girl who gets a slap on the leg and is told that if I ever do that again God will kill me right where I am standing. The little girl takes the touching. But today, they are more brutal than before. I stand on the bank and watch. I never feel it. I just see it from a distance. I am beginning to understand a little about these people that exist in my life. I did not make them up. My mother would say I had "pretend friends," and they laugh about my pretend friends. They are not pretending to be my saviors. They are saving me from dying.

The little girl gets the bottle pushed inside of her. I watch as tears in the dirt make mud. I watch as she twitches her fingers, taking my pain. Today, I realize how much these people love me to take on what I should be taking. It is not their fault but mine, and they love me that much to endure this.

I watch as Superman floats in the air. The little boy tells me that Superman's job is to make sure we do not die. Superman is like an angel. The little boy says that he is here only to protect us and give us life.

"Is Superman God? I ask.

The little boy laughs and says that he is not sure, but that Superman is strong, and that all we need to know is that he is always there.

The little girl takes my pain and when it is over, she pulls up the panties and we walk back up the hill. The little boy is holding both my hand and the little girl's. Superman is flying in front, and "he" is stumbling behind us, telling us how much "he" loves being here with us.

***

At night, alone in my room, I wait on them. Only Superman is flying around. Am I crazy or is this real? I cry myself to sleep because I do not know anything else to do. Sleep is the only thing I know to do.

Sometime during the night, the little boy takes over and we crawl outside on the cellar ledge. He wants to introduce me to the others. There is another little boy who says he is the "church boy."

"Know how the kids at church treat you badly? Always picking on you? Well," sighs the first little boy, "the church boy is there to listen to the preacher and protect you from being hurt.

"Like Superman?" I ask.

"No," says the first little boy. "It's a little different. He is protecting you from those kids by becoming the one who takes the pain."

The first little boy explains that they are like my Band-Aids: they cover up the pain.

"One day," he says, "you will have to pull the Band-Aid off: but, for now, we are here as Band-Aids.

Another boy is the athlete. He is the one who plays ball with my brother and his friends, the one who can throw a ball well for someone my age and can catch really well. He is someone I will need later, says the first little boy.

"For now, he plays when those guys get too rough with you."

The athlete boy is another Band-Aid.

The little girl only comes out during "his" touches. She is the Band-Aid for the touches.

"Why does she like those touches?" I ask the first little boy.

"She doesn't," he says. "She protects you so that you won't feel them."

Another one is the one that could hear for me. "He" slapped me one day, and I could not hear anymore. A doctor checked my hearing. All I know is that I cannot hear any more, so I make some excuse. The first little boy tells me to sleep on my bad ear to keep those bad voices away. He says sometimes bad voices will be screaming and I don't need to hear what they were saying.

"What are they saying?" I ask.

He says that the bad voices are the sounds of my uncle in my head, telling me I am going to die. I do not need to hear them, he says and if I keep my bad ear to the pillow, I will not have to hear the sounds. I will be protected from them. I didn't know how my pillow could protect me, but I believe in the first little boy. I know that he has protected me from my room being soiled in the same way that the creek is soiled ground.

Then, there is the little child who loves to play with army men. He is there to make me feel good and to play with me. It is like having a playmate when I don't have one. When my brother is playing baseball in Little League or playing with the boys and I couldn't, I can play for hours by the mimosa tree with my green men. Later, it is that same little boy who will ask for a Jane and Johnnie West set. That is many hours of fun too. Once, the first little boy tells me what the little child's Band-Aid role is. I am feeling better because I have someone to play with when I am all alone.

What I didn't know that night on the cellar roof is that these seven will tag along in my life for many years to come, many times saving me when I cannot save myself.

The little girl takes over again the next morning but, to my surprise, "he" is not drinking, nor does "he" bother us that day. The little child and I play out by the tree. We pick pears from the pear tree, and it is just a really nice day. Superman is always close by, and, for that, I start to feel the Band-Aid protection that the first little boy has talked about.

Knowing that the first little boy and the others are around me feels like, for this day, I can play without worrying about "him" pulling me from behind.

Chapter 2

Trick or Treat

Don't give up before the miracle happens.
Alcoholics Anonymous

One day, the first little boy tells us that he needs to talk to all of us. He says that he is scared that things are going to get worst with "him". He says that he saw a knife and is not sure if "he" is going to use it on us or not. The little boy says that he has heard stories about "him" when we are asleep and that "he" is a very bad man, with some very bad things "he" does to people. The little girl is crying. The church boy says we need to pray. The athlete is saying that he is strong like the little boy and will kill "him" first if "he" tries to kill us. The little child and I just continue to play with the green men. As long as I have my green army men, no one is going to bother the little child and I. Superman continues to fly. He will protect us all. I just know that he is stronger than all of us and will not let "him" do that to us.

That afternoon, "he" gets really angry about something and pulls us down to the creek. The little boy is out first, kicking and fighting "him." As "he" slaps the little boy, the little girl takes over to take the beatings. We know this is going to be a very bad day. At the creek, "he" slams the knife into a piece of wood and says that will be me if I do not do what "he" tells me to do. As the little girl takes off her pants and then the panties, "he" takes out something that looks like a long stick. The little girl screams and falls on her hip. She is crying mud again as I watch. This time, she cries for a very long time.

The little boy holds me and says it will be okay, that we are strong, that if the little girl can take it, so can all of us. I can hear everyone screaming, screaming very loudly, and then, the muffling of screams. "He" has "his" hand over the little girl's mouth, telling her to be a big girl and that she will like it. I am not sure how long it takes, but I remember seeing white stuff all over the ground. "He" takes out a red bandanna and wipes the stick off and puts it back inside "his" zipper. Just like that, "he" is nice again, telling us "he" is going to catch us a catfish. The little girl is wiping tears and she is walking funny. "He" tells her that she is to go take a bath and tell everyone she fell into the creek.

"You are so damn clumsy, you know," "he" says.

I hate "him" and wish that "he" would go away.

Later that evening, the little boy tells an adult that "he" is not a nice man. The next day, and for many days after that, we never see "him" again.

***

I get bigger but they never leave me. Whenever someone does something to me at school, being a bully or whatever, the little boy takes over. At recess, it is the athlete. In the classroom, it is the little child. He is my listener.

School is tough because I always struggle. I do a lot of daydreaming. Sometimes, it is voices and, other times, it is just wanting to be with the neighborhood and no one else.

Kids really don't want to play with the fat kid. I am different. I like playing with boys instead of girls and I can play just as well as the boys, thanks to Paul.

As my siblings go on with their lives, one constant thing in my life is the seven people in the neighborhood who protect me at all times. From falls to unkind words, they always protect me. I always have the little child to play with, and the little girl, who has not been around recently, is always there to take the physical pain.

Because the little girl has not been around for a long time, I almost forget about her. One summer day at the school, my brother and his friends are playing basketball on the blacktop. One of the guys is always telling me that he needs to see me later and talk to me a little bit. I never knew what that was about. The little boy quickly steps in and tells me to stay away from him. I think maybe things are okay with him. He always picks me to play on his team, always brings something back from the store for me. I think of him as nice and feel like he is like a brother to me. I have heard stories about how he steals church money and is a bad kid. But I was told that too, at the creek, by "him."

That summer day, I have my bike at school and am now very good at riding for long periods of time. I am 12. This guy is about 17. He catches me by the boxwoods in the front of the school. No one is around. He asks if we can go behind the boxwood and smoke a cigarette and drink a beer. The little girl comes out immediately and wants some beer. The little girl stays out as he tears at her pants and sticks his fingers inside of her. Later, the little girl says that it does not hurt because she is used to it. "He" always told us before that this is what little girls are for. The little girl believes it, or so she says. The little boy is angry and so are the others. I hear screams and the guy runs.

The little girl and the little boy get into an argument about drinking beer and smoking cigarettes.

"We are not supposed to do that," the little boy screams.

Where is Superman? I thought. *He is supposed to protect us.*

"He is protecting you. You are not dead. That is his sole purpose. You will never die as long as you believe that Superman will take care of you," the little boy cries.

I can tell that the little boy is hurt. Later, the little boy admits to being able to feel that guy as well. I could too, and I do not understand. What has happened to the Band-Aid?

I am getting really scared and tell someone about that guy. I don't remember what happened, but I did not tell the whole truth about it, just that the guy was talking bad words to me. If I tell the whole truth, no one will believe me, just like no one would ever believe that seven people live in my world and protect me from feeling pain.

The little boy says that we are getting older and need more help. I do not know what he means. He says that we have taken all the pain we can, that something else has to happen. But what? It is as if the little boy knows there will be more pain to follow. But what does he see that I, or the others, cannot?

***

My thoughts return to that October day. It's Halloween and I am 12 years old. I remember waking up and feeling very strange. I am looking in. All night, I have been thinking about wanting to be a boy. I want to dress up like a boy: but, for me, it will not be dressing up. It will be what I wish I could magically turn into. I wake that morning very early, knowing full well, from the plans made the night before, what I am going to be doing. Today, October 31st, I want to make a statement. I want to either do it or get help. There are periods when I want to die. I have all these things swirling around in my head, all these images telling me what, and what not, to do. I am afraid that I am going to live such a miserable life. I want so badly to have all the parts that 12-year-old boys have, to finally be accepted somewhere. Sad thing about it is that I don't know where I am supposed to be accepted.

I struggle daily thinking I should be a boy, or why not just let me enjoy being a girl. Trick or treat! If it is going to be a treat, I will get what I want, to be sent to that place my mother had talked about when I was 8, that place, in the hospital, where they are going to attach a penis to me, cut off my breasts, and I will be okay. Or will it be a trick and I will die, that there is no place where they can do that to me, that it is all a trick. Nothing ever seems to go my way, so why do I expect for it to happen now?

I started my period the week before. That was devastating. I remember being scolded all week about wearing the pads that were provided for me. I don't want to wear the pads. It is too girl-like. I hate the blood, the smell, the thought of what it is all about. It is painful and a reminder that I am going into womanhood. It is difficult to stand and pee with blood coming out. I just want to bleed, like the blood that is coming out of my vagina. I want to die.

So, that October day, for really no reason at all, I mix up plant food poison and start drinking it. It is me, but it is not my mind or actions. It is the little girl, who is mixing up the plant food poison. She says it is time to die.

Where is Superman?

Someone is screaming inside my head, but who can it be? I want so badly just to be normal. I wonder, at the age of 12, if the other kids are thinking I am different. Do I act different? At school, there are some weird kids that people make fun of. I seem to have escaped that. I'm not sure how, with all these voices and all these people. I am beginning to hate the thought of the people in my head. Sometimes, I lose time, forget that I am some place only to be told I am there. What is that all about?

The girls from elementary school are all giggles and stuff about boys. I am scared of them. I know what the last boy tried, and I want no part of it. Furthermore, I have boy in me, or so I feel. So, I pretty much am a successful loner. I have friends and they sometimes want to be around me, but they also have a great way of kicking me to the dirt whenever they want. I guess I *am* different.

The screaming is getting to the point that I have to do something about it. It is as if there are more people in the neighborhood, but they certainly only want to come out at night. Sleep is getting difficult. I am losing more and more time. I am losing whole days, but I can track things back and see that someone has been there. I am not hearing people say I am strange or that I am doing anything wrong, so I must be okay. But I am still the brunt of everyone's jokes. I can hear the laughter behind my back when I walk away. I am getting fat, so the athlete is not as good as he used to be. The little child does not feel like playing anymore because I am getting older and do not want my family to see me playing pretend outside with a figure that they can't see or hear. The church boy is praying, but what is the use? Superman is not around. And what is the little boy doing? Life is getting a little crazy. I have to do something to make this crowd respect me. But now, why does it matter? The little girl is the only one active. She is taking care of this, and I believe that she just might be the one to kill us all.

Is it time for me to die? Is there a way to stop her?
Where is Superman?

The little girl says that Superman is getting weak, like all of us. That he knows it is time. That I am only supposed to be here for 12 years. That it is time.

So, there is no struggle as the little girl mixes the plant food poison—the potion of death for me and the others—into my cereal and also my juice. There is no struggle as I gulp it down by the spoonful. I want a change and know that if I go to that hospital, they will change me to be a little boy. I don't know any other way to do this. Deep down, I don't want to die. I need more time to live. But I just want to make a change. I have to ask someone for help. I can't ask them at school. They will think I am crazy and, besides, I don't trust them. They will tell my mother too soon, and it won't happen.

"Drink this," the little girl is telling the others, and me. "We all have to agree, or it won't work," she says.

The little girl is getting anxious that one of us is going to back out. She pours the green mixture on our cereal and puts some in our juice. We eat and drink it all. We also make a pact to go to school and die there. We will show them, all those who make fun of us! Never again! They will pay! The little girl is angry. There is nothing to do about this but have it her way. She is convinced that this is the only way. As I eat and take in the little girl's mixture, I look around for Superman. Nowhere. This, then, is our time to die, our time to exit. I still have not mastered the bike: I have not given myself enough time to ride my bike.

But then, the little girl says, "Who cares? No one cares. It's just here one day and gone the next."

Almost time for the bus. I should have stayed at home, faked a sickness, and then called the ambulance. But I go to school because I want to make a big statement, to pass out from the poison and be whisked away in an ambulance. I want people to remember me, to talk about this. I want the attention that I think it will give me.

So, I board the bus. I am beginning to feel a little different, a little strange. The voices on the bus seem so far away. No one talks to me and that is okay. I just pretend to be reading, pretend that it is just another ordinary day. They make fun of my hair and are joking and playing. But, all the time, they are serious. They even tell me that I need to have some sex so that I will lose weight. Again, all joking. I just smile and laugh with them knowing that something is going to change the course of how they treat me. My point will be made.

My friends are all happy about Halloween.

Why? I think. *It's a day to pretend to be something that you are not. I play Halloween every day. I am always pretending to be something that I am not. Nothing special, except that, in a few hours, I will either be dead or in the hospital.*

I am hoping for the hospital. It will be there that I will ask if I can go to that special place and get the surgery—cut off the breasts and add me a penis. It will be that simple. I regret that my mother didn't take me there when I was 8. This would all be over with now. I would be a healthy, fun-loving boy, right now, something that I have always wanted to be. But today, I have to go through this to get what I want, to no longer have to play Halloween. No tricks or treats, just living my life the way I know deep down it is supposed to be.

As we get closer to the school, I am not sure I will be able to get off the bus. I am feeling very different. Is that also all in my mind? I have eaten a lot of the stuff so, by now, it should really be taking effect. The little girl is happy. The little boy is screaming and so are the little child and the athlete. The church boy just keeps praying to God that he will keep us safe. I think that church boy is also tired but knows nothing else to do but pray.

I get off the bus with no problem and head to class. I realize now how easily I can hide, even in a school full of people. It has always been something that I could do, just hide myself and not even exist at times. But still be in existence. I don't know if it is all in my mind or if it is something that I do very well. Either way, I feel it. I also sort of like being able to live this way with not really any expectations from people. All I need to do is just not make any close friends and keep my distance, a skill that will stay with me for many years.

I know that the longer I can keep that green stuff in my system, the better it is going to be. It is now a matter of strength, of how strong I can be. Will the will to live outweigh the will to die? How much do I truly want out of this world? I haven't really given it much thought. Haven't really thought about how much I love life. I just know that I want out of this misery. I want the visitors in my head to just stop. How can I stop something that has been a part of me for so long? How can I stop something that, more than likely, saved me from that mean man? If it were not for them, where would I be?

My stomach is feeling like it is on fire. I get a little scared thinking that maybe I have really done it. But, since I was 10, all I can think about was what it will be like to kill myself. I never think about the outcome, just the act. The act is what is attractive. The act is what keeps me thinking, almost every day for 20 years, about how to stay alive. Every day, from that day on, now that I know what suicide is, I am attracted to the act, not so much wanting to die but the action behind it.

But today, I have done the ultimate act. I have played out the scene. I am not scared, but I also am getting a little on edge about dying. What if something better is out there? What if I can truly find a good life? A life with people who don't always make fun of me. What if I can find a life where people want to be with me just because of me? Would that, or could that, happen?

In middle school, I hear people laugh as I walk by. I am fat and can't wear up-to-date clothes like everyone else. They just don't fit. My clothes are always bought, or made, like an older woman. I, especially, don't want to be wearing women's clothes. But I have no choice when it comes to my mother. I want to get to an age where I can wear men clothes like I am supposed to. Even then, will they still laugh at me? Will I hear that word "bulldagger," like I hear on the bus? Is life just going to continue to be tough for me because I am in the wrong body?

I want the answer to these questions before I throw up the green stuff. I just need a sign that I need to live. I need to hold on until something better can be worked out. Will I always be looking over my shoulder, wondering what was going to happen to me next? I want a life of fun, a life where I can be on top for a change. Will that ever happen?

***

In the first period, nothing seemed to be happening. The little girl is screaming during class that we did not take enough. The others are quiet.

All I could think about is, *What if someone finds out about me and this crazy stuff I am thinking? What if someone knows that I talk and play and sleep and pray with spirits I have names for? I will be laughed off of earth! I need to die.*

I am now beginning to see what the little girl is thinking. It *is* time to die.

As first period ends, I begin to feel a little light-headed. So many questions are running through my mind as I glide down the hall.

Where will I die? How long will it take? Will I just pass out and that will be the end? Or will I be hooked up to tubes, waiting for a slow death to take me away? Will "he" be at the funeral? Will "he" ever know what "he" did to me? How, if it were not for "him," I would not have these people, these spirits, running through me? Would I have been crazy like this after all? Even without "him" in my life?

The green stuff is beginning to make my ears ring, and now, I am scared. I have to tell somebody what I have done. I don't want to die, but I can't throw the stuff up any longer. It is in my system and is probably doing whatever damage it is going to do. I begin to wonder why I did this.

I don't exactly remember what happened but, all of a sudden, I get scared and know it is time to get some help. I walk past the guidance office. My counselor just looks at me. I have been in her office before, telling her that I am not happy. Or was it the little girl? I just know that, one day, I was there, not sure how or who put me there. I could hear her telling me that everything is going to be okay, that I just need to give this school a chance. I think everyone just thinks that I am the sick, little, fat girl who needs attention. I am attempting to tell this stranger that I need help, but I do not know how to go about it. I am afraid to tell anyone about these people or spirits in my head.

As I walk down the hall, I turn back and, in just that moment, I change my mind. I want to live. I do not know what this plant food is going to do to me. So, I walk into the office and tell my guidance counselor that I have taken something to make me sick. It is Halloween, a day I should be looking forward to going out with friends and having fun. But I am always the one lagging behind, the one they talk about but want to be with. I am tired of that too. I am tired of living the way I am living, both with this neighborhood of people and this neighborhood of spirits. I do not know which ones to trust at this moment. It seems like the ones I think I should trust are giving up.

I don't think anybody believes me at first. This is one of the reasons I don't want to tell anyone. Everybody always thinks I am just saying things to be saying them. It is something I have struggled with for many years. Even at 5, when I told what "he" was doing, all I wanted was to be heard. All I wanted was a way out of the craziness.

It is no different that day in the school guidance office. I want to be heard. I want people to know that I am tired. At 12 years old, I am just plain tired, tired of not being heard, tired of the laughter, tired of being bullied, tired of not being accepted. Most of all, I am just tired of all of them in my head telling me what to do. I just need space from everything.

I don't remember a lot about the ride to the emergency room. Someone is there, but I am sure it is not me. In the ER, I am treated like a criminal. I feel like I have committed a crime. My mother does not believe me. The doctors don't believe me. I am just lying on the gurney, feeling sick, and wanting some help. I need help with getting this shit out of my system. I need help with living life. All I want is to be away from this place. I don't really believe that this place is for me. I don't fit in. I don't even fit in the clothing that I have to wear. But if I am allowed to wear the clothes that I want to wear, I will be called a freak, a bulldagger. These are the same names I am being called right now. So, I guess it really doesn't make much difference if I am called names anyway.

I don't know if strangers are calling me that or not. But I sure know that the people I know are laughing at me, calling me names behind my back, just loud enough for me to hear. I feel like a stranger in a strange land. I don't understand what it is like to really be happy, what it is like to really laugh and have fun.

Later on, though, when I discovered drugs, that would all change. I knew what laughter was like. I knew what acceptance was like. I knew what it would be like to live. But, for now, I have to endure the pain of being different.

I remember hearing the doctor outside the door saying that I am too young for the mental health unit, but that I need help, that I need to see a therapist. Of course, that is going to be out of the question. I would never tell a stranger how I feel. We never tell people how we feel. It is the law of the land (or, at least, of our family). Always act as if nothing is wrong no matter how hard things are. Never show your true feelings. I remember my mother telling the doctor that I made a mistake and thought it was Kool-Aid. Denial everywhere. I am denying that I am crazy and hearing voices and talking to spirits. My family is denying that I am hurting so much that I want to kill myself. The spirits are denying me life. They have given up.

After much discussion, they decide to pump my stomach to see if I am telling the truth. So, for them, it is questionable if I have truly done what I say I have done. As they prepare to pump my stomach, a nurse, who is not very friendly, tells me that I have one last time to tell the truth. I look at her through the tears.

I wish I could tell the truth.

I don't even know what the truth is. All I know is that, since the age of 5, I was taught to lie. Lie about what has happened, lie about my feelings, and lie about my gender. Just lie.

So, what is the truth? I know that it is Halloween, that, while most other kids are out having fun, I choose to die. It is the best thing that I can think of doing for myself and for my family. I know the truth is that I don't know how to live even if I am 12 years of age. All I know is that, for no particular reason, I woke up this morning and wanted to die. No real reason why I picked Halloween. It just seems like the thing to do. I know I will never be what I truly want to be. I can never be that boy beneath my skin. I can never live life the way I feel that I am supposed to live it. In church, they say people like me will burn in hell. I hear the laughter from friends and family about people who are different.

"Sugar in their tank" is what gay men are called. "Bulldagger" was what lesbians are called. But what am I? The sad part about it is that I don't fit in either of those categories. Where will I go? I think back to that day when I was 8, when they threatened to drop me off at the door of the hospital so they could sew a penis on me, like a boy. I remember the feeling of "Yes! Yes! That is what I want." But I also feel the fear of loss, that if I do this, I will be dropped off and never picked up again. So, I can never be a boy physically. Only in my mind. But I have several of those little boys floating around in my mind. That is as close as I will ever get to meeting that boy beneath my skin.

I watch the little girl throw up green stuff in a pan. I hate the thought of throwing up all that green stuff. It means throwing up my desire to die. Every heave of green stuff means that I was going to live. Every bit of green stuff shows them that I am not lying. That nurse, the one who was so nasty to me, is now a little bit more compassionate. She keeps asking why I wanted to die.

"You have such a pretty face," she says.

But what about the rest of my body? I thought. *It is fat and out of shape. So, just my face is okay? How many times have I heard that in my life?*

As many times as I've heard, "Why don't you just stop eating?" They don't get it. What I am doing is building a shield around my heart. The very thing that was destroyed when I was five, I am now shielding with fat. I cannot be what I want to be. So, the next best thing to do is to just eat my way through. A short time later, I would discover another substance with which to hide. Only this one would make me popular.

The ride home is quiet. Like everything else that ever happened, it is never spoken about again. I don't go to a therapist. One week, I am called into the guidance office to check in, just the usual once a week, "How are you?" and "What can we do to make you happy?"

I think, *Can you make me a boy? Can you change the way I look? Can you give me my heart back?*

At that time, this is what would have made me happy. No one understands—not even me—about this confusion I have about who I am. I have so many ideas and people running through my head that all I know is I am different, strange, and people laugh at me. I am the bulldagger on the bus. I want to be popular. I want to be a great athlete. I have the skills to play any sport I want, but, like everything else, I have to prove myself 100 times more because of the way I look. People never believe in me, never believe that I can play basketball, or any other sport for that matter. At 12 years old, I am just the fat girl who wears old people's clothes because I can't fit into anything else.

If there was ever a time that I could have just walked away from school, I would have. Learning is a problem, especially numbers, because of all the stuff going on in my head. What am I to tell the teacher?

"Excuse me, I can't hear you at this time because there are others talking to me, but you can't see them."

Who would believe me? They don't even believe that I tried to kill myself. I know they cannot believe that I am walking around with a huge committee of people in my head. I want to tell someone that it is hard to learn. It is hard to understand what a teacher is saying in the classroom. I just have a difficult time concentrating. What if they are right? If I had been allowed to see someone, would it have made a difference in my life? Would I be behind in life the way I am today? All these things rush through my mind as I continue to try to succeed at this thing called school.

I manage to make it through those first few days at school without anyone asking me what happened. The school made it a "don't ask" thing. I feel ashamed to feel depressed. It almost feels like it is dirty to be sad. That is a feeling I would carry with me for years, that no matter how badly I feel I can not mention it because it is such a dirty word. Even the counselor at school doesn't want to talk about my suicide attempt. She talks about everything else. It is like it is a big taboo. In some ways, I guess it is. Suicide and thinking about taking my life are things that no one should have to listen to. No one wants to hear that I am sad, that I am done with this thing called life. The thought of suicide becomes my number one friend for many years. I study and research suicide as if it is a school project. I consume many years wanting to kill myself. When I think back now, I wonder, if I had put as much effort into school, living, and being happy as I did into suicide, would my life have been different?

That night, I go out on the cellar roof, but no one comes with me. As much as I need a friend, I am all alone. No one to talk to about why this is happening. No one to cry with. I cry alone for all those hurts. I cry alone, missing my spirits from the neighborhood. I cry because I just do not know what else to do.

Chapter 3

The "In" Crowd

If you don't want to slip, stay away from slippery places.

Alcoholics Anonymous

The next morning, I decide to join the "in crowd." I will steal beer, wine, whiskey, pot, anything I can get from the house and from my sibling, and I will let this crowd of people know that I have arrived. I start drinking between classes. The thing about drinking is that I do not need those spirits to become something I am not. Drinking does it for me. The more I drink, the more self-assurance I have. The more I drink, the more I say I need it. What I do not know is that every day, for the next 35 years, I will use something to alter my ego. Alcohol, drugs, food, something will be my addiction for many years to come.

The church boy is doing a lot of praying these days, and it is nice to watch him. He is a lot different than the type of praying people at church. He just prays simple prayers for us to be helped and stuff like that.

As I am getting older, I always think the neighbors will get older too, but they stay the same. I am beginning to question my gender: I always think that I am a boy trapped in a girl's body. I like everything a boy represents, their clothes, shoes. Almost anything that a boy does, I want to do, and want to do it better. The little girl is not pleased with this, for she wants to have a lot of sex with men. I do not even know at 13 or 14 what it feels like to kiss a boy. "He" kissed me before, but it hurt, and it was nasty and stinky. I do not want that if this is what it is all about. As far as love, "he" always said "he" did what "he" did because "he" loved me. Love hurts, and I want no part of hurt. For now, when I feel hurt and pain, I just go to a bottle, either liquid or pill form. I am fast learning how to become an addict.

And so, at almost 13, I find my way into what will become a new friend for the next 30+ years: I have discovered drugs and then, alcohol. And I make my first friend in school. In Spanish class, I hook up with a girl who doesn't make fun of me. She dresses differently with torn jeans and patched up jean jackets. She always looks like she has just woken up and started her day. Her dad is a doctor, and she says the only reason that she is still around is that she can steal drugs from him. Something called "Valium." It is the first time I have ever heard anything about drugs. She says that they will relax me and make me feel good. I really want to feel better about life. She says she will bring me some Valium the next day.

She keeps to her promise. The next day, in Spanish class, I take my first Valium. I am not sure what it is supposed to do, and I remember waiting for the feeling from this little pill. After about an hour, near the end of the class, I feel this sense of relief. It is like this little pill has taken away the committee in my head. I no longer hear the voices. I am feeling very at ease and don't care what people say or how they look at me when I walk down the hall. For once, I feel like a part of some world. Walking down the hall with my new friend, I feel that I have finally found the answer to what is making me feel so bad. I need this little yellow pill. Instantly, I want more, even before the first one has run its course.

My friend says that she can get more of them, but it is going to cost money. Money is not a problem for me. I always hold onto any money that is given to me. I don't eat at school because I don't want anyone making fun of me. I feel that because I am fat, if I eat lunch, the other students will make fun of me. Most times, I do not buy lunch. I am tired of being the center of the "Watch out! She is going to eat everyone's food" jokes. I always go to the gym and watch the guys play pickup basketball during lunch time. No one notices and I am glad. So, I always have my lunch money.

I usually spend it on walks to the neighborhood store. There, I buy cakes and soda, and stuff them in a bag. I have a secret hiding place in my bedroom where I hide treats. Then, I binge and eat all through the night. When I run low, I either buy them at the store or steal them from the cabinets in our kitchen. I almost never allow anyone to see me overeat. That was what I thought was a secret that I carried on through years—hiding food and eating it later, all by myself. It is comforting to stuff cakes and chips down and, sometimes, get so sick that I throw everything back up. This becomes a ritual for me. I just stuff the food, and later, I can simply throw it back up. This way, I can say I haven't had anything to eat. What I can't understand is why I am not losing any weight. Instead, I am getting fatter.

So now, I am almost thirteen and have found the wonder drug for me. Those little yellow pills have me relaxed. I am able to speak up for myself in school. I find my voice. I am talking and acting out in school. The more I take, the better I feel. I wish I had discovered these a long time ago!

One morning, my new friend informs me that she has a flask of bourbon in her bag. I had been forced to drink this brown stuff once before, when I was five, by "him." It burned my throat. "He" made me drink it or, "he" said, "he" would cut my private area. The committee in my head told me to do as "he" asked because I did not want to be cut there. So, at five years of age, I had my first drink.

Now, at thirteen, I am feeling that scared feeling all over again. Although my friend is not threatening me with a knife (like "he" did), she says it will go better with the pills. I remember feeling the same burning going down my throat. Only, this time, I am not scared of blood and pain. I am looking for relief. It works instantly. I am feeling even more relaxed, and I ask for more. She laughs and says something about not wanting to get drunk and draw attention. I just want to drink and feel good about the day. Those words and those feelings are what I longed to have every time I took a drink for the next 30 years. Only thing, I never got that feeling back again. Many years later, smoking crack made me feel the same thing. I was running after a feeling that I got the first time, but it never happened again.

Still, that morning, in the bathroom at school, I found another formula to success in my life. Alcohol. Mixed with those little yellow pills, I become what I have always wanted to become—a part of people. All I ever want is to be liked and loved. Now, people want to be with me and that is all that is important. I am someone. And, from that day onward, at the break, we take Valium and drink some bourbon. By the end of the class, we both are sleep on our desks. So, she gives me something called "black beauties" to bring me back up. At age 14, I am learning how to manage my addiction with uppers and downers.

***

The summer that I turn 13 is the summer that I become an addict. I am able to get Valium from my mother, who has been prescribed Valium after an accident with her back. I learn very quickly how to become a pill thief. I also learn how to steal beer and wine from the local store, and I discover pot through kids in the neighborhood.

My food addiction is out of control, and I am getting bigger each day. My life is that of a full-fledged addict. I am slowly becoming a part of the neighborhood group. I am smoking pot and drinking and feel like I have arrived! It doesn't matter to me if people are making fun of me behind my back. They are accepting me because I am using just like them. Even though I feel a part of a group, I always feel like I am looking in and not being in. Sometimes, I feel the disconnect even though I am in the room with a bunch of people. The committee in my head is telling me all sorts of things. Say this. Do that. I think that sometimes they just want me to act different so I will stand out more.

What I discover is that I have to drink more than everyone else, to be the clown when I am drunk or high, to draw more attention to myself that way. I am getting a reputation for being able to drink or drug a lot more than most people. I take pride in the fact that I can hang with the guys drinking. I am not going to act girly drinking. I want to stand out and this is the only way I know.

***

That summer, my Spanish-speaking friend runs away from home. She is found dead in Florida, hit by a car while hitch-hiking on the interstate. They say she just stumbled into traffic. I wonder if she just stumbled. I know, a lot of times, we talked about killing ourselves together, about how we both feel a difference in our souls. Did she have the spirits like I have? We never talk about it, but we both just know that we have connected souls.

So, here is the first of many people who will come into my life only to be jerked out of it, never able to connect again. It will become a pattern with which I have to learn to live. I can't cry because I have already cried all the tears of pain from "him" for the moment. I do not know how to cry for someone I am supposed to care about. I am not sure how to do that. To cry means weakness. To cry means caring. I am just not going to care for anyone. Never.

It is at 13 that I, once again, have to have my committee protect me. That summer, one of my brother's friends catches me playing by myself at the school. He pulls me behind a boxwood bush and proceeds to tear at my clothes. I just give in. What is the use? It is just a way to say he loves being in my body. It hurts, and I bleed, but I never tell anyone about it. I remember how he bit my nipples and how, during the pain, the committee is telling me that I will be okay. No one needs to be told and no use fighting it. I am getting what I deserve because I am trying to be like a boy. It lasts only minutes but leads to a lifetime of pain.

That night, on the cellar roof, I step out of myself and, for the first time, meet the older guy. I am not sure what the older guy's role is but, in a few years, at 15, I learn why he is placed in my being. The older guy comes out a lot. He is gentle and can take on a lot of hurt that people are dishing out to me. As soon as the older guy comes out, I also meet the addict, who is a total drunk and drug addict. The addict wants to drink and drug all the time. The addict also loves to eat, and loves being thought of as "the fat slob." The addict ignores the laughter directed toward me and just continues to eat.

The athlete also comes out and, despite my weight, becomes a very good athlete. The athlete helps me with the shotput and with volleyball. I play well, and there is a look of amazement on people's faces about how graceful I am. During some of my best games, I am drunk. It is as if this addiction has its grip on me, and I can't let it go. One time, I was drunk and took a nasty fall on the blacktop playing basketball. I know the coaches know that I am drunk, but no one ever says a word. It is as if I am getting a message from everyone in authority that it is okay to be screwed up. It does not matter.

Once again, my thought is, *No one cares.*

***

By the time I am 14, I am drinking at school, trading pot for alcohol. I am also getting a reputation for hanging with the older students in high school. I am riding to school most mornings with older students and getting high before class. One of my favorite times of the day at school is in the early mornings. We gather in a bathroom and the older girls get high and drink. I am right there with them. I always have money, so I am the one buying. It never occurs to me that they only want me around because I buy the goods. I always thought they wanted to be with me because they like me because I can drink and smoke, like them.

At 14, it is more important that I be accepted, more important to be loved. I want to walk in my brother's footsteps, to be popular, cool, and, one day, have a cool car to drive. I yearn for acceptance. But my addictions cannot be controlled. I continue to eat out of control. I am very active and, for the first time after playing with boys on the basketball court and baseball field, I am accepted as one of the guys. I am the only girl who plays with guys during lunch time at school on the basketball court. Fat as I am, I still am a decent athlete. I never have any dreams of doing anything else: all I think about is drinking, drugging, and eating. I also discover that I can eat a lot of food and throw some of it back up. That is a practice that I would suffer with for many years.

At 14, I am just entering the high school years. It also means more exposure to drugs and alcohol. Those next few years are the start of me becoming an addict. It is also the start of my destruction of ever wanting to be anything in my life. As long as I have drugs, alcohol, and food, I am set. I basically use the bus as a taxi to get to school, rarely attending classes. I never study. I don't care if I pass or fail a test. I have convinced myself that I am dumb, and that school is not for me. I continue to have that "I am all alone" feeling. It doesn't matter who I am around, I always feel out of place. Walking in the doors of high school makes me feel like I am just another number. I don't have a lot of close friends. People like me because I am learning to be the class clown, always something funny to say but never producing anything as a student. I skipped so many classes that teachers don't even know who I am in the afternoon classes. "O" on my report card is common.

By spring of my first year, I discover that I can do sports. I try my hand at throwing the shot put. Discovering sports saved me from being put out of school. I start attending classes, doing the work. Afternoons are spent on the track. It feels good to be needed. I excel in shotput and even break a few records along the way. I really think I found what was going to be my saving grace and keep me focused at school. But the summer is approaching and that means a lot of time on my hands. That also means going back to the same routine—drinking and drugging. I am getting popular because I always have drugs.

Somehow, at 15, I am able to buy alcohol at one of the local ABC stores. I never did figure out how I was able to get away with it. But I always have money because that summer I was pumping gas at the local store. I am also dabbling a little at selling pot. I do a lot of stealing that summer from the store—mostly beer and wine—so that we can all have plenty in the evenings, hanging out on an old road in the neighborhood we call "the Rock." We all gather, drink, smoke, and just have fun. I always feel left out. Guys are hitting on the girls but never on me. I guess because I am just like them. I have not explored sexually on my own. It has always been that someone violates me. Just those two encounters, first when I was 5 and then again at 13.

While everyone else is expressing themselves sexually, all I want to do is get high and have fun. I never thought about a future. I am not thinking about how to lose weight and feel good about myself. I just know that when I drink and drug, I felt "a part of." When I have stuff to share with others, I am popular. It doesn't matter if they are talking about me or making fun of me. I just want to party and have fun. It never dawns on me that I need to think about life after the party. I vow that I will still be smoking and drinking in a rocking chair!

That is what drugs are doing for me. It is taking away any dreams or goals I have for a future life. I am not even thinking beyond the next high. I am working and plotting my next drinking adventure. I think life is good, money in my pocket, easy access to drugs and alcohol, and fun times.

Still, I have that feeling of not being accepted. I am in my room at night, eating food that I have stored in my room and feeling very lonely. Even at the Rock, with a crowd of people, I am alone. I catch myself drifting off, looking into space and wondering when I will die.

That summer, I am able to get a car. I can't count the number of times I come home and do not know how I got there. My drinking has quickly escalated to black outs. It is never social drinking for me. I drink in order to get as drunk as possible, to be numb from the drugs and alcohol. What I also don't realize is that I am doing the same thing with food. It is never eating because I am hungry. I don't know what hunger is. It isn't just one hamburger: it has to be three. Everything, food, drugs, alcohol, is to the extreme. I only know one speed, from 0 to 60, as fast as possible.

I am also known for my fast driving and have a very fast car, even at 15 years of age. Everything I do has to draw attention. I need approval at all times.

My life is steadily getting out of control. I barely attend school. Even when I can't find anyone to skip classes with me, I go off by myself, driving around town or just sitting in the car alone for hours, smoking and drinking. In fact, most of the time, it is just me. I skip so much school that nearing track season, I don't think I will be able to be on the team and throw the shotput. The school makes one of the worse decisions they could make. They bargain with me that, if I write papers for each subject, I can be on the team. They should never have allowed me to be on the team. I feel like I have won in this battle of doing what I want to do. I never have a problem with writing. When I write, I just let the words flow. It is the one thing in school that I love doing. So, I write papers for Math, Science, English, and Art, and get "As" and brought my "0s" up so that I am able to throw the shotput. Even then, no one sees that I really truly need help.

***

I like throwing the shotput because it is a sport that I can practice all alone, yet still help the team out at the same time by winning my event and scoring points. I can still be all alone, never having to answer to anyone. The big plus is that the big strong guys are my mentors. They help me out and show me pointers. It is like I am part of a guy group, and I like that. I don't have to hang around the girls. There is always that fear that they will want to do something to me—like before—but they never do. All they are interested in is that I do well in my event. Workouts in the weight room with them are fun, and I am beginning to drink and drug less. But I still have the weekends when I am having problems. Even then, I am craving the drink. Since I am not drinking and skipping school, I think that I will not have to drink, drug, and eat like before. But I am wrong. When the weekend comes, all those demons come back. I can't wait for Friday nights on the Rock. I manage to find some friends from school who like drinking and drugging, like mc. Although, deep down, I don't want to do it, my mind and body are telling me otherwise. It is not long before the drinking carries over into the week while I am in school. I learn how to skip just a few classes and come back with a fake excuse at the end of the day.

It is self-destructive. As soon as I hear from one of the coaches that if I keep getting better, I might get a scholarship to college in the next couple of years, I get scared. I don't want to go anywhere. All I want to do is drink and have fun. I wish I knew, back then, that the drugs and drinking were taking away all my drive to do something better for myself. I just didn't want to do anything but smoke, drink, and eat.

Pretty soon, I am drinking and drugging before meets. One of my best meets, I don't even remember breaking the record for throwing the shotput. I was so drunk that I was in a black out. It wasn't until the next day that I realized that I had not only placed first but broke the school record!

When I realize that I can drink, drug, and still do okay with the shotput, my drinking and drugging goes right back to the level where I left it when I quit to join the track team. I am now also dealing pot. I learn very quickly that I can make some money by buying extra pot and selling it at school. I also learn that I have a whole new crowd of people who like me. I feel like I have arrived. I have the jocks liking me because of the shotput and I am liked by the drinking and drugging crowd as well.

Another addiction is slowly coming into play and that is my anger. I am having outbursts in the classroom and am being put out of class because of them. I am told by my coach to save it for the track. But it is just like the drugs and alcohol that I am using. The more I get away with it, the worse it gets. I get angry with anyone at any time. Because of my size, it makes it that much more frightening to see. I know that when I drink, it fuels the anger that much more.

The committee is still meeting in my head and there are times when it is getting worse. The one thing I learn is that drinking and smoking pot calms the committee down. I used that remedy for the next 30 years. What I didn't know was that it would make me a slave to an addiction that would only get worse.

***

By the time I am almost 16 years old, I have never dated, never kissed anyone, and all I am interested in is my love of food, drugs, and alcohol. Nothing else matters to me or so I think. Deep down, I want to be like everyone else. I want to walk down the halls with a guy carrying my books to class. I want to go to the school dances and dance with a guy. I just really want what I think is a normal life for a high school student. I am still being laughed at for how I look but not to my face. The only clothes I want to wear are men's clothes. I know that must be a topic of conversation for my so-called friends too.

I want to be popular. I want people to like me because I am smart. I want to be in the advanced classes. But the truth is that I can't be in those classes. I have not prepared myself to be there. I rarely open a book at home to study. As soon as school is out, if it is not track season, I am just drinking and having a good time.

By the age of 17, I know that I am different. I know that people are going to start talking about why I always want to wear boys' clothes. Why I always want to smell like a boy. I am always so afraid that when I die, my family will dress me up like a woman. Even today, I don't want to die as a woman. I want to die as a man.

As a child, I never wanted to wipe myself with toilet paper after I peed. Sometimes, I try to stand to pee. I feel like wiping myself is a girl thing to do. I know that I am not a boy, and it is always such an effort to go to the bathroom. I learn to hold it all day. I know if I don't wipe myself properly, I will more than likely have an odor. So, holding it all day until I get home becomes the normal routine. I look back now and see that I truly was born in the wrong body. I always thought that something was wrong with me mentally, but now, I see that it was gender dysphoria.

At 17, I'm not even thinking about sex. All I am thinking about is sports and drinking. Sports is what is keeping me in school. I really don't have the desire to further my studies. I am not even thinking about college or what I am going to do with my life after I get out of high school. All I want to do is drink and drug. Looking back, I realize that I was an alcoholic who needed treatment, probably more then, than when I did actually walk into the rooms of AA.

I have a reputation for always having something to drink and the best drugs around. I always have money because of selling drugs and I am considered one of the biggest partiers on the high school campus. As others are acquiring a skill or taking classes to prep them for college, I am drinking, and growing and selling weed. I am proud of the reputation I am getting. At least it is something. I am getting the attention I want.

No longer am I being made fun of. I am accepted by a group of people who, I believe, really think I am cool. I feel like I have arrived. I am not interested in sports, school, or outside activities. I just want to drink and drug. Looking back now, I see that, even at 17 years of age, I was in need of rehab from drugs and alcohol. So much had happened in my life already. If I had truly sought out the help back then, what would my life be like today?

Life is a big game, and I am in the center of the circle of games. But they are making fun of me behind my back. Everyone acts like they want to be around me and want me around them. I am always the first to be asked to parties. I have parties, and hundreds of people come. Is it me or the booze and drugs that they want to be around? Many times, when the kegs run out, so do the people. But it doesn't matter because I feel popular. Those days as a kid at the playground, being laughed at, are over. Being the one who cruel games were played on in the outside bathrooms are over. I have something that people want, and it is making me popular. In the school, everyone knows who I am. But I am not popular because of my grades, or athletic achievements. I am popular because I buy alcohol and have access to drugs. It doesn't matter what the reason is, I just want to be a somebody.

My weight is spiraling out of control. I don't care what I look like. I am drinking, drugging, and eating. I don't miss the days of throwing the shot put. I am even given a scholarship for college to be on the track team. I visit the school but decide that I would rather stay home and drink and drug with the neighborhood people. Nothing in my life encourages me to want anything better. I never think about the future. It is all about drinking, drugging, and fast cars. Life is about living at 100 miles per hour. Nothing in between. When things become too much for me to handle, I learn that I can just check myself into the mental ward and take a break.

I don't know what love is. I don't even know what it is like to admire someone and be interested in them. For me, life is all about a party. I dislike my body so much that I can't even think that someone else might want to touch me. I never touch myself in any intimate way. I hate my body so much that loving me and taking care of me is entirely foreign. I don't care whether clothes look nice on me. I am a girl wearing men's clothes. How nice could they look? I don't feel worthy of looking nice. I just never imagine anyone wanting to love me for who I am. Given what I look like, I know that boys are not interested in me, and I am not interested in them either. I also know that no girl will want someone who dresses, looks, and sounds like I do. Even at 17, I am having little children ask me what I am. It is so embarrassing to get the "Are you a girl or are you a boy" question from them.

There are many times I just want to hide and not come out, especially if the school is having dances. I don't have the clothes to go to a dance. I have never really danced so why would I go? I push that fear and guilt aside and hang out in the parking lot with the drug crowd. We say the dance is for losers and the happening place is with us. I think we are all a bunch of misfits just trying to find a place to fit in. I know that I have that feeling in my stomach that I just want to fit in with everyone, even those losers at the dance with their dates. I don't know what it is like to go out on a date. I have never kissed anyone, and I am always wondering what it would be like to have someone touch me, hold my hand, and kiss me. Whenever I think about those feelings, it is never with a boy, always with a girl. In my dreams, I am always the one acting like the boy. I want so badly for those feelings to be different.

***

At almost 17, I am still into sports. I play volleyball and throw the shotput for track. Even though I am still drinking, it is not to the out-of-control point. At that time, sports are my lifeline. It is the only reason I am still in school. If I am not busy in the afternoons with sports, I would probably quit school and join the Navy. That is another dream. But I am told by friends and family that I am too fat to join the armed forces. So, I stick it out in school. I am not really learning because my mind just cannot grasp what they are teaching in the classroom. Even with the sports program, I skip a lot of school and get in trouble for skipping. I missed so much time at school that it is hard to catch up. Even in grade school, I didn't learn a lot because I was always hearing those voices from the creek.

In my junior year, despite my size, I try out and am selected to play on the school's first volleyball team. I play the game fairly well and have a great serve. I am also becoming popular at school because of my connections for getting pot and my ability to buy alcohol. I am never carded at one of the ABC stores and regularly buy bourbon and grain alcohol. Kids have me buy for them as well. I will do anything to be their friend.

I feel proud that rich, white kids are wanting to be my friend. Being on the volleyball team exposes me to more of them. What I never realize is that, although I think I am just like them, they think of me as being different. I think they are just as interested in drinking and drugging as I am, and that studying is out of the question. Then, I realize that I am not in the same classes as they are. They are talking about life after high school. The life they are talking about is college. I have never even given that a thought. All I think about is drinking and having what I think is fun. I want that to last forever.

That year, I become friends with one of the girls on the volleyball team. We do a lot of drinking and drugging together. I am even invited to come to their home. I like hanging around with her and, even more, I like hanging at her house. She has the coolest mother. We use her house as our hangout spot. We go into the basement of her parents' home and smoke and drink, almost like we don't have to hide. Her mom is laid back and very accepting of all of us. She knows we are drinking in her house but never says anything. She reaches out to me, and we develop a bond. She is very open and accepting of me, and I am always made to feel "a part of." She is someone I can talk to, and I feel that I can confide in her as I should have been able to confide in my own mother but cannot. Many nights, I find myself at the kitchen table talking to her about my feelings of being different, my fears of not being good enough, about being fat, feeling bad about myself, and feeling like I don't fit in my body. She listens and never judges me or acts as if she is making fun of me. She is the first person to whom I have ever expressed my fears. I feel safe, as if, for the first time, I can express myself. She doesn't want anything from me. She just listens. And I need someone to listen to my fears, someone who doesn't judge me when I say I am in the wrong body. Yes, even then, I felt as if I was in the wrong body.

My mind drifts back to the day I was told that I was going to be dropped off at the hospital. I was going to have a "thing" sewn down there, all because I don't want to wear a dress. I want pants. I want to dress like a boy, wear baseball caps, and look like a boy. It is my lifelong dream. I am always wondering when I am going to wake up and have all my boy parts.

Every person that I had met up to that point in my life had an agenda. My uncle had an agenda. He was fun and friendly at first, only to do the things he did to me later. Whenever someone wants to be my

friend, I am always on guard. But I am beginning to let my guard down
with her. She appears to have no agenda, nothing except being willing
to listen and be my friend. Her house becomes a safe haven for me. It is
a place where I see people talk openly about their feelings and fears. I
also see people openly expressing their love for each other.

At my house, we always just assume that we love each other. No
hugging, no expression, we just move through our days "as if," never
expressing any emotion, except anger. It is just like that. To express
emotion means being weak. And we are not weak. We are strong Black
people, who achieve success from the hard work that we do. We never
go on vacations, never have family outings. All I see my parents do is
work. I want us to be different. I want us to be like other families, to go
on planned vacations, to talk about our feelings, to say we love each
other, rather than assuming that we do. But it never happens. They were
born in a different era. To them, providing for their family is the only
thing they know to do. And provide they did. For what they do, and how
hard they work, we never go hungry, never go without.

But I need more. I seek that through her family. I want to suck up
their environment. I dream of the day when I live there so completely
that I become a regular part of that family. But any way that you look at
it, I am different. I am Black, and, in so many ways, this life is foreign
to me. I don't know how to receive it. Still, as uncomfortable as it
sometimes is, I want more of what that family has to offer.

I will be turning 17 soon and school will be over. I talk to her about
my fears of what am I going to do after the ride of high school. I trust
this woman. I feel that she won't hurt me, that she doesn't have an
agenda. What I will soon realize, however, is that, as much as I don't
want to admit it, she is a predator too. What I thought was safe was not.
Many years later, I realize that she is no different than any of the other
predators in my life. She is just like my uncle, only her package is
dressed up a little more attractively.

***

School is going okay. I am not skipping as much because I realize
that skipping school is yet another addiction that I have developed. My
drinking has slowed down a little, but I am still smoking pot and hash
on a regular basis. My food addiction is completely out of control.

As volleyball season starts, it is pretty certain that we are not going to have a very good squad. We are new to the league and don't know a lot about the sport. But it doesn't matter. We are having fun.

The only Black person and overweight, I feel, for once, that I am being accepted. I am popular! I don't realize my being popular has more to do with my access to drugs and alcohol. Some want to be around me just for me, I think, but the majority want something else. I guess I do too. I just want a friend, someone who is not going to judge me, someone who is not going to ask why I am not attracted to boys.

It seems as if being involved in sports is my saving grace for staying in school. It keeps me responsible because I know without getting decent grades, I cannot play. I start going to class and not drinking as much because I have a responsibility to the team. The league rules are clear: no drinking and keep a certain grade average. I have to do just that. I want to be able to play. Still, I don't really study and never think about life after high school. All my other friends are thinking about what they are going to do. College or whatever. Even the so-called hardcore drinkers and druggers are acquiring a skill. The guys are in shop or auto mechanics class. The girls are taking business classes and learning a skill. But, for me, it is just drinking, drugging, and having fun. I don't realize that I need some sort of skill to prepare myself for life after high school. This is the one piece of my past that will haunt me throughout the rest of my life.

As the volleyball season continues, an amazing thing happens. This team that has never played the sport before turns out to be somewhat successful. We get better with each game. We are winning, and we are a team that the other teams respect. I have a wicked serve and, in one game, served 9 consecutive serves! I am one of the team captains, and, finally, I feel like I belong. Now, I know what it is like to play a team sport. It is different than throwing the shotput, being alone and scoring points. This is a team effort.

I never really realized how much those two years of sports in school were my saving grace. They keep me somewhat disciplined, and I am a lot happier when I am playing sports. It slows down my drinking, and I can concentrate on being an athlete. When I am playing volleyball, there are practices and games, and they keep me out of my head. I still have my moments of needing a drink but, many times, I don't act on it. Still there is something missing. I am not like everyone else. I feel different. I need more out of my life. I am not complete. But, at least, I don't have the committee in my head telling me what to do or not to do. My committee always seems to believe all the negative stuff people want to tell me, things like: I don't have to go to school, or that I'm not good enough to be a decent athlete. The committee always wants me to accept the worst, that I just am not good enough to succeed at anything. I believed it for so long, convinced that I would never get anything good in life. I struggled for a long time before I would finally see my worth.

***

Although I am not drinking as much during the week, on the weekends, I am still drinking to blackout. But it isn't every day. I have something to look forward to. I am responsible to my team to stay clean and sober. We are doing well, and, for the first time, I am having fun. I have friends who want to be around me, not just for drugs and alcohol, but because they like me. I even begin thinking about how I can lose some weight to get into better shape for track season. I am feeling like, finally, life is turning around for me.

Then, comes homecoming and all the hype behind that. I am asked by several girls to buy some booze so that we can party a little before going to the homecoming game. They can party for one night and it is okay, but, for me, a one-night party can last for many days. It is just how drinking and drugging are for me. As long as I am not doing it, I am okay. But the minute I start, it is like a faucet I cannot turn off.

We get a lot of alcohol, and someone has beer. We proceed to drink at this girl's house. Some of the girls have never been drinking before. They get really drunk, and their parents find out. A few of the girls dime me out as the one who bought the alcohol, and I am kicked off the volleyball team. What I can't understand is why others are still allowed to play when they have been drinking, but I am kicked off the team. It really doesn't matter though. I go back to drinking again and never look back. Now, I can drink until spring when track season starts. I have time to just drink and not care about anything.

I start drinking in the mornings, smoking pot before class, and drinking during our morning breaks. I don't ever remember going to the lunchroom for lunch my entire junior year. I am always out in the parking lot, drinking and smoking. I leave the school a lot of times with people who have already graduated but are back to hang out and sell pot.

All of my addictions kick up to higher heights. With no sport activities in the evenings, I begin to hang out with my other friends more and more. I feel betrayed by my sports friends. I feel like they have dimed me out to save their own skins. Deep down, I really miss the game and the responsibility of trying to stay clean while playing a sport. The last thing I want to do is go back to drinking. I really want to quit, but my mind is telling me something else. It is telling me that I need the drugs and alcohol.

The sad thing about this is that, for the first time, I began feeling like I might have a future. I am listening to the other girls on the volleyball team talk about applying to college.

For the first time, I think, *Maybe I too could go to school.*

I even think about going into the Navy. But the others tell me I can't because I am too fat.

"Just get a good job after school is over," they say.

I wish I had never listened to them.

We have just won the volleyball regionals and are heading to the state finals. The misfit team in the league, we keep it together long enough to be a contender. We have made a name for ourselves in the volleyball world. In the end, when I watch my team lose the Regional Championship, there is a part of me that is glad that it ended that way. I am still hurt and angry that they turned on me but relieved that now I can drink and smoke and not have to worry about being dimed out by anyone.

Chapter 4

"Her"

It's always easier to take somebody else's inventory.
Alcoholics Anonymous

But for now, it is time to have a party and celebrate. The team won the district championship, and it is time for us to have a big party. Being that "she" is the "cool mom," the party is held at my friend's house. Her mom even buys us a keg. No one thinks there is anything wrong with that. "She" makes us all agree that if any of us get too drunk to drive, we will camp out there at her house. "She" is not going to have anyone driving home if they have been drinking. So, all week, we plan the big sleepover. We get some grain alcohol, and, of course, I score some pot and hash.

We have a great crowd: there are about 25 of us at the party. Not surprisingly, being the drinker that I am, I get drunker than anyone else, and I don't remember a lot about the party. I have not been drinking as much for almost 4 months, and I pick right up where I left off, drinking to black out. And I *did* black out. That turn outs to be one of the worst mistakes of my life. It is a decision that haunts me for many days to come.

"She" is the one person who came into my life at a time when I think "she" is what I need. But "she" turns out to be just another piece of destruction, one of many to come. I have been hanging out at their home, thinking it is safer than my own. One night, after one too many drinks, I confess to "her" my fears about my drinking, my fears that I might be crazy, and my fears about life in general. It starts with a hug and ends in 10 years of insanity from drugs, alcohol, and all-out drama. I want someone to share all these things with. But "she" is not going to be that person. Like others, "she" also has an agenda that does not include being only a listener.

What I can't figure out is how I get downstairs. I am in a room all alone when I wake up. I have been left on the sofa in the basement to sleep it off. Where is everyone else? What have I done to be put down in the basement? I soon realize that I have done nothing. It is all a setup. A predator's game. "She" knows what "she" is doing long before that night. "She" knows what "she" wants, and I am thinking, all along, that it is because "she" cares about me.

Sometime, during the course of the night, "she" comes downstairs to supposedly check on me, to make sure I am okay. "Her" checking on me leads to "her" touching me. Being that I have never been with anyone sexually, either man or woman, I am not sure what "she" is doing. The touching leads to kissing and, before I know it, we are having sex. Here I am, at 17 years old, having sex with my friend's mother! At the time, I respond because it is new, and it feels good. "Her" touch and "her" telling me that "she" has loved me for a long time only makes things more complicated later. This woman has children, a husband, a career, and I look up to "her" as a mother figure. Now, we have crossed the line, and life will never be the same. I don't know how long it lasts, but when it is over, I feel the same guilt and shame that I felt with "him" (my uncle) and that friend of my brother.

"She" tells me that I am not to tell anyone. That it is our little secret. Here we go again, except, this time, I am not being threatened with being killed or losing my pet as my uncle had threatened me by the creek. But is "she" the same as "him"? Many times, I have been told to "keep this a secret," to keep this as something wrong. This *is* wrong! "She" has a lot to lose, "she" says, if anyone finds out. "She" says that "she" just wants to be my first, to be the one to show me how to love, not just have sex.

I am so confused. "She" is the first one I told about my uncle. "She" is the first one I told about the guy behind the bushes at school when I was 12. "She" is the first one I told about my feelings for women but didn't know what to do about it. It is the '70s and being a lesbian is not something you just blurt out. It is a "don't ask and don't tell" life back then. It is still considered a mental illness by a lot of doctors as I would find out.

Who am I going to turn to now? Lately, I had let out all my dark secrets to "her." "She" keeps telling me that it is safe for me to talk to "her," to tell all my secrets about how I feel about myself, my life. They are all safe with "her." But it is different now. We have crossed a line that is confusing, a line that I will never again have my life back. I didn't plan for this.

That night, as drunk as I am, I become another statistic. That night down in the basement of "her" home, I have no choice. I come around naked, knowing that I have been violated. Sex against my will—again. Just like being at the creek. Just like being in the bushes at the school. I have been given no choice. The only difference, this time, is that it lasts for about 3 years. For three years, I let this woman feed me drugs and sex, and I do nothing about it. I just stay there. I become a victim.

Once again, I am back to feeling scared, angry, and alone. Who can I tell this to? Who can I talk to about why this happened? I quickly blame myself. I should not have gotten so drunk that I could not drive home. I should never have come to the party. I am no longer one of the team members anyway. I feel like I am not a member of anything anymore. I don't have a family that understands. Church says my kind will burn in hell. I don't have anything in common with girls and despite the things that I feel I have in common with boys, they still will not accept me into their world. It might have been different if I wasn't fat. If I am more athletic looking, they might accept me more. But I always have to prove that I can hang with them when it comes to sports. I never am good enough at anything. I learn that just getting by is okay. I never really have to excel at anything. For many years, that attitude keeps me from being the success I could have been.

***

Now, in this strange relationship with "her," life is going to take on a whole new meaning. I learn very quickly that isolating and drinking and drugging is the way to go for many years to come. I am still the one at parties who has more to drink than everyone else. I am still the one who is the clown of the group. It is better for them to laugh with me than to laugh behind my back. I always want the laughter to be *on* me, not *at* me. So, I always act out to get attention.

And it starts all over again with those people in my head. They tell me that I need to kill myself, that everything bad that has happened to me thus far is my fault entirely and that it is time to just end it all. This thing with "her" is going to get messy, and I don't need to be in the middle of all of this. I am 17 and don't know which way to turn. All I know is that this thing with "her" doesn't feel right. But, all the time, I am craving the attention from "her." "She" is the only one who really wants to be with me. "She" is the only person who says I am beautiful. Through the layers of fat, "she" says that I am beautiful. Through all the insecurities, "she" says that "she" wants to be with me. But it is wrong!

I have to remind myself that I didn't do anything wrong, that I was minding my own business, that "she" came after me. Could I have stopped it? I know deep down I could have said "no." But I didn't. Just like I could have said "no" when I was little. I should have said "no" both times. Maybe then, I would not have this group in my head telling me to do all these bad, horrible things to myself, and I would not be so angry. Anger would not become one of my friends. I might not have been fat. I might not have been a lesbian. So many might-not-have-beens.

Am I blaming myself for stuff I should not be blaming myself for? I remember someone saying once that we are responsible for our own actions. I feel that I am responsible for these things that are happening to me. I have to do something about these people taking advantage of me sexually. I wish I could have found therapy and gotten some help. I wish I could have found AA. Maybe my life would have had better meaning.

So here I am at 17, not sure where my life is headed. Not really gearing myself towards anything, just drinking and drugging. Not thinking about the life ahead of me. Not even living life a day at a time. I am struggling to find my identity. I am teased a lot because I want to wear boys' clothes. I am working a part time job, so I am able to buy my own clothes. I always want to wear boy clothes even when I can't because, when I am in girl clothes, I feel like a fake. I am so uncomfortable. At 17, I can pretty much wear what I want. My dream is not to have a girlfriend or anybody for that matter. My dream is to become a boy. Many nights, I dream of dying as a girl and being born all over again as a boy. Nights when I am in a struggle with myself about killing myself, my thoughts are, *If I kill myself tonight, could I come back as a boy?*

This will be a struggle I will deal with until my late 50s. I don't care that people are making fun of the way I look. I think I am accepted in school because of me just being me. The truth of the matter is that people want to be with me because I can get the good drugs. I can buy the alcohol. I have a car. They really don't want to be with me to be friends.

I know something is wrong when in my senior year, I refuse to participate in any sports. The coaches are coming after me for track. But I am telling them that I am not interested. It is then that I should have had an intervention in my life. I think back today and so much heartache could have been prevented if I had gone to a therapist and gotten the help I needed then. I was walking away from everything in my life that interested me. The one thing that kept me alive during my junior year was sports and that was the one thing I was walking away from. Drugs and alcohol were taking over. It was more important to stay high and skip school than to be a part of something constructive.

Sports might have saved me, but I watched from a distance and then, eventually, it got to the point where I would not even attend any of the sporting events, leaving school, instead, to drink and drug, then coming back to meet with my so-called friends after an event to party even more.

I tie together the thought that it is sports that has me confused about "her." If I had never been in sports, I never would have connected with "her." Could my life have been different? All these questions. One day, I would learn that I should not regret the past nor wish to shut the door on it. What happens, happens, and I should not dwell on it. Instead, I should just learn from my past and move on. But at 17, these are the thoughts going through my mind. It is a constant moving picture that, many nights, I cannot turn off. The only way to turn it off is with drugs and alcohol. In many ways, the combination of these substances saved my life. If I had not been able to drink and drug, I would certainly have blown my brains out.

"She" and I continue to see each other. It is secretive, behind closed doors, and "she" keeps telling me never to tell anyone. I am "her" dirty little secret. I learn very quickly to lie and to be invisible when needed. "She" has "her" life of bridge, tennis, and golf friends and, by night, "she" has "her" dirty little secret.

I am progressively getting worse with drugs. I am taking just about anything I can get my hands on, and "she" introduces me to cocaine. With coke, I can smoke all the weed I want and then, get that boost to make it through the day or night. Sleep is something that I rarely do. I have all sorts of drugs, cars, and gadgets at my disposal. "She" makes it all available to me. Money is not a problem. Abusing my body is the problem. My self-esteem is the problem. I am convinced that no one wants me.

Previously, I would skip school with a group of people but now, I am beginning to learn the art of being a loner. I am beginning to just ride around all day drinking and drugging. I learn how to hide off in the woods with my drink and my drugs and my music. For many hours, I just stare off into space, my mind wandering, and playing with my gun, wishing and hoping that I would have the nerve to just end it all.

I don't have a clue about loving and being loved, but, at the time, in some strange crazy way, "she" does teach me about love and being tender and kind to someone. What I don't realize is that "she" is just another predator in my life, simply dressed up in a different fashion. We become lovers, haters, and drug addicts. Again, to me, this is what someone caring about me is about. Abuse and craziness. "She" walks away from "her" family, "her" life of being a stereotypical Mrs. Brady, for drugs, crazy living, and what would end in total destruction.

"She" thinks that showering me with material things is what I need. Driving fast cars, having money, and loaded with drugs is the life I live with "her." I never commit to living with "her", but I go for days and weeks hiding out with "her," as "her" hostage, living on cocaine, pot, alcohol, and food. The crazier life gets, the more my addiction kicks in. The more my addiction kicks in, the more the neighborhood goes completely out of whack.

I am in and out of mental institutions, taking their drugs, taking my drugs, and allowing "her" to be my Higher Power as a drug as well. Life is out of control, but I know nothing but this life. Life, as I know it, is jumping from job to job, periods of being in hospitals, and lots of suicide attempts. At this point in my life, a suicide attempt is almost a daily ritual for me.

I wake up every morning and think, *This is the morning that I will kill myself. This is the day I will just end it all.*

Every morning, I wake up with one bullet in the gun and pull the trigger. That it never goes off, I think is luck. But it is God doing for me what I cannot do for myself. He is keeping me alive because I have not finished living yet. I do not know that then. I still have not mastered riding my bike.

***

"She" and I continue our drug-crazed life. Cocaine and uppers by day, pot and downers by night. I am also using Thorazine, Haldol, and Lithium to maintain my sanity, or so I think. With all these drugs, I am just a walking zombie most of the time.

The first real fight that "she" and I have is over drugs. I want to stop. I want to come clean and try to gain some sanity. I always prefer to admit that I am crazy, rather than an alcoholic or addict. Crazy seems to be more acceptable. I just use drugs because it is something to do. Never once am I going to admit that I am using drugs because I have a disease, that my usage is an allergy. It would take another decade or more before I admitted my powerlessness over substances.

"She" is angry about my cutting back. I am angry because I cannot cut back. The more I try, the more I use. I go through extreme withdrawals. My mind is spinning with the spirits and spinning with thoughts that are just not making any sense at all. I know that when I do more drugs those thoughts are more intense, more of everything.

I have to get out of this, but how can I? I don't have a job and no real training for a job. Every job I take, I keep for a short while, and then, it is off to the races of being in a mental unit. Sometimes, it is over-dosing. Other times, I just can't control myself in the real world. I just need a break and to slow it down. Most times, I really just need to get away from "her." "She" was toxic for me. But "she" was also the one drug I wanted to put down but couldn't.

It was because of "her" that I found all those other drugs. Cocaine and uppers, prescription drugs. They are always within reach when I am around "her," always ready to take me on what I think is the ride of my life. I never know on which path the ride is going to take me. Bumpy, smooth, it doesn't matter as long as I am riding on the road of addiction.

Finally, it is beginning to get old—the drugs and the drinking. I want to go to the place called AA but don't want to go alone. I didn't want people to think I am different, didn't want to be all alone after I stopped. I really don't know anyone who doesn't drink or drug. I am tired of always being the loner. With drinking and drugging, people want to be around me because I am fun—the clown, the one they laugh at. Are they laughing because I am funny or laughing because of the way I look?

By now, I have ballooned to well over 300 pounds. I don't care what I look like. Clothes are impossible. Still, I always want to wear men's clothing, and I am always being teased by friends because I am wearing them. I am still not out to anyone about "her." I am just laughing with the others when they made jokes about 'those people who are funny.'"

I feel like a sellout. I am afraid of not being "a part of." I keep everything about "her" a secret. And "she" keeps me a secret as well. I feel dirty and ashamed for being with "her." And I feel like I am being punished by God for being fat, for being a drunk, for having this mental illness. I feel like all of the things that happen to me are because God is not pleased with me for being, and wanting to be, with a woman. I think God is angry with me because I only like dressing in men's clothes. I hear the laughs and see the stares from people. I think they are trying to figure out if I am a man or a woman. Or perhaps the stares are about me being fat. Whatever the reason, it just starts pushing me into the house.

I never know what "she" sees in me. My self-esteem is low. I don't care how I look. I am more concerned about where the next drink or drug is coming from, instead of appearances. So, here is this woman saying that "she" loves me and wants to be with me. Am I just a companion for drugs or did "she" really love me for who I am? Everyone wants to believe that they are loved for who they are. I am no exception. The one thing that I don't know, at the time, is what love really is. I go from being told love means pain, to being told love means addiction to drugs and alcohol and constant chaos.

The one thing I know for certain is that I don't want to be in this relationship any longer. I want out. There is no one else. It is just that I need to be with me. I just need a break from people putting their hands on my body. I need a break from drinking and drugging. My body, my mind, and my spirit tell me that I have had enough. But why am I so afraid to speak up and say that this is what I need? I want to say that to the shrinks who are treating me with their drugs. It is not working because I am not taking them as prescribed. I mix this with that, and my solution to the problem is being like a zombie all day from the mixture of my drugs and theirs. Nothing is working. I cannot, or will not, hold down a job. I am just all over the place emotionally. I am angry all the time. I am like a ticking time bomb. And I have found a new addiction—anger.

With anger, I can blow up and calm down at a moment's notice. I never think about the consequences of my behavior. No one calls me on it. I will say and do whatever. People are afraid because my anger is so out of control, and my size is an intimidating factor as well. The anger is like a cork being pulled quickly from a bottle. Loud pops in my head, and then, it is a tornado that rips through the town. Loud noises, lots of destruction in a very short period of time. Then, the sun comes out, and I really cannot realize that the destruction has just been a part of my life.

That is how I feel almost every moment of the day, waiting for the button to be pushed, waiting for the wind to whirl. And then, I take it to the next level.

The thing about the rage and anger is that "she" has just as much as I do. So, for both of us, our communication is always at a chaotic level, all the time. There is nothing loving about us being together. But, in some sort of sick way, I love "her" for that chaos. It is the only attention someone like me can get. "She" is an attractive enough woman that "she" could have had anyone "she" wanted, but "she" picked me—me, who cannot even look at myself in the mirror and accept who I am, me, who is getting bigger every day. My binge eating is also getting out of control.

I don't know, then, that it is binge eating. I just think it is what I need to calm the emotions. If I am scared, I eat. If I am happy, I eat. The only time I really don't eat a lot is when I am in and out of the mental units. There, I would eat healthy, and I would lose a few pounds, get my life back on some sort of track with food. Then, when I get out, the insanity with food starts all over again.

"She" doesn't care that I have poor eating habits. "She" never once tells me that I need to lose weight. "She" never once calls me any bad names about my weight. I think "she" truly wants to be with me for what "she" sees inside. Being a drunk and an addict helps with other things as well. "She" has someone who will stay with "her" because "she" can never be alone. "She" always says that "she" has a great fear of being alone, of being unloved. Funny thing. I feel that when I am with "her," I am unloved. I feel cut off. I feel like I am not in my own skin. I feel like the skin I need to be in is that of a man because, even then, I knew I have been born in the wrong skin. Even then, I knew that underneath this skin is a completely other person, who is not a female. I am a male.

But how to get to that skin? What do I do? I do the only thing I know and that is to drink, drug, and eat. There is no fixing this. I have already been told it is a mental disorder, that in order to have it fixed, I have to do what I have done before—shock treatments. I don't want to go through that again. I feel like I am being punished because I am in the wrong body. I take their drugs because I want to be free from the bondage of the skin I am in. I do the only thing that I can: continue to destroy my mind, my body, and my soul with food and substances.

I bounce in and out of mental units. Sometimes, I need to be there and, other times, I just go to escape from the world. Sometimes, the world just gets to be too much for me. So, instead of dealing with things, I just check myself into whatever unit will take me.

A lot of times I am running from "her." "She" always wants to do drugs to escape from reality. I am really getting tired of being high all the time. I don't have an answer to how to stop it. I know I can go without it in the mental units. I even feel better when I am off alcohol, drugs, and food binges. I eat healthier, and I am walking around the grounds, so I am exercising, playing volleyball, doing normal stuff that people do. My life is not all about drinking, drugging, and eating. I like that life but know, deep down, that as soon as I leave the contained environment, it is right back to destroying myself, with others and with "her." I don't know how to change.

I am told a couple of times that perhaps I need to try AA, that maybe I need to transfer to the 28-day unit upstairs in the facility where I am staying. But I am having no part of that because I don't want to quit. There is a part of me that just needs to be high. It is the best way to mask the confusion about my body. If I just keep drinking and drugging and eating, I do not have to deal with the lie I am living.

Sometimes, I wake up from a dream and hope that it is real. The dream is always that I am a man. Nothing to change, nothing to be ashamed of. I am who I need to be. Sometimes, the dream is really a source of comfort and, other times, it shakes me to the core. What am I fearing? Why is it so real but, when I wake up, it is just a dream? I feel like I am going to be one of those people who everyone talks about. The old lady who wears men's clothing, living alone and dying alone, the one who people whisper about. I do not want to die an old, lonely woman. As much as I fear dying, I also fear living. I am a drunk, a drug addict, and am tipping the scale at 400 pounds. At the rate I am going, I just might die from a heart attack, stroke, or some other medical condition. Perhaps, I will be one of those people bound to the bed, weighing 800 pounds, and never leaving the house again. I am already knocking on death's door. Playing around with overdosing, eating, and drinking like I am, something is going to happen, and it is not going to be a pleasant ending.

I toy with the idea of suicide a lot. I always say that I will kill myself when I least expect it. It will be one of those times when I take too much of something, and it works. I won't get to the hospital in time. I won't call someone until it is too late. The truth is that I don't want to die. I just can't and won't continue living like this. The sad part is that I continue to live this way for almost another 20 years before I finally surrender.

Chapter 5

The Man in the Car

Suicide is a permanent solution to a temporary problem.
Alcoholic Anonymous

At this point in my life, I am 17 years old and learning how to be a loner in this world. To the world, I have a ton of friends. To me, it is just me in this world, all alone. Skipping school alone and traveling around the streets during the day becomes a custom that will be very costly to me.

I totally miss 3 years of my life. I am not sure who I am or what I am doing, but I know that drugs and alcohol play a big part in it. The little girl comes out every now and then and plays with men, never going all the way but playing just the same. It sickens the others because we all know what men have done to the little girl and we wonder how she can even stomach the idea of being with one. She, however, always wants sex or, at least, she tells us that she does. Of course, most of the men are the scum of the earth because of the way we look and how we carry ourselves. We think that we don't deserve any better.

The addict is out in full swing, always drinking, always drugging. By 16, almost 17, the addict is taking us on runaway excursions, always having the police or fire department finding us sleeping in the woods, never with anyone, just being a loner. Family friends think it is all about getting attention. But it is the spirits in the neighborhood telling us to run. The older guy, who is the most sensible one, always wants us to stay on course. I like the older guy. He is strong, kind, and loving. He never says an unkind word to anyone. Soon, though, we learn that for every side of these spirits there is a flip side.

The little girl is becoming more forceful and one runaway day turns into a costly trip for all of us. The little girl gets herself into a situation that none of us can handle. It could have been a horrific experience, but the older guy steps in and, as that happens, another spirit emerges.

One cold, rainy day, the little girl decides that school is not the place to be and decides to skip. We start out going to school, but she wants something to drink instead. Sometimes, the addict and the little girl work together, and when the two of them work together, it always spells disaster. The little girl leaves school, driving in the car that my parents got for me. I have little money and cannot afford to buy my usual drink of bourbon. So, she stops at the local 7/11 to try to get anyone to buy her some beer.

A man pulls up in a very fancy car.

"What are you looking for?" a voice comes from the very fancy car.

"Beer," the little girl replies. "Just some beer. Nothing else. Okay?"

"Why just beer when I have something stronger here in the car? Care to ride and have a morning eye opener?"

This man is dumpy looking, the little girl thinks.

But then, those are the only kind that give her the time of day. She decides that this might be the best offer she will have all day, and she has only been in front of the store for about 10 minutes.

She proceeds to lie and says that they will not sell me wine because I don't have my ID with me.

He laughs and says, "Why not buy something a little stronger?" that he too could use a little drink.

So, she parks my car in the nearby shopping center and proceeds to get into his car. As she slides into the nice leather seats, he gives her the bottle of bourbon right away.

My kind of drink, she thinks.

He asks if she does drugs.

She tells him, "Yes."

He asks if she would like some. The little girl and addict both think that they have hit jackpot! I can hear the screams from the others.

"Stop, little girl. Don't do this! This is trouble," the little boy screams, and I can sense this *is* real trouble!

The little girl won't hear of it. She wants sex and she is sure this is what this guy wants too. He makes her feel special. The addict is happy to come along for the ride to feed his habit. The little girl knows exactly where to take him to get some pot, which is all he is willing to buy.

"Nothing strong," he says. "I don't like kids taking strong stuff. I am a father, you know," he says with a sly smile.

There is something creepy about him, but the little girl wants to play with him, then let him down easy, not go all the way.

***

We start to ride around and drink. We talk a little but mostly it is quiet, just like I want it to be. We then start heading towards the parkway. He starts to drive out of town, which makes everyone a little uneasy. He says it is time for a little fun. I don't know what fun he has in mind. So, I pull out the weed and start smoking. He drives into the mountains where there is lots of snow and ice. He stops the car, and they start drinking and the addict is smoking pot. The little girl feels a hand on her knee.

That is okay, she thinks. *He is giving me attention.*

He takes a big drink and proceeds to tell me that he is going to get his money's worth for buying the bourbon. Being very high and almost drunk, I really don't care.

Do to me what you want, I think. *I got what I want for the day. Something to drink and to ride.*

But what happens next, no one sees coming. He slaps her across the face. This gets everyone's attention. There is nowhere to run. We are on the side of a mountain. He tells her to get her fat ass in the back seat and take her clothes off or else he will kill her.

What I don't know is how brutal he is going to be. Tearing at my clothes, he tells me that I am his bitch, his Black slave, starts biting my nipples hard, and putting his hand over my mouth to muffle the screams. It is then that they come out again. Just like they did when I was at the creek with "him." They are back to take the pain.

This is a white version of "him," thinks the little girl.

She begins to get scared and wants the others to help her. Nothing anyone can do now. The little girl freezes. I watch from the outside, not able to do anything at all. I watch as my body and someone else's spirit are going to be killed. I look and Superman is nowhere around. He has not been around for a very long time. The church boy starts praying. He asks God to protect us all.

He tells the little girl to get over in the back seat, "right now or else." He starts pulling her clothes off. He tells her to take off the panties and get on her stomach. She feels him grab her breasts and pull them hard. He stops her before she can get over the back seat and bites her nipple so hard that she lets out a scream. Was it the little girl screaming? Or was it the others? Or me? I can see the fear on her face. She knows there is no turning back. This is going to be just like "him" when they made "him" mad, when the little girl first came out and protected me. She is going to be hurt like this again. Could she take this pain again? Her face is full of terror: she knows there is no turning back.

As he grabs her and throws her into the back seat, he smacks her on the back and tells her that she is going to be a good, Black bitch and do as she is told. Just as the smack happens, the little girl disappears.

"I will take this," a strange voice says. "You do not have to take this on. I am strong and I can take it."

The street thug lays on his stomach and takes the thrusting, the in and out, from this animal. The thug never cries, just digs into the nice leather seats and takes the beating and the raping. It seems like hours, but it is only minutes. Then it is over.

***

When it is over, I have bruises and bites all over my body. He has brutally raped me from every end. I am bleeding and sore. But I still feel like this is what is coming to me, what I deserve.

He says that if I tell anybody what has happened, no one will believe me. I am skipping school. I got into his car. And I am drunk. What he doesn't realize is that I could have killed him long ago. I had a gun in my bag all the time. But the bullet is not for him or anybody else for that matter. The bullet is for me.

All the time he is talking, I just zone out. I am thinking about getting back to my car and killing myself. Now, I am drunk, hurt, and confused. Again, here is someone who took my body and did what they wanted to it and never once asked if this is what I want. When it is over, I feel like this is what I deserve.

"Get out, you Black bitch, and get home the best way you can."

The thug gets out with pride, looks at him with a stare that even that animal knows is scary. The thug takes on the pain for all of us that day. The thug becomes what we all want to be, strong, in your face, and angry.

The thug pulls on our clothes and gets out of the car. The car speeds away. The thug vows that he will find that bastard one day and, when he does, he will kill him with his bare hands. No one deserves what has happened.

The thug takes ice from the ground and places it between our legs and butt. It hurts and stings, the touch and the feel of the ice. He cleans himself up as best he can. There are scratches on our back, bite marks on our chest. But he cleans us up with pride. He looks at us all and tells us that, from here on out, he is going to take care of us.

We start down the mountain in the cold. The little girl is shamed, and the spirits in the neighborhood tell her it is her fault that they are in pain. The thug knows that he is going down the mountain with pride. He knows one thing and one thing only, that if he had gotten to his backpack, "Doug" would have been dead. He knows that guy's first name and nothing else. But, one day, the thug knows that he will encounter Doug again, and he will take care of him, once and for all.

We get down the mountain and, just as we thought the thug is going to be in control, we are introduced to another spirit. He wants us all to die. He talks about the gun in the backpack that has one bullet in it and how he can convince the hotel clerk to give us a room and then, he can just kill us off. He says we are a disgrace and what about this man? He can come after us anytime. If we are dead, he will be just another one to think about how badly he has treated us all. We are worthless, the spirits keep saying. In school, but not really learning. Not really a good athlete, because we are fat. No boyfriend. No girlfriend. Just no life. Let's die!

Somehow, we all are pretty beaten down and agree with the spirit that wants us to die, agree that we need to get a hotel room and let this new person take over. The thug is hurting, you can tell. In just one day, the spirits in the neighborhood are introduced to two new spirits, one who took on our pain and one who wants to take it all away. Which spirit will win is the important question.

I am now more convinced than ever that the best thing for me is to just die. This sex stuff is scaring me. People are not loving me: they are just using me. I think about calling "her." But what for? I have confided in "her" before and look what happened. I have no one to tell this to. It is best that I just kill myself. I take the bottle he has given me. I know that with the $50 he has given me, I might be able to get a room at a hotel and kill myself there.

I am thinking that I love my car too much to do it in my car. Deep down, I love my parents too much to do it in my room. I think the best thing would be a place where I can be all alone, and then, I will be able to do it.

No one will believe that I have just been raped. I had it coming, like he said. I got into the car with him. I was drinking with him. And I am underage. I skipped school. It is all my fault. So, once again, I take the blame, just like I did with "him," like I did with my brother's friend, and like I did with "her."

I always wanted the first time to be with someone who I could say that I loved. Then, we would live happily ever after. But it is not like that for me. I will never experience what it is like to date, what it is like to fall in love. I will struggle with that for the rest of my life.

I spotted a hotel when we were leaving for that horrible mountain drive. I will go there. No one will know. It will take a few days for them to find me. I can take my time and figure out just how I am going to do it. I have about 10 bullets. Only one will do.

I know, deep down, that this is for the best. I will not have to worry about "her" and "her" demands on me. I will not have to explain to the world why I want to be a boy. The laughter will stop. People will finally take me seriously for once. This will be the final statement. No letters, no explanations and, most importantly, the voices will stop. I have had all that I can take of people staring. What I haven't realized is that as I continue to get fatter, the stares will turn into people laughing and people shaking their heads like I am some sort of alien from another planet.

***

I cannot see myself in college, have never prepared for it. I cannot think. All I can do is drink and drug. I can't remember things and am too afraid to tell anyone about the creek, "her," or my fears. All I can do is just keep stuffing it inside and move through life. That day is the final straw. When he was raping me, I knew this would be the last time anyone would do what they wanted to me.

More than anything, I want to remember what it is like to be a child. Was I happy? Did I ever truly have fun? I can remember all the bad parts but there have to have been some good days. I am always the outcast in my family, living in the shadows of my popular brother. I am forever trying to fit in. Fast cars, drinking, and drugging, I think those are the elements I need to finally be accepted by other people. I have friends who I think want to be with me because they just want to be with me. But I find out later, it is the access to drugs and booze that keep them around. As soon as we graduate, I will never hear from them again. Amazing that, during my senior year, I am voted most unforgettable. Is that because of the weight? Is it because of my ability to get drugs? I wonder if that is sincere.

So, here I am, headed back up the mountain to get a room to check myself out. I am not feeling scared. In fact, I am not feeling anything. I want to know what it is like playing under the Mimosa tree at my house. What it is like to crawl into the cellar and play in the dirt. What it is like hiding in the old garage with my Collie dog named Mike. I loved him, I think. I only remember what he looked like through pictures but not much else. I don't remember the feeling of being with an animal. So much loss.

***

Somehow, we manage to get a room. I am not sure how they can rent a room to someone who is drunk and covered with mud, but they do. The spirit takes over immediately, getting out the gun and loading only one bullet into it. We all know this is the closest we have ever come to wanting to die. I know we all want relief from the pain. The thug is shut down or perhaps this is his normal behavior, although, somehow, I doubt it. Also, we don't know him very well. All the others are just crying. Church boy continues to pray that God will do for us what we cannot do for ourselves. He is praying for guidance. I look for Superman, but he is not around.

The spirit takes the gun and puts it close to the back of our head. I can still hear crying. I still have not mastered riding the bike. I still have never been in love. I still have not made love to someone. I still have not started to live life. But now, it is going to be over. Maybe it was never meant to be. Maybe this is all that life has to offer me. I want to know more about life, but too much has taken over—drugs, alcohol, rapes, and torture—nothing good is coming out of this life. I am not one to believe in life after life, never really gave it much thought. But somehow, I want to believe it will be better than what I have now. I can only wait and see.

The spirit pulls the trigger with no reservations at all. I can still hear the humming of the bullet. I feel no pain, I only hear screams, and then all goes black.

***

From a distance, I hear sounds and see some lights. Where am I? It takes many minutes for me to realize that we are not dead. The little girl says that, at the last minute, church boy pushed the gun behind our head. The spirit says that he was not really going to kill us anyway. Church boy says that God is doing for us what we couldn't do for ourselves, that he wants us to live.

Bits and pieces are all I remember about that night in the hotel. I remember locking the door. I remember hearing the bullet. I remember thinking I am dead. From the report, I understand that I fired the pistol, but the bullet slipped past my head and struck the wall. Whatever happened, the bottom line is that I am alive. I still have a chance in life to master riding that bike.

Police and lots of people fill the room. We are taken away to a hospital for teens. There, we let the thug take over. Tough, not caring, and just shut down, we finally get a good night's sleep. All the spirits need rest. I need rest. The next day, we are told that we have a gender problem, that we need help finding our true identity.

"What a crock of you know what," says the little girl. "Don't they know that they are dealing with more than one spirit, and that's okay with us?"

We all explain to the little girl that we cannot tell anyone about the neighborhood. They will put us away for sure. They see different sides of us each day. Thug one day, little boy the next, and so on. We lay awake and hear them talking in what is called "report." We hear the words "schizophrenic," "borderline," "manic," lots of terms we do not know. The thug says it is all bullshit. We are just protecting ourselves. He says to just play the game, and we will get out soon and life will be back to normal, as normal as we can have it.

I quickly realize that it is important to ask for help. I have to, or I will possibly be headed to juvenile hall until I am 18. Having a gun, getting a hotel room, lying about my age, drunk, and having drugs on me. Funny thing they never once consider jail. I think those policemen can see how very much I need to get some professional help. I am sent to an adolescent center for mental disorders to see what is wrong with me. I am almost 18 years old, and this will be the start of my professional career for many years. I live in and out of these facilities for the next 15 years.

I know that I don't think like everyone else, or so I think. I don't think anyone else hears those people talking inside my head. I am afraid to tell them about that because they will think I really am crazy. During the physical exam, they find all the bites and bruises from the day before with that guy on the mountain. The doctor never once asks about them, and I never tell. Again, it is like some dirty, dark secret that I have to carry with me. I never speak of him doing those things to me. It will take years before I am able to speak to anyone about what happened. I am also keeping quiet about "her" and my involvement with an older woman. Again, I know it will be looked down upon, and I need to keep quiet about that too. I am a master at keeping secrets. Never once do I realize that talking about my experiences might help me. What I discover at the hospital is that they don't really talk to me a lot. I just fade into the woodwork. When asked how I am doing I respond. Even when I want to talk, I don't. A couple of times when I do try to talk, I am told to just go to my room, and someone will be there shortly. Shortly never came. What I come to realize is that I am just there because my parents have great insurance. When it is used up, they send me on my way.

Someone asks me to draw pictures of what I look like. He asks that I draw a picture of what a man looks like and what a woman looks like. He asks a few questions that don't make any sense to me. But I answer them the way I think he wants them answered. He asks if I get sexually aroused by men and I say, "No." He asks the same question about women and, again, I say, "No." I am not going to let anyone know about "her" or about my feelings toward the same sex. Deep down, I feel like I am not having feelings for the same sex. Anyway, I always feel that I am different than other women sexually. We finish up the meeting with me cutting out pictures and pasting them on paper. This is supposed to be some form of expression as to who I see myself to be. What I don't realize after I am finished is that all my pictures on the paper are men doing sports. That is how I see myself, as a man.

The whole time I am in the hospital, I feel like I am never being truthful about things, until that moment. I do this without thinking and when it is finished, I want to throw it away. He doesn't let me do that. He thanks me and takes me back to the ward. There is something that doesn't feel right about this, and I know that I am going to be in trouble for doing this.

***

A few days later, the same man meets with my mother and my doctor. My doctor is a very strange man who never talks to me. But he has a lot to say in the meeting. When it comes time to talk more in depth about me, they ask me to step out of the room. I can still hear the conversation and am very curious as to what they are saying. The man who gave me the test says that I am confused about my gender. That it is a mental disorder, but they have ways of treating it. What he tells my mother is that I think that I am a boy, that it is a very bad disease that I have, but, again, it can be fixed. He says a series of treatments will help, along with some medication. The secret is out.

Being a family that lives off its secrets, this does not go well with my mother at all. She wants to take me home, but they tell her that they will just get a court order because I am suicidal. I was when I came in, but that was a couple of weeks ago. No one has asked me anything about how I am feeling for a while. How can they know now?

***

Again, I feel like I am out in the world alone and cannot really talk about my true feelings. I am learning that the one thing I need to do is just keep quiet. It seems like I am only heard when I am angry, threatening to hurt myself, or drunk. It is those three things that I take with me for many years to come. It is the only way I know how to get people to listen to me.

One day, out of the blue, they tell me that I am going to a place where they will do some treatments to help me no longer be depressed. I am a little confused because I am not even sure what depression is, but I guess I have it. I remember feeling down when I was in a car accident earlier, during the school year. I had been given pain meds and am spending a lot of time alone at home, out of school, due to the accident. I would sit in the rocking chair and just look out of the window. I am not sure, now, if that was depression or the pain meds making me into a zombie. I remember taking a lot of them and even learning how to complain to my doctor to get more. I had a few broken ribs and a leg injury from the accident. My pain was not extreme, but I liked the way the meds made me feel. It was almost like when I was 12, and my little friend in Spanish class introduced me to Valium.

I don't know what these treatments are going to be, but they affect me for the rest of my life. They eliminate many of the memories of my childhood. I don't remember what it is like to feel happiness as a child. I don't remember playing games. I do remember being the outcast with my cousins, the one they laugh at all the time. I remember going down to the creek with "him." What I don't remember is the pain. I don't remember the feel of "his" touch. The treatments take all of that away. Sometimes, I wish I had those days back. That I didn't have the treatments. Maybe, it would have been better to feel the pain. This is something I learned to do for many years. I teach myself that when things start to feel bad, or if I have some emotion come up, I can just eat, drink, or do drugs. Since that is most of my existence, it is not surprising that I became addicted to drugs, food, and booze.

As I look back today, I really wonder what would I have been like without all the pain? Would I be in a successful relationship? Would I not have to rely on the 12 steps to keep me alive? I have often wondered if I would have had a successful long-term career. Too late to focus on that wondering now. The treatments happened and it is what it is.

***

The treatments don't hurt. They just make me really tired. Most of the time, after I have them, the staff leave me alone. I just stay in the bed. It isn't like I am a zombie or anything. I am just tired. I lie in bed and try to remember things that hurt, to remember playing as a kid, remember their laughter at me. I can pull up bits and pieces, but to say I know what it feels like? I can't recall.

As the weeks of my stay turn into months, I stop the treatments. I just say whatever they want to hear. It is almost time to graduate, and I wonder if I am going to be able to get my diploma this year or not. Like everyone else in my life, they just want me to be pretty much nonexistent. I don't think the school system wants to deal with me any longer. What I don't know is that, during one of my black out states from taking too many drugs and drinking, I brought a rifle to school, telling the other students that I was going to use it on myself. They tell the school officials. But before they can get to me, I leave the grounds. Calls to my family and, of course, they take it all in stride. Denial is a big gift in my family, and we use that gift well.

So, it is never talked about. Someone takes the rifle but never asks why I have it or what I am planning to do with it. That all occurred right before I went into the hospital. I remember being angry with the man who took me to the mountain. I remember being angry with "him" for doing what he did to me, angry at "her" for not being my friend but wanting to be a lover. I think the gun was for all of them—not to kill them, but to kill myself because of them.

I remember the feeling I had when I heard that "he" had been killed, stabbed by a stranger who he made advances toward. His desires had not stopped. He was still trying to take advantage of young souls. This time, it backfired, and he was the victim. My guess is that he left far too many victims during his lifetime and that is why it finally stopped in such a brutal manner.

I remember standing at the funeral as family members were upset, thinking that I had no feelings at all. Death should scare me, but I do not feel fear, don't feel sorrow. I finally realize that "he" had been stopped. "He" can no longer take away the innocence of youngsters or others again. Somehow, I think that, on that day, my life will be free. I will no longer be hounded by those demons. But as I get older, I discover how wrong I am about that. It is like I tucked it away. The same way I tucked away my feelings of not being in the right body. I am convinced that I will die early and that I will take all these secrets to the grave. But I am not hiding anything from anyone but myself. At the end of the day, it doesn't matter if I tell my secrets to anyone. I have to admit them to myself first. The more I want to forget the secrets, the more I drink and drug. Amazingly, it takes almost 20 more years for me to start the journey of healing by putting down the drink and the drugs.

I think back to that child walking down the road to the creek. Every time, I would be so happy because I believed "him" when "he" said we were just going to fish. How stupid I was each time being happy to be spending the day with someone who would let me do boy things. Most of the time, fishing never happened. Ironically, the creek was the same place the church used to bring people to be baptized, washing away their sins. The creek had an entirely different meaning for me. It was there that I began to feel that I was the sinner. I always thought it was my fault. If I had spoken out more about this, if I had really had tantrums that I didn't want to be left alone with "him," would it have mattered? Somehow, I think no one would have listened because I was not explaining. I was not speaking up. But how much could a 4 or 5-year-old say? Most of the time, people did not understand what I was saying anyway because of my speech impairment. Just another thing to add to my list of being different.

Chapter 6

Labels

God don't make no junk.
Alcoholics Anonymous

I think that it will be easy to just walk away from "her." I think "she" will understand that I just need to find myself for a little while. I don't have a clue as to who I am, what I am, or what I want to become. I always have some sort of label on me.

I am a "mental case," a "drunk," a "druggie," a "dyke." I even accept the label "bulldagger," which I hear behind my back. I am always called something. In my younger years, it was "stupid." All through school, I thought that I was, believed that I could not learn like everyone else. I have this fear that I need to be in the special classes. My friends tease me that I can't hear out of one ear. They don't know why. Eventually, I sort of figure it out, that it is because "he" hit me really hard one day when I would not spread my legs. The sound in my ear just rang out. From then on, I am never able to hear things the same. I never tell anyone because I think it is just for the best. My circle of protectors know, and that is all that is important.

When it comes time to tell "her" that I want out of this very sick and destructive relationship, I think I am doing this for all the right reasons. There is no one else. I don't want to be with anyone but me. I want to go back home and stay in my bedroom. I just want to escape. I want to try going back to school, maybe even find some sort of career. It is time to be like other people, to work rather than work the system. I am truly not a mental case. I just need to stop the drinking and drugging and see what is beneath the surface once I sober up. Something deep inside of me is telling me that it is going to be difficult to leave "her." It is going to be a lot of drama and fighting. That "she" is someone who, if "she" doesn't think of it first, it shouldn't happen.

I try everything I can think of to push "her" away. I try for a few days not to take any drugs or drink. What I find is that I am truly addicted to this stuff. My body needs it to function. Apparently, stopping cold turkey is not the answer. I am struggling to sleep, struggling to think straight. Just another label to add to the list—a drunk *and* a junkie now. I think, deep down, that this is exactly what "she" wants. "She" wants me addicted to everything, including "her." But there is something about the connection with "her" that is not the same as before. Somehow, I feel that we are not going to survive. That we are headed toward death. I fear that someone is going to overdose. I am also convinced that "she" really doesn't have the will to live anymore. The funny thing about this is that the one who keeps going in and out of mental units saying they wanted to die is me. But, when it comes right down to it, I don't want to die at all. I want to see what this world has to offer. I want to live a good life. I have dreams of losing weight, getting healthy, and living life, of having a life that I want, not a life that someone else is telling me I need to have. I almost had that life, if only I had gone away to college. But I listened to all the outside sources telling me life would be much better just doing what I am doing now.

I never really know what fear is until I decide to walk away from "her." Something in my gut is telling me that fear is going to win this battle, that I will not be able to speak up for what I want, that I will not make it to live that dream of losing weight, getting sober, and having a simple career. Fear will win because I am not bigger than the fears. I have no faith in anything but drugs, drinking, and "her."

***

My thoughts go back to when I was 17 and was told that I was confused about what sex I was, that I had a mental illness, and that they had a treatment for that. Shock treatments. I guess they wanted to erase all the bad behavior from my life. After a couple of treatments, they are stopped. Am I cured? Doesn't seem to do anything but make me realize that those people are not to be trusted, that I have to be careful what I say. Everyone, who says they are there to help me, are just out to hurt me. I cannot trust anyone.

Life just continues with a series of admissions, in and out of the one place that I know I cannot trust. But it is the only place I know to run. Whenever I don't want to deal with life, I just check myself in. Whenever I am too afraid to deal with life, I simply run to the mental unit. Whenever I don't have anything else to do, I just run there.

This time, I decide that I will not run there. I have to tell "her" that I cannot stay in this relationship. It is killing my soul. It is taking away the last piece of love I have for myself. I am eating more and more each day and getting bigger. It is beginning to affect my thinking. I don't want to go anywhere. I don't care how I look. Most of my clothes are soiled with food and holes from smoking pot. I just don't care what people think of me, or so I tell myself. I hear people in public places laughing and staring. I retreat, but even the stares and laughter don't stop me from eating. I am topping 300 pounds at that point. My body is beginning to tell me that it cannot carry this weight. It is years before I surrender to that as well. Amazing how I just continue to beat and destroy my body. I just have not hit my bottom with anything, not even "her." I am not even thirty years old.

Every day is the day that I will leave "her" and not have "her" in my life. I know, deep down, that we can't have a lasting connection. I have to make a clean break with "her," at least for a while. I know that "she" is not someone I can see occasionally. She is a drug on which I have overdosed way too often. "She" held me like a hostage, like a slave. "She" is my master, along with food, drugs, and alcohol. The sad part is that "she" knows this. So, I question all the time if this is love or just another person in my life punishing me with what they called love.

Just like "him," "she" is a predator. "She" is an abuser. But I am no longer a child, unable to take care of myself. Still, I feel like that child on the creek bank, the child who needed the aid of others to protect me. As I get older, I realize that they are not real: rather, they are there to protect me. But what has happened to them? Why don't they come out again to protect me from "her"? Why don't they step up and help me now? I am in a struggle just like I was before. I am lost, and I want so badly to be found. I want someone to come along and save me, someone to tell me that it is going to be okay. But I have no one. There is no one in my life that I can tell about this. "She" made sure I have no close friends. Also, I learned, from an early age, that I don't need anyone, to never trust anyone. I learned that lesson very well. So, by trial and error, I discover that even if they say they love me, it is not true. It is always them trying to get something from me. But what do I have to give?

Book II

Visiting the Dark Side
(Writings to Myself: A Therapeutic Diary)

You can't think your way into a new way of living.
You have to live your way into a new way of thinking.
Alcoholics Anonymous

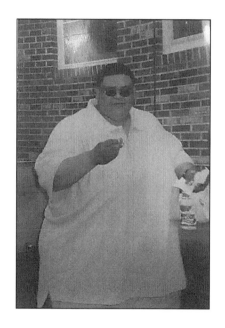

Chapter 7

Humpty Dumpty

Sobriety is a journey…not a destination.
Alcoholics Anonymous

If someone is reading this, I could very well be dead by now. This world is just too much for me. I don't think I belong on this planet. I keep wondering, what is happiness? What is peace? When do I have these things, and can they be sustained for any length of time? Sometimes, there are glimmers of rays of hope. Hope, something I should have faith will come. Hope and faith that God is with me at all times. Am I with God?

So many questions. Am I supposed to be gay? Am I supposed to be in any kind of relationship? Maybe my life is supposed to be solo, alone. My soul is supposed to be dark, soggy, no ray of hope. These are the things that riddle the thoughts in my mind. How can I move on when there is no hope?

It's all about Humpty Dumpty. Did they put him back together again? Why was Humpty just hanging on the wall? Why did it take Humpty falling apart before anyone heard him and tried to put him back together again?

***

I feel that my life has been over some time ago. Today, I just move through the motions because I don't have the push to kill myself. It would just be so simple if I could just die. Nothing is simple and if I want out of this planet, I need to take action. If I really look at it, my soul died a long time ago. Rage took over. Now, the rage is gone, and I am not sure what is left.

I am so tired, so drained. Where is my energy? It's Sunday night and I am so depressed about having to get up and motivate myself for nine hours on this job. I don't ever recall feeling so unmotivated about work. It would be so simple, so easy, if I could just die. What would happen if I got the death ticket? Would I fight to live? Or would this be my out?

I watch a fellow AA member know, or so he has been told, that he has six months to live. By summer, he could very well no longer be here.

He deals with this with grace. I have never heard him speak about being angry. He keeps going to a lot of meetings. He has not given up. Could I do this? Would I even want to? Shit, I just want to stay in the bed. No food, no water. Just the bed. How long would I live if I just went to bed and never got out of it? That is such a dream. Maybe next day, next time I write in this journal, I will make it more positive. Would I be living a lie trying to be positive when my soul, my mind, my being wants to be just dark. I want to live in the dark. I want this lonely, dark life, or do I?

Why do I go to Jen every week? Why do I take meds? Why do I keep trying? I have to want some sort of light. In some way, I want to see a better life. I would not be doing this if I did not have some level of hope.

Am I uncomfortable feeling good? Will I feel good? What does being happy and feeling free and peaceful feel like? Thought I had it with Constance in my life. Thought I had it when I first got sober. Those first two years, when it was not about the drink anymore, when I was living life not for anyone but me. There was still that hole. It's like a raw flesh eaten hole. It's red, raw, and so deep that all you see is flesh. It's dark. It stinks. It's the raw eaten flesh of a hole. That is what I feel like most days. There are moments when this wave of raw eaten flesh mood feels like it is going to eat me alive. Other days, it's just there. I always know it's there.

***

It's almost Christmas. Will I make it through these holidays? This would be the perfect time to kill myself. Blame it on holiday depression.

I am so tired of traveling alone, coming home alone, being alone. Why can't I tell Jen or anyone about this feeling? I need to appear strong or so I think. God, I pray I can make it through Christmas. I know how it will be. Go with the family and, then, home by myself. No gifts, no present to open. No Christmas cheer.

Might be easy to just fucking drink. I could find some people to be around. What difference does it make if I take a drink now? Who would know? I could not lose any more than what I have already lost. Girl gone. Soul gone. Respect for myself gone. Love for myself gone. What do I have left?

I really need to step away from these feelings. Why are they so strong? Why do I write this shit down? Who is going to read it?

Am I physically sick? Is this emotional sickness? This huge destruction to my heart and soul? I am so tired, so drained. Not sure how much longer I am going to make it. Getting up every day and attempting this normal life shit.

***

Sort of funny. I am at work and the only comfort I get sometimes is saying over and over "Soon, I will be dead." What a relief I get from knowing that it could very well be true. How simple it could be if I could just lay down and go. Not having to take any effort to do anything about this. I might not even have the energy to kill myself. Fucking Humpty Dumpty.

***

What is the reason behind me not staying happy for any length of time? Why do I go to that dark place so quickly? Am I going too far with no reason? I really wish I could answer these questions. Why do I keep this journal? I think just in case I live. I want to be able to really see how dark I can get and that there is hope. Maybe I am writing this so that people will understand that I am just not giving up. I am just going on to another level.

My favourite children's book is the *Little Prince*. What a beautiful soul that child was. He just didn't belong on this earth. He was different. I feel that I am different. I just don't want this. If I really look at this, I just try because I am curious about what life can bring. The truth is that I go to work, come home to dark, quiet, alone. I don't want to try to start new friendships. I have slowly cut people away so that I am just with me.

I believe in what Jen has shown me thus far. She is slowly showing me that I am someone of value. I am worth loving, worth living, worth being loved. I get it. But I go to that place when I am alone. I hate the quiet times. The voices in my head just won't stop. The truth is that I miss Constance a lot. I miss our conversations. I miss her being here in the house. I miss our quiet times together. Those were the good things. I miss the butch and femme dynamic that the two of us had.

I really never had that with anyone before Constance and I really feel I will never have that again. I miss being with my, or our, Black friends and the understanding of our culture.

Will I have to move to get what I need or want? I can truly believe moving would not be healthy for me, unless I really am more stable with my emotions. Why am I so fucking hard on me?

***

It's been a while since I have written in this book. I told Jen a little about being in a bad space. It was important for me to tell her. I felt like I had been keeping a huge secret from her. Truthfully, she needed to know, and she was still understanding about this.

I am so scared of my in-the-dark-of-the-night emotions. When it's 3 AM in the morning and there's no Jen, no AA, nothing but me and God, and me and those dark thoughts. This fucking scares me.

Last night, I put on that damn music. It's dark, about death. Sometimes, it's not the music. Last night, I needed the music to help me get dark. I was craving the darkness like I crave the drink. How fucking sick it that? I crave death the way I crave drinking.

Last night, it woke me up. Telling me to just die. Don't have a plan. Don't have a gun. Got a bunch of pills but that won't work. It has to be hard, quick, devastating. Nothing with the risk of my stomach being pumped. That's fake ass. I don't want to die. Shit. Been there. I am not interested in the white coats. I will not do that. That is why it's important that if I am going down, it be quick.

I am tired. It's time to stop writing this stuff. Maybe I just need to try and write brighter stuff the next time I write.

***

Things I want to do before I die:

1) Fall in love,
2) Have a home of my own,
3) Lose weight to 225,
4) Play golf,
5) Play volleyball again,
6) Hot air balloon,
7) Own my own company,
8) Be fit enough to work out every day,
9) Help someone every day,
10) Truly love myself.

***

You know what? Fuck that bucket list. It's just a dream. False hope. This is the best it's going to be. Dead-end job. No life. No friends. No desire to have them. My family keeps telling me that I don't need a relationship, that I always did better alone. They don't know what goes on in my head. Hell, I am not sure anyone really knows what goes on in my head. I am not sure I do. I really just want to die. Can anyone understand that?

***

Keith Urban has a song about "Tonight I Wanna Cry." Don't know why I know that song. Country music really is not my thing, but I relate to that song. At night, most of the time, I just want to go to the bedroom, get in the bed, and just cry. It takes all of the energy I can muster to go to work. By 6, I can't make it anymore. When I go to the gym, it destroys me. It's those nights that I have the darkness more than other nights.

Tonight, I just wanna cry.

I am so thankful to God that I have not taken a drink or used drugs behind these feelings. Spite has a lot to do with it. If and when I die, they will not say it's because of my drinking and drug use, or let me give the proper respect. It's God who is keeping me sober and clean.

***

It is 3 AM on Sunday. I have made it through New Year's. I made it through the holidays. I really truly did not think I would. So much for what the mind will allow me to think, huh?

I really need to talk to Jen about this shit. Everything does not have to be pink clouds. But when will I get better? Will I always have these deep dark moments? Is there something I can do to stop these thoughts? I think I can use what I am learning with Jen. I don't have to give these thoughts so much power. But that is easier said than done. I can think about how positive I need to think, how I need to act my way into feeling instead of feeling my way into feeling. But there are days when I say that is total bullshit. When my dark feelings come on, there's really no stopping them. They have to happen. Maybe it's just a part of who I am. Who knows? I can't say.

I used to think I might have all those different personalities and this dark side was one. Could that be true? Well, bullshit! I am addicted to death, addicted to dark, addicted to sadness. I remember Constance told me once that my soul was miserable. Is that true?

I am getting tired. It's 5 AM. I have to work in the morning, or do I? Why not just take all the pills and maybe I will just go to sleep and not wake up? There has to be a way to do this. If I hit the streets for a gun, I might get addicted to the power in the street, and then, all bets are off, and I am drunk, drugging. Can't risk it. Not that my program is weak. I will not go out not sober.

***

The truth is I miss Constance a lot. I miss all the good. We really were good friends. I am not sure I can or will be able to allow myself to get to a level with someone like I did with Constance. She knew. She just knew. What's the use? She is living a life with someone, and I am here alone every night in this house. Alone with these thoughts. Alone with a broken heart. Alone with this dark soul.

I remember when I used to get really suicidal. When I was going to do something to uncork the pain, I would write, smoke pot, drink, and write. Write for hours about darkness, sadness, and no hope. Have things changed? Yes, it has on the drinking and smoking end. I write today not under the influence. I write today with raw feelings. The biggest question I have is will I kill myself? I can't see myself living another year like this. As much as I work with Jen, it's nights like this that all the work becomes meaningless.

I can't even imagine life on this earth for another year. Crappy-ass job, money always tight. God, I ask you every day when do I get my break? I know, through the program, that I am only to pray for God's will. What is God's will for me? I know that my program of recovery is trust God, clean house, and help others. How can I help others when there are moments in my life when I can't help myself?

How do I love again? How do I totally love myself? Is this my life? Working a crappy-ass, 12 buck an hour job, going home, and waiting. Waiting for darkness. Waiting for the loneliness to come and engulf me, like gas to fire.

I believe in what Jen has done for me. It has actually kept me alive. It has kept me from flipping out. Keeping me from just saying fuck it, going home, giving up, and just losing everything. House, job, everything.

Something keeps me going. Something gives me hope at that moment. Why can't I carry that feeling of hope with me all the time? Why can't I keep that push a little longer than a day? A flash of the moment?

***

I don't blame my childhood shit on my life today as much anymore. What happened back then just fucking happened. I am so tired, just so fucking tired. I battle my mind all the time. Do I need different medicine? Do I just need to fucking give up? I just want to close off and leave people alone. No Darlene, Day, or Janice. I don't have the energy to shuck and jive with these women. I am just tired. Is the sex because of childhood shit? I really am afraid to find out. What if it is too much for me to handle? My life is just so fucking pathetic. I am so disappointed that at 50 years old, I make 12 bucks an hour at a job I hate. I am out of shape, fucked up, and nothing of any hope on the horizon. God gave me love and took it away. Is it because I am gay, and I am not supposed to be? Is this punishment? Everyone has someone but me. My life is really no different than my brother's. Alone in a bedroom, low pay, life fucked up. The only thing I have managed to do is stop drinking. Should I start back? Could I? Would I be okay with the drinking now? I am really feeling like an outcast with the people in AA. I have truly managed to stay away from them. I am different than them. God, please help me.

***

I know that I still don't know how to pray correctly. I know that if my prayer life was a little more solid, maybe life would be less miserable. So, why don't I do the next right thing? I don't want to. In some sick way, I think that if I don't pray, I can die. How crazy it that thinking? Why do I wake up in the night and think this stuff? Why can't I have more thoughts of hope?

I get so afraid of someone loving me again. I don't want it. I want to be alone. I don't want to be alone. I love life. I don't love life. What is this? Is it normal? I don't think so. God, please help me.

***

If I die, I really don't think it would sting that much. If people realized how my heart is broken, my soul is damaged, and my spirit is just dead, they would say this is the best thing that could ever happen. It's not giving up. It would be moving on.

I need to move on with my life. I need help to die. It's like I am struggling on life support. Therapy is the machine. I need to have people see that my heart is broken. The only thing that is keeping me alive is that machine.

***

So, the secret's out. Jen finally got all the dark secrets out. I have wanted to tell her. Pull out these secrets, these skeletons in my closet, and lay them out. I've kept these for so long. The depression, the missing Constance, my gender. Oh, yeah, the gender, probably the biggest of all. I live in a body that functions in two worlds. Most of the time, I am not ever sure which world I am supposed to be in. It's like going to AA day after day, seeing no black faces. I feel so different. It's like I have released a little part of my maleness to take over my outer body. All my life, I have hated my body, my voice, my look. Even after losing some weight, I still was not happy.

So many nights, I have wanted to take a knife and cut my breasts off. Why did I have to look like this? Why did God create me in this freakish body?

Will God punish me for wanting to have a body different than what he created? I really wish I could find someone who has or is going through this. I feel so alone with this.

***

Somehow, I knew this day would come. Jen is leaving in July. I feel numb, scared, and I have moments where I don't feel much hope for my gender issues without her help.

She says she will pick someone who will continue to help me with my issues of gender. But they won't understand like her. No matter if the dream team is still around. They might not have my back like Jen. I came to Jen broken, lost, and dark. She helped me mend, finding myself and seeing the light. Will someone else go to the lengths of walking beside me, like her?

I just have to make these last few months productive. Even more., dig deep, work harder. I have to trust Jen with who she picks to be the next therapist. She has not let me down yet. I trust her completely.

***

I am missing Constance more. Not sure what is going on. Why am I thinking about her more?

I have to stop with this underlying false hope that we will get back together again. I have to stop with this yearning for her. So many things remind me of her. I have to move on. I have to know that this too is a closed chapter in my life. Too many people stay just a short time in my life and then they are gone.

***

So, I had this dream. I was male, fit, with muscles. Light fade of a beard. Confident, living life to the fullest, loving myself, looking in the mirror and seeing this strong, confident male. I was not fat, not feeling uncertain. I was a good-looking Black male with the life of a good healthy male in my hands. Life was my choice. Not thinking those dark thoughts. Gone were those dark depressing days of wanting to be something I never thought I could be.

My name is Christian. I am a confident man. My life if filled with some close friends. No longer did I spend most of my life alone. I was someone who was helping people, reaching out, being a friend to many.

This is a dream. But I know it can be a reality. Anything is possible.

I know anything is possible. I am sober today.

I know anything is possible. I survived when "she" didn't.

Anything is possible. I survived my heart being torn apart when Constance left.

Deep down, I worry about not having Jen around. I can be a runner when in fear. Fear that I have to keep under control. I am right at a crossroads. I need to educate myself about gender issues and be able to make my move towards this life with support, even if it's not from friends and family.

***

I have been listening to Eminem's *Recovery* CD. He raps about how he is not afraid to take a stand. That has to be me. I have to take a stand with my gender. I have a right to be who I am comfortable with.

I have to be happy. This is what life is about. Living it, enjoying it. Will I have a chance at a happy life?

***

So, I am excited about what my life looks like down the road. My only sad part is that Jen will not be a total part of this as I travel down a new path. So much to think about: a name, finding where I will work, and what will my friends think. But if you really look at it, I don't have a lot of people who are a constant part of my life. Who cares what people think? That is part of my fear—what people think—if I break this down. What will my family think? I have been putting some thought into this. I am really not involved a lot in my entire family's life. So why should I freak out about what anyone, including my family, thinks?

Start with what is best for my life. For so long, I lived for what others think. Time for me to take care of me. Jen has taught me that—to take care of me. I am learning how to love me. It all comes from being in therapy. Being willing to listen to Jen and the dream team.

I really see my life moving where I have always wanted it to be. I feel spiritually fit. I feel emotionally healthy. My physical body is taking a new twist.

***

I have been reading *The Testosterone Files*.[8] I am learning slowly what will happen if I ever were to start hormone treatment. He talks about how his muscles are getting hard, facial hair. These are things that I fear thinking about. Why? What is it that makes me feel fearful, shy, about my body changing? About thinking about me being referred to as a man. Are these normal things?

I need to get a journal together where I have questions, like this. Sometimes, I have so many thoughts that I feel like I am on a manic run. Thoughts, visions of what I might look like, run through my head at fast speeds. I have to slow these down. What's the best way to do that?

***

I'm not feeling the best this week. Kidney infection, again. This shit makes me feel so damn depressed. So low, no energy, drained. I should have never called Constance today. Bad move. So, I have to tell on myself, talk to Jen about it. At least, I can see why I made the initial contact. First time I have done that. I was feeling lonely, sick, needed someone to give me some attention. It was a big move for me because

---

[8] *The Testosterone Files: My Hormonal and Social Transformation from Female to Male*, Max Wolf Valerio, Seal Press, 2006

of the risk of rejection. I never thought about the rejection factor until it was over, until after the conversation.

I need to make a contract with myself, make relationships right now that have no sexual energy involved. I need to concentrate on the issues at hand.

***

In the book I am reading, *The Testosterone Files*, Max talks about no longer having the mood swings. I had some big swings in mood today. It's Mother's Day. Why do I feel depressed? Could it be I still am not feeling well? I also need to get back to the gym.

Maybe I just need to recognize that every day is not an up day. I refuse to become a man who is not taking care of my body. I want to be a fit, healthy man. Can't believe I am beginning to think of myself as male. Something clicked last week when Jen asked if I wanted to be addressed as a male. It really scared me. I felt fear, felt like I was dancing around the question. I really didn't know how to answer. I still don't know how I feel being referred to as "he."

I have been called "Sir" on the phone. Even been called "Sir" in public. But now that I can do it with ease, I am scared. I am embarrassed that I think like this. So much guilt that I can't just live life without having to go through this. Angry that I was just not born male. Would not have to go through this.

***

I was really excited to watch Oprah today and see Chaz Bono. It was like I was hearing my story again. He got sober, and then, with a lot of therapy, he made his decision. God, did I hear my life! It was what I needed to hear. Tomorrow will be his documentary, and I will go out and get his book. I needed to see and hear his story. Today, I have been feeling so alone and scared. Most of my free time is spent alone. I need to find like-minded friends. I need to find things to do with people. I am scared that if I can follow through with the change will I be alone? Who will turn their back on me? Who will accept me? Can I accept me?

***

I need to create a game plan. Need to work on what my path is going to be. I have to accept that the path will sometimes stray off on a different course. I have to go slow, but I can't rest on my laurels with this.

I have to take a realistic look at what route I want to take and how I am going to exercise that plan. Am I being too disciplined on this? I think that I have to know what I am going to do next. I will pray on this and work on this tomorrow.

Today, I felt more male than ever. There is really nothing different except my acceptance of what I need to do with the next stage of my life. Every day, there is a new path I can take. I need to start making small decisions about my gender identity. I need to start somewhere. I know everyone is saying take it slow, that I have plenty of time, but I need to take more steps than just talking about it.

I feel like I need to take care of bigger issues with Jen still here. I trust that Jen will pick someone who is good for me. But will they take those extra steps like Jen? Jen truly has my back. She works beside me, not ahead of me.

***

Just finished watching the documentary on Chaz Bono. Again, fear came over me. My mind wandered to recovery if I had top surgery. Who would help me? The pain pills and my life being sober. I know this is crazy to think about right now. But what would it be like to be on pain pills? Could I handle it?

I can feel what it's like to have my breasts gone, to never feel like a freak having them. I realized in the last few weeks how my breasts make me feel so different. One thing that scared me about taking testosterone is the list of risks. But driving in my car is a risk. Tonight, even though I have more fear, I feel hopeful.

***

Today, I left Jen/therapy so hopeful. I just get a little sad when I think about the months to come and there will not be Jen riding shotgun. I trust what she says. I trust that Jen has my back. I simply just trust her with my life.

I was so broken coming in the door at The Family Stress Clinic, and Jen allowed me to stay broken until it was time for me to heal. In AA, they say, "Let us love you until you can love yourself." Jen did that with me. This weekend, I will create my plan of action. I need to think about names, get the foundation application filled out, think about what is next for me.

***

It's 1 AM and 100 different thoughts are going through my mind. What about acne? What about the aggression being on testosterone? Am I attracted to lesbians or straight women? How much pain goes along with top surgery? Will the next therapist offer to me what Jen has offered? So many questions. I have got to slow my mind down and get some sleep.

Tonight, I feel some loneliness. Some disconnect. Not sure what is stirring this up. It's 2 AM. I have played enough video games. My mind is slowing down, and 100 different thoughts have dwindled down to a few. I feel sleepy. Perhaps, it's time to try to go to sleep. I will pray myself to sleep. Pray that God removes me from this bondage of self and try to think about helping someone else.

***

Book III

Finding My Way in My New Life
(A Transition Blog)

Sometimes the only thing between an alcoholic and a drink is his higher power.

Alcoholics Anonymous

Chapter 8

2011

Easy Does it.
Alcoholics Anonymous

Monday, July 4, 2011
My New Journey to A New Life

I am in the process of changing my name. Amazingly, I am having a hard time changing my voicemail. What is that all about? I am so ready for this new life. So ready to move forward. Why is it so hard to change the voicemail?

It is almost like I know once I change it, I am out in the open with this. This will be one of the next steps to my new journey to a new life.

When I bought my binder, it was like it was one of the welcoming pieces I have missed for so long. Why did it take 51 years for me to get to this? It was all in God's time. God was not ready for me to move through this until now. Succeeding through the stillness. I have learned to be still. I have learned that it's okay to feel lonely.

Today, I feel really lonely, really all by myself. I will just move through it with no drama. I tried to reach out to a few people, but everyone is busy. So, I will just get productive with starting this new blog and putting down my thoughts.

Tonight, I will just read a little, pray a lot, and rest my body, mind, and spirit. I will be okay feeling a little lonely tonight.

Wednesday, July 6, 2011
Saying Goodbye

So, one more hour with Jen and we say goodbye. The last few months have been a tremendous growth experience for me. I don't know where I would be right now if I had not found Jen. We taught each other a lot. I know Jen has taught me to be secure in who I am. When I first came to Jen about my gender issues, she went right into "let's teach each other about this." She helped educate me on who I was going to be, what to expect, and where to go for help. She never stopped trying to learn as much as she could about the man I want to be. As sad as I am about Jen leaving, I am at peace with what she is leaving with me. With how she taught me to play well with others.

I don't have anger about this, just sadness that she will not be around to continue to watch my progress unfold. But I will never forget her for what she brought to my life.

Thursday, July 7, 2011
Serenity and Peace

I am feeling something this evening, just not sure what it is. I am thinking that I am just at peace in my life and serenity from time to time. I keep thinking about the 9th Step Promises. We are going to know a new freedom and a new happiness. We will not regret the past nor wish to shut the door on it. We will comprehend the word "serenity," and we will know peace. We will suddenly realize that God is doing for us what we could not do for ourselves. I love this and try to remind myself of this daily. My life is taking a new step, a new phrase of my development. I will become a different person, the person I was always supposed to be.

Saturday, July 9, 2011
A New Man

Today, I have been thinking about how I will soon become a new man. I have a little fear about what I will be like. How I will react to things in life as a new man. My mind can sometimes go so far to the left that it is scary. I have been thinking that since I am becoming a man, I will be able to drink a beer from time to time or have a drink from time to time when I get home. Then, I come back to the reality that I am an alcoholic. No changes in my body will take that away. I guess I need to crank up the meetings a little more, talk about it with this new therapist guy.

Damn, how I just don't want to start a new relationship with a therapist. Why can't Jen just stay? Well, that is all just me wanting things my way. Her leaving is not about me. That is what I have to realize and keep reminding myself about. This is not about me. It's about change and how I need to change the things I can, accept the things I cannot change, and have the wisdom to know the difference.

I cannot believe how my life has changed since accepting my gender difference, how I feel more at ease, how I am just happy with what life has to offer. It amazes me how I handle situations while, at the same time, it baffles me! Am I in some dream world? Is life just this good for me right now? I mean, I still have little money from month to month. I am in a job that is the least favorite job I have ever had. But I just keep moving through.

As a new man, I want to be a gentle soul like my Daddy. Someone who just takes life as it comes. Charley means "free man." I have to smile when I think that, say that. "Free Man." I am free.

Sunday, July 10, 2011
Fear

Last night, I got sick at my stomach. Not sure what was going on, and I had this cloud of fear surround me. What will happen when I have surgery and there is no one there in the night if I get sick? What happens if my body has a hard time with testosterone? Will someone be there to help me? This is the lonely, fearful part of my mind. I was really in my head last night when I woke up sick. The mentally sick side of me felt like a victim and wanted to feel sorry for myself. But deep down, God was doing for me what I could not do for myself. He quieted the disturbance in my head. I was able to awake this morning not feeling well but still able to take care of a few things, and then, take care of me. Sleep, eat well, rest, and pray. Those were the essential things that I needed to do. I have the tools today to make my day good or bad. I took care of me.

Tonight, I am preparing to meet with the Fan Free Clinic (FFC)[9] on Tuesday and take that next step towards becoming a man. They will talk to me about testosterone, an intake, and I am officially on my road.

How I wish Jen could be a part of this next step. I have to recognize that this is some of what is going on with my emotional self. This is going to be a tough emotional week, and I just need to accept and move on. Relationships change and end, and new ones begin.

Tuesday, July 12, 2011
Being A Black Man

So, I am watching this YouTube video on Facebook about this brother who is trans and how he is being treated now as a male, that when he is walking down the street, White people fear him. It struck me that this very thing could happen to me as I continue to transition. I mean, I sort of kind of get it now but a little different. Before I got the binder, people could not figure me out from a distance. They looked at the chest first. Now, they still look at the chest, see barely anything, and then, try to figure it out. Right now, this is what I am having a hard time living with, this see-saw gender living. At work, I am Charlotte. To family, I am Charlotte. But, to some, I am Charley. I just will be glad when I can finally step over and just be me! The African American brother I am supposed to be.

You know, this would all be so simple if I had just been born a man. As a child, I can remember dreaming of being a little Black boy. I would climb up in the tree in the front yard, armed with green army men and GI Joe. I would play for hours as the little boy I wanted to be. Amazing, how many of my childhood memories are coming back now that I have taken this step. I keep thinking about that tree and how, when it was cut down, I wondered if those green army men were still in their cave? Today, I have some of those green army men on my bookshelf. Some of them had parachutes, and I would drop them from the tree. Those hours I spent playing alone must have been the happiest moments of my childhood. I was all boy. I was just being me.

Today, I can play with those green army men like a young boy if I want to. I don't have to feel ashamed or that I am being different. I won't be laughed at by classmates at school or made to play with Barbie dolls.

---

[9] Now Health Brigade, https://www.healthbrigade.org/.

Today, if I want to play with green army men, I can be who I want to be.

Being a Black man, will I be feared? How different will it be? Am I afraid of being a Black man? Can I handle being a Black man? So many questions circle around in my head about this. What will I be like? I want to have the gentle soul of my father, his honesty, and his character. Can I live up to being the man my father was?

Tonight

A little disappointed in that the clinic called and cancelled at the last minute. Once I got over the first response of disappointment, I realized that everything cannot go my way. I have to learn to go with the flow of life. It is so amazing how, these days, I can recognize my feelings, address them, and move on. Wish I had learned this months or years ago. Things could have been so different. Or are they coming to me at the time they are supposed to come? I talked to a good friend tonight who feels like he does not need AA. I listened. I never made a statement until the end. I just shared my own experience, strength, and hope with him. My experience is that I have to go to a certain number of meetings. If I don't, I start spinning out of control. I don't overdose on meetings like some, but I have 3 or 4 that I go to every week. My strength from this is that I stay in control with a mixture of AA, the fellowship of a certain few people, and my own self-worth from helping someone else by being there. There might be someone that if I take just a minute of my time, I can give them something that they are missing or don't even have. My hope is that by going to meetings, I am helping someone else who helps me stay away from the drink and the drugs.

I have learned the hard way that I cannot put all my trust in AA, that there are other things that are going to help me have a balanced life—AA, therapy, work, my home, taking care of me, just to name a few. Tonight, I listened to my friend struggle with issues with an ex, struggle with allowing sick people in AA to rule his comings and goings. I take what I need and leave the rest. I am grateful that we are all not sick on the same day, that someone with 30 minutes of being sober and clean can help me, just like someone with 30 years. We all are the same, just a daily reprieve.

Wednesday, July 13, 2011
Tomorrow

So, tomorrow is the last session with Jen. I am having some mixed feelings about all of this. A little anger that she is moving and feeling like she is leaving me. Some sadness that she won't be a part of the next part of my journey. Jen has been riding shotgun with me for a while now. So, now it's time for her to jump out of the car, and I am allowing someone new to ride in the car with me. How will the ride be from here on out?

Jen saved my life when I did not even know where I needed to start to begin to live a good life. I didn't have a clue as to what life was supposed to be like. So, tonight, I am going to pray that our last session will not be very emotional, that saying goodbye is only a start to something new.

Sunday, August 7, 2011
Making A Difference

Yesterday, I saw what it means to make a difference in someone's life. I was at a meeting, and this guy comes to me after the meeting, shakes my hand, and proceeds to say he heard my share over a month ago about changing my name. He asked if I was going to transition from female to male. I swallowed hard, not knowing what to expect from my "yes" to his question. But I did answer, and what happened next was earth shattering for me. He proceeded to tell me about his daughter who is ten, who they were taking to a specialist to help her become a boy. He spoke of his daughter/son with such love and caring, how all he wanted for his child was that they be happy. He asked if I was willing to meet with his daughter/son. It was the first time through just my short life of attempting to live as a male that I felt I could be of service to this father and his child.

Amazing what happens when we put ourselves out of the way and let our Higher Power simply move through us. We *can* make a difference.

Thursday, August 11, 2011
August 23rd

I have my prescription and the next step is to get it filled and move on to the next stage of my life. This is yet another new journey. I feel alone with this, like I am the lone wolf out in the field away from the pack. It's not that it's a horrible feeling. I just will be glad when the changes really start to take effect. Then, I will not feel so much like the freak that I feel now. I can wear men's clothes and feel okay. I will be looked at as the male that I am. Right now, I feel like I am caught in-between. Is this what it is like when one dies? People talk about them being present in the earthly world and present in the Godly world. Am I waiting for Charlotte to die and Charley to emerge and bring new life?

I will just keep moving towards being healthy, eating well, exercising, and keeping my head clear. I keep my head clear by forever remaining teachable. It's hard work living healthily. Every morning, I take the responsibility for what my day is going to be like. How am I going to treat people? How do I want people to treat me? I think that by practicing these principles in all my affairs, they will keep me healthy.

I need to make a commitment that I will blog my feelings and thoughts. I can't go back to the old routine of keeping them closed in. I have to write this out. I do a mental 10th step daily. I need to do this as well.

I am going to apply the steps about my transitioning. I was a little shocked that they gave me these meds so quickly. So many thoughts running through my head. Am I ready? What will it do to me? Will I die from this? Is God pleased with what I am doing? I need to settle down and just go with what God is doing for me. He is doing for me what I can't do for myself!

Wednesday, August 17, 2011
Name Change

Tomorrow, I go to get the official name change with the court. Just filling out some paperwork, then waiting, and it's all done. How do I feel about that? A little scared, but I'm not sure where the fear is coming from. I can't really pinpoint the anxiety, but I feel it in my stomach. Many times, I wonder if this is the right thing. I know in my heart and soul that it is. I know that in order for me to be a complete person, I have to move forward with this.

There are days when I want to shout this out from the rooftops. Other days, I just want to hide. I am in the peeking-out-of-the-hole stage today. Just like the groundhog, peeking out to see what I see. But, unlike the groundhog, I am not running back in. I can't, I won't. I should not have to.

Sunday, September 18, 2011
On The "T"

For one week I have been on "T." Every day, I look for changes. I feel like I did when I was eight. It was Christmas, and all I wanted was a Johnny and Jane West set. Of course, the complete set! With the ranch and the horses. Deep down, I wondered if I would be allowed to have this boy toy. There had been no debate about it when I asked for what I wanted on that special day. I thought it would be safer asking for Jane West as well. After all, she was a girl doll. But she wore western wear and, looking at her now, she was nothing near the femme world of Barbie. She wore pants and a shirt very much like her husband, or could it have been her sibling? I got the entire set, including Johnny West, that Christmas. I think it was the best Christmas present I ever got. It certainly is the one I remember. All the accessories were included. I spent hours playing with Johnny and Jane, riding into the sunset on Thunderbolt, waking up in the morning having coffee over the flames. As I recall I was always allowed the boy toys. I had GI Joes, etc.

I write all of this because, last Tuesday, I felt like that little boy. Excited and anxious, all at the same time. I am crossing over to being the man that that little girl of eight wanted to be.

Sunday, September 25, 2011
Sunday Morning

Here I am on a Sunday morning. The house is quiet, and my thoughts of my new life are swirling around in my head. Two weeks on "T." I wake up every morning thinking something has changed. But change takes time, and I have all the time in the world.

I realized this morning what a calm, peaceful life I have going on right now. I am content in many ways. I miss being in a relationship but that too takes time. I love Sunday mornings, quiet, easy, no rush, nothing on the agenda.

I have been thinking a lot about what will I look like on "T"? Will my looks change? How much will my body change? How soon? So many questions. I have some fear and doubt at times, fear that this will just alienate me even more in this town, doubt if I am doing the right thing. I just keep coming back to the core of all of this. What is making me happy? Why am I so content in my life right now? I am content because of the decisions that I have made thus far. I am content because

I know I am not a lesbian, or a straight woman. Where do I fit? Who am I? I am a transman who happens to be attracted to lesbian women.

Will I be accepted by the lesbian community? I really need to connect with more Black transmen. How do I do that? I have to be willing to step out of the boat and walk on the water, to have faith in what I believe and move forward. These words sound great, but can I do this? Can I step out? I have to. I have no other choice. I don't want my life to be alone, no good friends who like me, etc. I have to do what I need to do.

Saturday, October 8, 2011
Caught in the Middle

A lot of days, I feel caught in the middle. Am I male or female? When do I become completely male? Will it be when my name change is official? Is it when I feel more emotionally fit in my new world? I feel like I am walking this alone. All I have to do is reach out to others. I will go to the support group Tuesday night and get back, at least, with transmen. They are different. No Black transmen. No one my age. At least, we all have one thing in common. We are men trapped in another gender's body, and we are traveling a new journey to create ourselves. I miss Jen more the last few weeks. As much as I am trying, I am not feeling a connection with Michael. I have tried more and more, but there is a wall. A barrier. Is it me? Can I try harder?

I just don't know how much longer I need to give this before moving on. I will try just a little while longer. I have to keep reminding myself that he is not Jen, and he will not be bringing what Jen brought to the table. He is bringing something different. I am not one to give up on anything any longer. I will not give up on therapy with Michael

Thoughts

I spent time today when I was cutting the grass thinking about all the changes in my life that have taken place. The changes that have happened and the ones that are coming up. I felt a sense of fear, for just a moment, thinking about the challenges ahead of me. Today, I felt the loss of not being in a relationship, of not being able to come home and share details, both intimate and the just whatever moments. I realized that it could be that I will be even more alone as the changes happen with my gender. I have to keep reminding myself that I am okay with where I am right now, that it is okay to be alone, that it is okay to be single going through this, and that I am healthy and free to move around the universe today.

I am who I am because I chose the path of being healthy instead of sick. I read Jen's letter that she wrote me today, and it made me sad but hopeful. The last line in her letter is that the rearview mirror is smaller than the windshield for a reason. I need to buckle up and drive without fear, look at what's ahead, but always pay attention to what is happening now. The now is that I am happy, I am healthy, and I have a sense of freedom.

There is more I will write in the days to come about therapy and how it's just not working for me right now. But, for today, I am going to enjoy that freedom I am feeling at this moment, looking out the windshield at the road in front of me, feeling okay, and knowing that I am making the right decisions about my life

Sunday, October 16, 2011
In The Middle Part 2

I am beginning to get stares when I'm out in public. It was the same stares when I was larger with more weight on. Weighing in at close to 500 pounds, seven years ago, I got stares and eyes rolls and laughter. The last few days, I get the stares like, "What is that?" Is it a man? Is it a woman?" Could it be me being more sensitive to what I am trying to become? Could it be a mixture of both? I am feeling a little uncomfortable in my own skin at the moment. I am operating off a little more fear

I got word that my job is suffering like every other company during these times. They are cutting back our hours. I think, right now, I don't want to look for another job. I just came out to these people as to what I am doing. They have been very accepting. Fear about money, fear about applying for another job. I just am trying on a daily basis to take these fears and give them to God, to have faith that my Higher Power is going to ease my fears, and things will work out the way they are supposed to.

Funny thing about fear, it always seems to come on me at different times. It's like a big ugly bird that swoops down and tries to grab me. I am trying to figure out which direction to go, and it just keeps flapping its large, dark wings. If I just close my eyes and then open them, it's gone. Just my imagination. It's never as big as it seems or as dark. I just have to stop, take a deep breath, and recognize that it will be okay.

I feel stuck in the middle with therapy right now too. I know with this cut in pay, I am going to have to cut back on my time. Co-pays are too high to pay every week. I am a little fearful of that too. I am also trying to get into some sort of groove with Michael. It's just not clicking. It's missing something. It's not feeding me what I need or what I was getting with Jen. Again, is it me? What adjustments do I have to make? I need to talk to Michael about this, and I will. AA has taught me that your secrets keep you sick. I don't want to be sick any longer, and I am not one to keep secrets, not with something as important as therapy right now

Why did Jen have to leave? It's all a process of growth. I accept that. I just don't like it.

Tuesday, October 18, 2011
Early Morning

I woke up early. Guess I have a lot to think about, with job and future and stuff. But I keep reminding myself what Jen said, "The rearview mirror is a lot smaller than the windshield for a reason." So, I am going to keep reminding myself of that. Amazing though, I am not in freak-out mode about the job. I am just getting myself geared up to be in survivor mode. I have to take action to make up for the lost income I will have. I just have to step up and do the next right thing.

Last night, I was thinking that the timing for all of this is bad. How do I present myself at my job as one thing when I am becoming someone else? If I interview for a job now, who am I? Damn! These are the thoughts that wake me up. But I just started praying and started writing. It's the only thing I know how to do right now.

I have been thinking so much about Jen lately. What would Jen suggest that I do? That is a little saying I am repeating to myself when I feel up against the wall. No need to tell Michael. It's just not working with us. That is okay. I am giving it till the holidays, and then, I will look at things. I am okay for now with me and God, and God and me. If I need to bounce stuff off someone, I will. I have learned a lot about keeping those sick secrets. So, it's 6:30 in the morning and the start of my day. I am grateful to wake up and feel free. Grateful that I can recognize my feelings and work through them. Grateful to be a part of another day

I have to take the action that is needed to make my life complete. I will do that. I will move forward and not be crippled by the anxiety that life can bring.

Sunday, October 23, 2011
Peaceful Sunday

I woke up this morning and listened to the Sunday morning sounds. Quiet, peaceful, serene. A work week that was like the strong winds that blow. My feelings about work, future, etc. are just the strong wind blowing. The wind is going to blow, and I have to learn to ride the storm. I never thought I would be able to feel this way. I always thought that life was just a big storm. The reality is my life is good. I am just where I need to be. I am who I am because of the choices I am making. Life is good. I am going to have more storms and more craziness in my life. It's what I do with it today that will help my tomorrows.

I am okay.

Friday, October 28, 2011
Changes

I really thought I would have seen a few changes since starting on "T." I can't see anything but have been told that my facial features are changing. I guess it was sort of like when I stopped drinking and drugging. People were saying they were seeing a difference in me, but I could not see it. I am slowly feeling more comfortable in my body. So much to think about with my life. I am only at the beginning of the changes. But I fear what people are going to think. I have to admit my fear. If I keep it inside, it just festers and grows. In the past, I would keep all this stuff in, and then, it would just explode. I am beyond the exploding stage. I am all about what is the next healthy step.

I am so glad that I connected with the VA Chapter of Black Transmen. This is going to be a great support to me. I will be able to meet people like me, and I will be able to finally see others like me, others who think like me.

So, today, I watched two coworkers be given their pink slips. I felt a lot of fear at that moment, knowing that I have seen this before, letting someone go, and then, in a few months, everyone is gone. I can't just watch now and do nothing. I have to take action. I could step outside of myself so quickly and see that wave of fear coming over me. My first thoughts were, *Who would hire me now? What am I going to do now?* I stopped myself and went right to helping those two guys by talking to them and being there for them. I did what the AA program has taught me—to get out of myself and help the next sick and suffering person. I worry about one of the guys because he is also a member of AA. He could very easily go out and take a drink. I just have to pray that he does the next right thing.

As for me, them leaving will be yet another change at the job. But, for today, it is not me. I need to just keep doing what I am doing, and I will be okay.

Saturday, October 29, 2011
Frustrating

Before "T," I was referred to as "sir," or "he" a lot more than I am now. Am I more sensitive to it now? Was it happening all along? What do I need to do to "look" more male? I just want to feel comfortable in my skin and be comfortable with how people see me. I feel like I need to "man it up" more. I have to ask others if this is normal. I am learning to reach out more and ask for help. I am never going to step out of the boat and feel more comfortable unless I put myself out there.

So, it's Saturday night, and I am a little lonely being in the house all alone. I wish for more. But what more do I want? A relationship? Friendships? What is it that I am feeling like I am missing? This too is frustrating.

For tonight, I will just rest and find some peace.

Thursday, November 3, 2011
Becoming a Man So Far

So, here I have been on "T" since September 13th. Almost two months. Am I changing? Some say I look different. My face is not as round. I know that I am needing to use more hygiene products. But I have always used men's products. Nothing new with that. But I have had to crank it up because I have a different odor about me. Amazing how things are changing.

I am so fucking horny. I feel like I need a lot of sex. I have never had to get off like I am now. If I could, I would just stay in bed and play with myself all day. I think about sex. I look at women and think so many fucking sexual thoughts. Just strange women at the grocery store. But what is frustrating is that I still look female. So, what do I need to do to man it up? I think I might start by getting rid of the earrings, changing them, or something. Hell! Would fucking earrings make me a man?

I feel like I am stuck. I am not sure, a lot of the time, what I am. I feel such excitement about what I will be like, what I will look like, what kind of man I will be. I want to be this perfect man. But there is no perfect man. It's just a man striving to live in a perfect world but never obtaining that perfect status.

So, for now, I just have the hormones of a 17-year-old boy and live the life of the road I have walked for 51 years.

Saturday, November 5, 2011
Who Am I?

During my quiet times, this question comes to my mind. Who am I? Where am I supposed to be? After a few minutes of pondering, I realize I am just where I need to be. I am becoming comfortable with becoming a man. Everything else can come in its own time. I try to look more male. I feel fake. I try to man it down, and I feel like a fake. But when I just say, "Fuck it" and let it be, I am more comfortable.

I am more honest with who I am with people. I am not shouting from the roof tops that I am becoming a transman, but I let people know who need to know

I went to a local church function tonight. For a few moments, I did the "there is no one here like me" routine. Then, I finally relaxed and enjoyed the music, that old gospel music that I was brought up on. I always feel like, in church, I am going to be called out, that they are going to try to convert me into being something I can't or won't be. Again, it's all in my head. Everyone is in church for their own reasons. I am not that important that they are there thinking about me.

Amazing where my head goes. I can take those thoughts so far out into left field. I get scared of being dimed out. But who is diming me out? Them or me?

Saturday, November 12, 2011
Midnight

So, it's after 12, and the house is quiet. The world has taken a little break from all the hustle. I am in a quiet mood. Tonight, I want to be around people more than ever. I realize that I really don't know who to turn to without feeling like I am exposing myself. I feel like a lone wolf, that massive animal that stands on the top of the mountain and looks down for its prey. As much as the lone wolf is a hunter, it's very much alone, operating in life without the pack. I feel like that. I am separated from the pack. Do I do this just because I don't want to get hurt? Have I had enough of this so that I just don't want to try anymore? I am not sure which answer is the correct one. Maybe there are more than just two answers. Maybe I am right about people. Expose myself and get hurt. Every time. What is the reason for trying? I am not into this keep-getting-back-up-on-the-horse-and-ride mentality. I got bucked off the horse once. Don't get back up on that horse. Look for another one. Is that so wrong?

I miss conversations. I miss the closeness. I miss just regular conversations. Where do I find these?

Thursday, November 17, 2011
Childhood

It was not until talking with Michael this evening that I thought about the green army men. I remember playing in the Mimosa tree in the front yard. It had a hole in it that I would hide my army men in every night, neatly tuck them away because they were my boy toys. Two had parachutes that I would climb up into the tree and let them spiral down. Even at six or seven years old, I was that little boy trapped inside the body of a girl. Even then, I was living a dual life. I was the little boy romping through the yard by the week. But weekends at church, I had to become the awkward little girl. I didn't know how to stand or sit correctly in dresses. I felt like such a fake. I think back now about how unfair it was that I had to live that life in that body. I just wanted to be free to be who I always thought I was supposed to be.

I think maybe that is why drugs and alcohol became so important in my life. I could escape into a different world. Today, I don't have to escape. I am becoming more comfortable with who I am as a transman. Someday, I have to introduce the two—the little 6-year-old boy and the 51-year-old man.

Friday, November 25, 2011
Thoughts And Such....

Any day now, I should have my name change. Then, the work begins of contacting places and changing my name. But changing my name does not make me the man I want to be. It will take a lot more than that. I stumble today in a world of in-between. I have learned to live that way. When I was struggling with being a lesbian, a butch woman, I always felt I lived my life in-between. Sort of what it is like living in two worlds. One world had me as a woman, the other world had me as a butch woman. I didn't fit in either world. This is what it is like right now. I am shifting through two different worlds.

Some days, I feel like I am just floating between those two worlds. It's okay because I am feeling more comfortable just floating. I am confident about who I will become. It's almost like I am taking deep breaths and am finally able to exhale. For so long, I held my breath. Holding my breath, afraid of what people would think of me, afraid that people would think less of me, or that I would not be accepted.

Today, after making the decision to transition into the life I was supposed to have, I no longer have that fear of what people will think. I feel so much more comfortable in my skin. Life is good.

Wednesday, November 30, 2011
Changing

Every day, when I look in the mirror, I wonder when I will see the changes to the man I want to become. I realize though that the change needs to start from within. I need to step up my game and be more accepting of who I am. Sometimes, I operate from fear, fear that this is not going to be what I need to do, fear that I am going to be alone, just plain fear. But then, I stop and think about what I have heard in the rooms. "Stop telling God how big my fears are and start telling my fears how big my God is." Just that, plain and simple, and a lot of times, it slows my fears.

So, last night, I looked in the mirror and saw that I was getting more hair on my chin and starting to grow a mustache. I went straight to fear, fear that people are going to see part woman, part man and put me in a freak category. That fear came back. I am so thankful that I have developed a group of transmen friends from Richmond and other areas to talk to about this stuff. I have likeminded people who are going, or have gone, through this.

Sometimes, I think I need to just move so that I am in an area with more people like me. But I feel like I have more to do here before my journey in this area is over. Or am I just staying in this place because I am fearful of stepping out and doing something different. But, even through all the fears, I am more content with my life today than I was a year ago.

Friday, December 2, 2011
Changes Continue

Today, I feel more in touch with who I am as a human being. New job in the works where I can take a deep breath and exhale a little financially. It's still not within reach, but I can see some financial breathing happening in the near future. I will be okay. No matter what happens, I will be all right. I just have learned to turn it over to my Higher Power, what I choose to call God, and let the rest move at its own pace. I have no control.

I still feel like I am in the in-between stage, but that too is something I need to just accept and move through. Today, I am just me. I am someone who is becoming who I have wanted to be since I was a child.

My thoughts still go back to that tree with my green army men. There are days when I wish I could play with those green army men again. But then, why can't I? I mean there is nothing wrong with me going back and (re)living bits of my childhood again by playing with some toys. Sounds crazy? I don't think so. I just want to be able to get in touch with that which has been lost. Lately, I find that I miss my memories of my childhood. I want to remember more. I want to feel more. I try to reach deep down and pull out those memories but they're just not there. Am I trying too hard? Maybe, one day, I will buy me some green army men and play with them. I want to connect with some of my past. I want to accept some of my past. I want to be able to feel safe looking at my childhood. Maybe working with Michael, I can do that. Maybe, slowly going to the tree and climbing it, I will be able to see the view and feel safe about doing it.

Thursday, December 8, 2011
Name Change

All the official paperwork is in, and I can now move forward to change all of my documents to my new name. There is a little bit of sadness to losing the name Charlotte. It was Charlotte who endured evil at the hands of my uncle. It was Charlotte who watched her father take his last breath. It was Charlotte who walked into the rooms of AA and got clean and sober. There are so many milestones that Charlotte passed. What will the path for Charley be like? So many changes. New job, new name, new life. Sometimes, I wonder if I am doing too much too soon. But, you know, I have to take action on being in love with my life and starting to live again. I have never been so content in my life as right now. I am living the peaceful, serene life I have always thought I could never have. Today, I am truly Charley. The name means "Free Man." Today, I am a free man!

Monday, December 12, 2011
Stuff

Today, I started my new job. Working from home is very different. I have to pull out all the discipline I can muster not to just slack off. But I have incentives to make money to get the things I need in order to continue my journey. I want to set a goal to have top surgery by this time next year. So, I have to work hard and save the cash I will need to make it through this. I know if I put my trust in God and let him work it out, it will happen.

I am so excited about this job. It will allow me to test my marketing skills and also my sales ability to step up and perform. I just need to continue with the discipline and not become a slacker.

Chapter 9

2012

First Things First.
Alcoholics Anonymous

Sunday, January 1, 2012
New Year, New Life

I have had a lot to reflect on about my life these last few days, the path along which it is going, how much control I have in it. I know that I let my Higher Power, which I choose to call God, take control of the wheel. But I also know that I have to step up and take action. I can't just ride this journey for free! So many changes last year, some for the better, all for the good, is the way I am looking at it.

So, right now, I am in search of that next better job, in search of that next person to love, and in search of the man I am becoming. It's a new year with a new life. I am learning more and more every day about how to just remain teachable, remain willing to listen, willing to step up, and walk out on the water without fear.

I remember once being in so much fear that I was not going to ever love someone if I became trans, that I would forever remain alone. I have to take the action to get to know people. That is happening right now, and it feels good to have someone interested in getting to know me, for me. "Take it slow, boy" is the motto I am chanting to myself. Don't let the ego get in the way. Just move slow, get to know, and have some fun in the process.

I am approaching this new year with a new attitude. I am no longer that scared little boy hidden behind the shield of woman. I am no longer that lost child waiting to be saved. I am a man, moving towards my life in a direction that I control. I have the wheel. I can choose who to bring along for the ride. I can change passengers whenever I want and, sometimes, I can even step out of the way and let someone else drive. It's all my choice. This is a new year with a new life, and I am in charge along with my Higher Power.

Monday, January 2, 2012
Just Another Day...

Nothing special about this day. Just here chilling out and taking action to move forward. I am feeling hopeful about so many things: the possibility of some dating, a new career path, and really wanting to settle down and do some service for my community. I also have a goal of losing a few more pounds. Of course, everyone has that goal! I need to start doing more push-ups to strengthen my upper body for top surgery someday. So many things in my life, but I just have to keep reminding myself it's one day at a time and each day is just another day.

I've been listening to music again, which is a good thing. Music enriches my soul. I had stopped listening to music last year because I was in a bad space. When I did listen to music, it was depressing music. Today, I want to listen to the type of music that stirs my soul, that pumps me up to be ready to get through whatever task is ahead of me.

The last few days, I have felt more in touch with my maleness than ever before. I am feeling so confident in me. I feel like this is the right thing and that I am on the right path. Last Tuesday, when I first found out about the job, I questioned everything. I just went to that dark place. It was okay though because I didn't stay in the dark space. I recognized that I was there, and I just kept on moving. What do I owe this to? God doing for me what I can't do for myself. I simply turned it over to that power greater than me.

At this moment, at this time, I am me. I am confident in what I believe, and I am ready to move through life to do what I need to do to make a difference.

Thursday, January 19, 2012
Been a While

It's been a while since my last entry. A lot is going on in my life, but I just continue to try to have some faith that it will all work out. I feel like my hormonal changes are all good. I am gaining more confidence in myself and can speak up for me without getting angry. Could this be changes because of the "T"? Or am I just gaining confidence in myself because of who I am becoming? I feel so free these days even in the midst of all the changes. I might be isolating a little, but I think it's the down time that I need.

Here is a fear that I need to get out. As I am looking for a job, I have changed the resume to say "Charley." When I am getting calls, people are saying "he" and "yes, sir." What the fuck do I do when I get to the face-to-face interview? I have to check with the other guys in my group about that. These days, I am up for getting suggestions about any life changing thing that I am doing. I guess AA taught me that. Amazing what I bring with me through being in recovery.

While I am home, I try to stay productive and busy. Up to 100 pushups a day and 100 sit-ups. I work out with a couple of guys online through video chat. I never realized what a comfortable feeling I had, being able to see those two and talk to them. It was amazing. It was just like I was where I belong.

I need to be able to write more and get my feelings down on paper, on screen, whatever. This is my journey, and I want to be able to record it somehow. Just for my own personal keepsake. Perhaps, it could help another older guy, like me, new in transition.

It's been 4 months on "T." It seemed like yesterday I was given the script, and now, it's been 4 months. At 6 months, I can start giving the injections myself! I think for me, through everything that has happened and is happening, I am still able to stand tall and be the man I need to be. It is amazing to see this.

I am feeling down about the possibility of having to move and having no real job. But I still have everything I need to get me through. I am becoming the man I want the world to see.

Saturday, January 21, 2012
Coming To Terms

I have struggled these last few weeks about what are the next steps I need to take to become the man I want the world to see. Should I change my dress? Should I remove my earrings? Shave or not shave? I am learning that I can be any kind of man I choose to be. I no longer have to meet the standards of this planet that dictate how I should look. I am slowly becoming the man I want to be.

I now have women taking a second look and, of course, my paranoid mind wants to say it's because they wonder. Now, I have a whole new struggle to deal with. Who do I date? Will straight women want to date someone who has not gone completely through the change over to a man? Are lesbians wanting to be with someone who is stepping over the fence to be a man? Am I attracted to gay men? So many questions about my sexuality. I put it on the back burner as life-on-life's-terms come up. But I have to address this sooner or later. Am I a gay man? A straight man? What am I? Does it make a difference who I am as long as I am free and happy with myself?

So many questions but I have plenty of time to address them.

Monday, January 23, 2012
Choices

So, I am here researching the internet for items that I need. I am looking at packers, STPs.[10] Not sure which one to choose. The great thing about this is that I have brothers from Black Transmen Inc. to whom I can turn, who will guide me into the right choices of the items I need to purchase. I had a wave of anger come over me that I have to do this. Why couldn't I have just been born a man? Why do I have to find shit that will make me a man instead of just having the proper tools. I know everyone goes through this, and I need to express it, but I guess I reacted because of the fear of the unknown. Not knowing what to get and how to use it—all that shit.

I will learn and I will be willing to be taught. I just needed to vent.

Monday

Went to an interview this morning and think I did fairly well with the interview itself. Will just do the waiting game now to see if I get

---

[10] Stand to Pee.

called back for a second interview. As I was there, talking with the guy, I felt so confident as to who I am and what I have to offer someone in the workplace. As I walked in the cold, misty rain on the downtown mall, I never felt so connected with who I am. Even through my life-on-life's-terms turns up obstacles, I am moving through life at the pace my Higher Power wants me to move. The situations in life will always be there. I just have to take the action to change what I can and leave the rest. I can truly say that, for today, my soul, spirit, and mind are at rest. I just have to take it one day at a time.

I have been thinking about goals for the year and what things do I want to do just for me. I know I want to continue writing because I know I have something to say. I know I might be able to help the next person my age come out to be who they truly are.

So, its Monday, and I have accomplished a few things and will continue to move through the rest of this day in peace and serenity.

Tuesday, January 24, 2012
End of a Day

It's nearing the end of another day. I am grateful that I did not have the desire to take a drink or drug today, that I was of service to someone else. I woke up this morning thanking my Higher Power for the start of the day. I will end my day by thanking my Higher Power for getting through this day. I feel more confident in things today and feel more at peace again. I like it when I can piece together several days of serenity. So, for tonight, I can look back and see that today has been a good day. Confident in the man that I am becoming.

Another Tuesday

Another Tuesday and I am taking action to do what I need to do. I am up to 100 pushups and 100 sit-ups! I am determined to get rid of these last 60 pounds! Bulk up a little and feel good about myself.

I keep thinking what it would be like if I lived in a bigger city with more resources for my transition. Would I reach out for the help? I'm not one to ask for help up front. I keep trying to do it myself until I have exhausted all possibilities. I guess I have just done things myself all my life, so asking for help is hard.

I wish I could hang out with people like me—trans/gay and trans friendly/African American people. It's hard being here in Charlottesville. Most of the time, I continue to feel like that lone wolf, standing at the top of the mountain, looking down. I guess, at least, I am on top instead of looking up from the bottom!

Today, I am going to concentrate on looking for a job, writing, and getting to a meeting. I feel so creative lately, like I have so much to say that I really do need to put down on paper. Let my feelings flow into words.

So, it's Tuesday and it will be a productive day!

Thursday, January 26, 2012
Man Up

Today, I felt a little disconnected from becoming a man. Not that I don't want to do this. I just am trying to figure out ways to pass as a man better. It used to be that I was called "sir" all the time. Now, it's the opposite. What the hell is going on? What do I need to do to man it up more? I'm not sure what I need to do to change things. It is a little disappointing that I am going through this and even strangers can see that I am still female. Bad enough that I have to wait to go through surgery to have my gender changed. I am a man in my mind, a man in my body, and a man in my world. Why can't people see that? What do I have to do? I don't want to come across as hardcore. That is just not my style. Is it the way I am dressing? The way I carry myself? So many fucking questions! So fucking frustrating!

Wednesday, February 1, 2012
Hard Day

Today has been a very stressful day, but I have gotten through it. I realized just how much I miss not having a partner to help me with these types of things in life. As much as I think I can do things myself—don't get me wrong, friends are good—I just wish I had someone to hold me and tell me it's going to be all right. Of course, I go straight to that fear, that there will never be anyone in my life like that again. I quickly move that notion out of my mind, but, just for tonight, I wish this house was not so quiet and not so lonely.

There, I said it. The "lonely" word. I try to be strong and want others to think that I am okay, that I don't need anybody. The truth is I really do need someone in my life. But, for tonight, I will just take care of me and trust that on the hard days, one day in the future, I will not have to go through this alone.

Thursday, February 2, 2012
New Day

Amazing what a little sleep and some hope can do for the soul. This morning, I woke up without the pity party going on. Had a hell of a headache, but it is now better. Amazing what stress can do to the body. My life is so uncertain right now. I'm not sure where I will be living in a few months, what the job situation will look like. But, at least, I know who I am. I have accepted my life becoming a man, and I am clean and sober. Life is not all that bad. It's a new day and I just need to walk through each day 24 hours at a time.

Thursday, February 16, 2012
Life On Life's Terms

It's been a while since I have blogged. Call it lazy, but really, I just didn't know what to say. Life has been kicking my ass, and I have just been taking the punches, keep getting up, and moving through the shit. I still don't know where I am going to live by April. I just have faith that things are going to work out.

I really want all of this to be over. The move, getting out of this house, finding another job. All of it, to just be done.

I want to get back to adjusting my life, trying to live as a man. I want to save money to have my top surgery and face life as life is handed to me. Maybe that is too much? Am I trying to play God? I have thought that, so many times, about me in my transition. Am I playing God? I don't know. I know that I feel like a fake in this body, trying to pull it off as a woman. I know that I am tired of being a woman wearing men's clothes. I want to fit the part I am presenting to the world.

Damn, I knew this would not be easy. This shit is hard!

Sunday, February 19, 2012
Manning Up

So, I have now been on "T" for 5 months. I see changes that are beginning to take place and it's all good. Now, I need to become a man full time. Not that I was not trying before, but I need to change the look so that there's not any confusion with people that I am a man. Michael and I talked about this on Friday. His suggestion was a good one, about the earrings. Funny that it has taken me this long of a time to remove the earrings. Such a small feat to do but so fucking challenging. It's like another step in killing off Charlotte. As much as I want this, there is a part of me that misses Charlotte. Even though I could not see a thing that would be female with Charlotte, I still miss that softness. I still grieve the killing off of Charlotte. Charlotte went through so much and remained strong. Charley is walking through his own shit too, but Charlotte was the survivor.

So, this week, I will man it up a little more, make my appearance just a little more masculine. I have to because I believe in me. I trust where Charley is going to take me. Charley is going to be strong, loving, and kind—just like my father. Charley will be the man that people look up to. Charley will be balanced and stable, a sober and clean Black man who walks with respect.

I can't wait for the world to see the real Charley.

Saturday, February 25, 2012
Connecting

I hooked up with some brothers last night and had dinner. They were all transmen. I felt so connected, so myself for the first time in my life. It was my first time being with African American transmen. I can't even describe how comfortable I felt and how I felt like I had finally arrived.

Earlier this week, I was invited to dinner with a bunch of women. Other obligations led me not to go. But I was also thinking that what I and my female friends need to realize is that I am no longer one of the girls. If I am coming along for the ride, it will be as a male. More and more, every day, I am accepting my maleness. I am getting comfortable with becoming a male. Not sure what led up to this or if it's just a direction I was heading in anyway and finally have gotten there, but I am feeling much more like a free man these days!

Thursday, March 1, 2012
First Negative Response

So, today, I am doing some work. I had a cousin and his boyfriend (yes, they are gay) helping me. I thought it was as good a time as any to tell them about my transition. My cousin just went on and on about why would I want to do this, and he thought it was not something I needed to do.

His boyfriend was behind me 100%. He kept telling my cousin that it was because it is what I want to do. Then, he went on to say that they had been together for 35 years and that he had wanted to have a marriage ceremony but will have to wait until my cousin's mother dies!

I said that I was not waiting for anyone to die to be happy.

It really hit home because I thought that, of all people, they would understand. I have to look at them and realize that they have their share of problems and ignorance about what I am doing. I should not let it affect me, but it is just one more reason to remember that I might not have family and close friends to support me through this.

Thursday, March 22, 2012
Accepting Change

In AA, we use the Serenity Prayer a lot. I have been saying that prayer a lot these days. So many changes happening with me, changes that I see physically and mentally because of the hormones, changes that are happening with the move and with the continued faith that I am going to be okay through all of this. Turning things over on a daily basis, I am seeing and feeling the growth in me. I am becoming the man I always yearned to be, the one who I toyed with the idea of becoming at 16—*What would it be like to be a boy?*—the one shoved aside for so many years. I am emerging to become someone I truly want to be around.

I still have my extreme lonely periods. Where do I fit in? I no longer fit in with the women. I never really did. I feel like I don't truly fit in with the guys either, although I always was more comfortable around them. There is something different, some sort of quietness to my soul. Is it a mixture of acceptance of who I am? Could it be that I am just no longer depressed? That I am enjoying life even though I don't have anyone to share my joy with? Oh, I have a few people that I could share this with, but I miss the intimate person, the person who will know all sides. That too will come in time. Or maybe not. I am not the one to foresee what my future holds. That is where the Serenity Prayer comes in—to accept the things I cannot change and the wisdom to know the difference.

I am gaining that wisdom to know the difference these days.

Friday, March 30, 2012
Last Night in This House

So, tonight is the last night in my home in North Garden. I am sad, but it's what has to happen. This was the home that my ex and I created, and, in a short time, I found myself here alone. But so many things have happened with my life while being in this home. I arrived here a very confused butch woman, or so I thought. It was here, in the dark of night, feeling so out of place, that I discovered who I really am, that I am a man trapped in this body that is called "woman," that underneath this skin is the boy I always knew I was supposed to be.

Tonight, I have one final time in this home, reflecting and knowing that there is something out there greater for me. I just have to keep the faith and stay positive. God has my back.

Wednesday, April 25, 2012
On My Own

Last night was the last night that I have to go to the Fan Free Clinic for injections. Yet another change in my life that is good. I am on my own with injecting myself. I feel yet another form of freedom.

My life is so serene today for many reasons. I have settled into my sober life. I have accepted being a transman. I am at peace with being alone. I love myself. I could just go on and on about what this peace and serenity means to me. I never thought I would be so at peace. Last night, one of the directors at the FFC joked and said when we see you again, will you stop smiling so much! I have never been told that before. I always had this mad, serious, unhappy look on my face. Today, I can feel my facial expressions are different. I am not saying that every day is a great day. There are some days that I am filled with fear. But it does not consume me any longer. I recognize it, accept it, and move on

Today, I am grateful for the peace and serenity that fills my day. It has been all about acceptance of who I am.

Friday, May 4, 2012
New Job

Been a while since I have been here. I am feeling a little anxiety this evening. I got offered a new job. Not the greatest of jobs. For one reason, they do not offer health care. I keep feeling like I just settle for jobs because my back is up against the wall. So, I let my anxiety fly for just a little while, and now, it's time to bring myself back to reality. My unemployment runs out in 11 weeks. I have been unemployed since January. This is the first job offer. I need to accept this job, do well on it, and continue to move forward looking for my next opportunity. Who knows what it will be? I prayed for a job, and I got my answer. Just didn't tell God the specifics on what I wanted! ☺

So, here comes the next part of this anxiety. I have had three interviews with these men. I have passed as a guy for all three interviews. Next week comes the test as I have to show ID and my ID still shows female. What do I do? Well, I just suck it up and explain if I have to and move on.

I did not go through my transition thus far to be afraid. I am proud of who I am, and I should not let this affect me in anyway. I just needed to get this out—that I am having anxiety about it—and ask, What should I do?"

I took it to my VA group of brothers on the Black Transmen site. Will get some of their experience, strength, and hope on this. The beauty of having a support system is that one is never alone.

Sunday, June 3, 2012
Long Time

It's been a long time since I have posted. Not sure I had a lot of words to say, just living life one moment at a time. I did this 6-week workshop on Mindfulness Meditation. I have been incorporating that a lot in my life. Just being aware of everything I do and everything around me. I have gotten so comfortable with being the man that I am becoming. I am accepted as a male at my new job. As a matter of fact, the coworkers know nothing about my transition. It has been so comfortable just being me.

I don't know about other transmen, but there are moments when I am in the company of men when I feel like they are going to figure me out, that I am going to do something that will give me away. I don't know what that something is, but I have just a twinge of anxiety about that.

I take a deep breath and try to get myself centered into being who I know I am supposed to be, an African American man just trying to make a living in this world.

As I look back over the last year, I see how I have gotten stronger with every hurdle I have had to cross. I look at my spiritual level and how much it has increased. My faith is stronger than ever.

My next challenge is finishing my book. I have it in me, I just have to step out of the boat and continue the journey.

Thursday, June 14, 2012
9 Months

So, it's been 9 months since I have been on "T." A lot has changed in those 9 months. I have struggled financially due to loss of jobs, but I'm starting to pull myself back up slowly. I have mended a very good friendship, and it's stronger every day as a result of my becoming a good honest man. I feel more confident than ever with who and where I am.

The motto for Black Transmen is: "Becoming the change you want the world to see." That is where I am. I am changing and becoming that man. It has not been easy, and my anxiety level surfaces from time to time. But the anxiety is nowhere near as crippling as it used to be. Today, my recovery program is strong. I am physically strong and mentally strong.

You know, if I were to get into a relationship today, that person would be very lucky because of the secure, confident person I am evolving into.

I have so much to say about my growing up and where I am now. I have started writing a book but, somehow, I cannot put pen to paper. I have got to discipline myself to do better with that. As I need to discipline myself to do better with my daily blogging. I really need to get back to a daily journal here.

Life is good.

Thursday, June 21, 2012
Feeling Good

I realized this morning just what a good space I am in. I am moving forward with life. I still have moments of anxiety about what people think about me. Am I going to be figured out by people who just meet me? I really wish that I had moved to another area. I can't even imagine how freeing that would be. So, I have some long-term goals that I am going to start trying to shoot for, like being moved out of Charlottesville in the next 12 months. I realize the importance of setting goals.

On another note, I am constantly seeing changes in my body. Hair on my knuckles. I know it sounds crazy, but I love looking at my hands now. Hair is coming out on my thighs and little fuzz on my arms! I feel so much more confident. It is amazing to watch these small changes occur.

Still horny as hell and don't know why I just don't find someone and take care of that! I realize that I am not the kind of person who just does one-night stands. I want to save myself as a transman for someone who I will fall in love with and who will support me in this change, not someone who is just interested in seeing what it would be like.

Okay, so I am on the clock with work and need to get busy for the day. I need to come back later and write more. I just started writing again in what I hope will become a book. It's all about growing up and being confused about my gender. I am digging deep and looking into my childhood. Some of it is painful but many of the memories are so vague. I can't remember what it felt like to be a child.

I will keep working with that.

Wednesday, June 27, 2012
My Father
Today is the seven-year anniversary of my father's death. I remember it well, being there by his side. How I wish I was clean, sober, and healthy then. I always think of these last six years of being clean and sober. The one person who would have seen the difference was my father. No words would ever have needed to be spoken. He would have just understood and flashed that smile. He would have had peace knowing that I had peace in my heart. Today, I am moved by the mannerisms that I have that are like his. My actions and my words. I am often reminded of the things he said or did just by thinking about him.

Today, I miss my father and, today, I am proud to be like him.

Will I always be?
Man have I been sick all week, high fever, UTI. I got some antibiotics for it yesterday. This is when I get a little pissed about still having the parts of a woman, when I suffer from these UTIs. In the last two years, I've had a lot of them. But it has affected me more this time around. Perhaps because it has been the worst one yet. Usually not with a fever like this. I just don't have any energy at all. Will these be the things that will always remind me I am still a woman? Will I be fully able to walk this earth knowing I am the man I am supposed to be?

Now, when someone slips and says "ma'am" or "miss," it just spins my head a little. Thank God that I have a filter on my anger because someone who does not even know could be in my line of fire.

I often wonder what happened to that rage and anger. I realize that it's all because of the acceptance of who I am. I am finally living the life

I am supposed to live, developing the body that I am supposed to have, and loving the person I was always supposed to love.

So, today, I just praise God for bringing me this far and allowing me to be teachable, and to accept what he has in store for me.

Thursday, July 12, 2012
Just For Today

Again, it's been a while since I posted. I keep telling myself I am going to get better at this. But, of course, I slip. I have got to put my thoughts and feelings out here just to prevent me from keeping them all in.

I am doing okay. Work is good. My family is well, and I am adjusting to life. I never thought I would say I am comfortable being single. But it is not all that bad. I have a good life right now. Just for today. I am feeling good about losing almost 30 pounds and am going to keep eating healthy and need to pump up the workouts. Right now, I am going to work out at home since I am trying to save money and the gym is not something I can afford right now.

I was, at one point, doing 100 pushups and sit-ups and need to get back to that. Man, was I feeling strong when I was doing them! I don't know if it was all in my mind or if it was really happening, but I felt like I was bulking up!

So, I guess I really had not talked about the changes that I am seeing since being on "T" for 9 months. I am beginning to get more hair on my thighs and knuckles. I know that's a crazy thing to notice but hair on my knuckles was a big deal for me! I have to shave every day, or I have that teenage fuzz look. I really don't need a beard or a mustache to make me the man I want to be.

My time with my therapist, Michael, is ending this month. We are still having a hard time connecting. With me working in Richmond a lot, we really could not connect. I am feeling okay with just chilling out for a little while and shopping around for a therapist this time who will understand the trans thing.

I remember when Jen left, I was really sad, and it took a while for Michael and me to connect. I don't really think we ever really totally connected, but he gave me what I needed for the time that he gave. I needed to be with a male therapist to get some of the male take on things. I am going to take a holiday from seeing a therapist until about September, and then, I will find one through the Fan Free Clinic.

Just for today, I am good. I am feeling okay mentally and emotionally, and I am relaxed with my life.

Just for today.

Sunday, August 5, 2012
Drinking Dream

It's been a while since I posted anything. I have got to get better at my writing. I am feeling really good about my transition. I am comfortable where I am and even more comfortable with my manhood.

Often, I wonder where my path would be right now if I had been born a male. Would I have been a substance abuser and drinker? Would I be married now with kids and a house? What would my profession be? Making this change late in life is almost like a rebirth. I am starting for the first time. I feel the need to become a new person all over again.

I had this dream the other night that I was totally male, and I was having a drink at a bar with this woman. It was so real. I woke up thinking that was my glimpse into the world of what I would have been like if I was born male. I might have been able to drink. But this is real life, and I cannot drink. I am a recovering alcoholic, and, in this life, I cannot and will not drink.

In AA, they call that a drinking dream. I have never had one before in my six years of being sober. I have heard people talk about them, but I had never had one. It's tricky because I woke up thinking, man, was that a dream or did that actually happen? Thank God, it was a dream!

So, here I am, on Sunday morning, enjoying the quietness and getting ready to start my day. There's something about Sunday mornings. They're quiet and serene. I yearn for those serene moments. I love just being with me in the quiet. My soul is at rest.

I promise to write more, to become better disciplined with writing in my blog as well as my personal writings that I have started.

Monday, August 20, 2012
Grateful Monday

So many things that I am grateful for today. I think that life is going okay now. I am grateful to have a job, a place to live, good friends to turn to when I need it. I am so grateful for Black Transmen Inc. They are opening doors for me that I would never have stepped through. I am excited that I am going to run a Black Transmen booth at the Cville Pride fest. In the past, I would never have even attended this, let alone worked a booth! My self-confidence is getting higher. I am much more comfortable with who I am.

I still have my struggle about my transition from time to time. I still struggle sometimes whether this is the right thing to do. Will anyone ever love me, and I love them? Is this what God wants from me? Just questions that I am sure sometimes go through the minds of almost anyone going through this.

I will have to ask some more of the trans guys if this ever crosses their minds. I know it happens less than it used to. In the beginning, I would get fearful, and then, those thoughts would come to mind.

Today, they are less. But I still have them. I think of it like when I was getting sober and would second guess if this is the thing I wanted to do. Was I really an addict? The truth is that my life got so much better after quitting that I don't want to go back out to try it and see. I just cannot think of what my life would be like if it was like it was when I first came to AA.

I am grateful today just to be grateful. I still need to work on developing some stronger friendships with some trans guys. But I am reaching out more and helping some younger guys, keeping a watch on them to see how they are doing. Just putting myself out there more. It feels good to think about someone else, to be of service to someone other than myself. It gets me out of my head.

Today, I am so grateful

Monday, September 17, 2012
One Year

September 13 was one year of being on "T." I am a little late writing about this. I did a quiet celebration of my anniversary, but it's like it's not complete. I want to have top surgery so badly. It's hard trying to save money on the salary that I am currently making. But I just keep praying for a better job, praying that something will work out, and I can get the surgery that I need to take that next step into my manhood.

I went to the Charlottesville Pride and worked a booth for Black Transmen Inc. It is official now. In Charlottesville, those who know me now know that I am a Black transman, and I am living my life as one.

I still have moments that scare me a little with my family. What are they thinking? What are they saying? But I quickly let go of that fear and just know that I am living my life for me. It's time that I simply step up and be who I was supposed to be all along.

I fear that I might not ever love someone in an intimate relationship because there are no women out there wanting someone who is trans. But that too will come in time. What I want to do is finish my novel, finish those thoughts, and get them down on paper, to see if it can help the next person like me who is attempting to transition this late in life, to be their voice, to leave the print of my footsteps so they can follow me.

This week, I am going to a new doc for my "T." This will be at UVA.[11] I am not sure what to expect from them. If they are going to be ignorant to what I need and treat me differently, I am prepared to defend myself about what medical services I need. I am not going to be afraid to speak up for what I need, what I am supposed to get for my health.

So, for today, I am feeling okay. I am feeling like I am going to make it. I am on the right path, and I am moving forward to become the person I am supposed to be. After a year on "T," I am right on target.

Sunday, September 23, 2012
Sunday morning

I like Sunday mornings. Quiet and peaceful. I used to not feel the serenity that days like today give me. I was so caught up in my head that I just could not feel or see the beauty. Today is so different. I am so different. Does this come from taking "T"? Having some therapy under my belt? On meds? I think it might be a combo of all of them. I also think that I am just maturing into the person I am becoming. I don't worry about what people think of me.

This week, I have had a little inside battle about my growing mustache. It is becoming more visible, and I worry what my family is going to think. But after a lot of soul searching, I have to be me. This is what this journey is all about. I have not driven the miles that I have every other week to Richmond, long hours of therapy, and a lot of soul searching to be scared or concerned about what others think of me. It's none of my business what they think of me. They are going to be uncomfortable with whatever I do. First, they were uncomfortable about my lifestyle. Then, who I loved. Now, it's my transition. It's all okay. As long as I am comfortable with who I am, it's all that matters.

I have been writing a lot more lately and I am determined to write at least 2500 words per day. That is my goal. I am not sure that I will

---

[11] University of Virginia

meet it, but it's what I have put upon my soul to do. It helps to put those feelings from the past down on paper. I can feel it and just move on.

I have been packing more lately, and it is such a great feeling to pack. It helps with me feeling caught in between lives. It helps with being more in touch with my masculine side. It just gives me a better feeling all together. Hard to explain but it just does. I am saving money to buy a STP and will be wearing this at all times. It's another step towards being the man I am supposed to be. I really am excited and can't wait until I have all the money saved to do this.

I went to UVA on Friday and met with my Endo doc. She was very understanding, and I am actually the first transman who she will be seeing. We spent a lot of time just talking. I was afraid that they were going to require that I have more therapy. She was very impressed with my letters of support and, actually, everything took less than an hour and I was out of there.

Then, I went for a job interview. My goal is to find a better job by the end of the year, one that pays a little better and one where I have some health benefits. I pray every night that God will enlarge my financial and employment territory. I pray that I will have someone in my life to share these joys with. I pray that my life becomes complete. I am heading in the right direction, but it all takes time. Still, I am becoming the man I want the world to see.

Sunday, November 4, 2012
In My Head

Been sort of in my head the last few days. I just can't seem to get the fucking break I need with this damn employment. Laid off again from yet another job. This time, I really didn't see it coming. Last Wednesday morning, I woke feeling a little scared, having that fear that this might be my last day with this company. I guess my gut feeling was right. Within two hours, I was, once again, without a job, living in slight financial fear again, having to put on the song and dance routine for interviews.

What is God trying to tell me? Am I supposed to do something else in my life? I need to get quiet and await God's answer. I know He has one for me. I know I just need to wait this out and God will provide. I have this faith. I have this belief. But there is still that small amount of fear. Sometimes, it's like I have these moments of, "Oh, shit!" I have to catch my breath and remind myself that I have been here before, and I will get through this. I have to get through this. Fear and bad moments don't last forever.

I have to be vigilant about what I need to do with my life, moving forward. I just need to speak my fear about everything, job, relationships, money, life, stuff. The most important thing is to keep my sober life intact. For that, I need to continue to work my steps, go to meetings, and just live my life emotionally sober. I have to keep the faith. I have to know that God has my back.

I have been reading a lot about following my dream. My dream has been to be a published author. Could this be what I do with the free time that I am going to have? Continue to put my words down on paper? I know all this sounds so crazy. Here I am with no job, and I want to be a starving artist! It makes me smile. But it's my dream. I have a story to tell. I have words that need to speak out, to help someone and to help myself by putting the words down, the story of my journey to healing. I have come to a lot of healing moments but there will be more. I love the thought that I will always continue to heal from one thing or the next. But I have so much time to catch up on my healing, so much to speak about, so much to acknowledge that was not my fault.

Do I love my life right now? I do. I just wish it was a little better. But it's okay. It is what it is, for the moment.

Monday, November 5, 2012
Changes

I realized how much life has changed for me since I have transitioned. I am no longer a part of the lesbian world. I am now a man and seen as a man. It just sort of hit me like a ton of bricks. Living here in Charlottesville, I have alienated myself again with a new label. There are very few FTM people here, and I am feeling the loneliness today. I really need to decide if this is the place where I am going to live out the rest of my years. Maybe it's time to move on to another place, Maybe God is telling me the changes that are happening need to happen in a new place. I sure am not getting anywhere in this town. Always one step ahead and three steps backwards. Always struggling. When does this struggle stop for me?

I am trying to keep the faith with these employment changes, but I really need a break. I am feeling bits and pieces of fear, but I keep trying to turn it over. Turning it over is what they tell me in AA. Turn it over. This weekend, I felt a little bit of fear whenever I would be alone. Fear that I am here, in this time, all alone. Here, with no job, no social circle of FTMs, just alone. I know it sounds like I am feeling sorry for myself, but it's true. I am like a fish out of water when it comes to my transition. More prayer and more faith, that is where I need to be. Changes are going to happen. I have to accept that. Change will change my life. I just have to hang on.

Wednesday, November 7, 2012
Still on the Path

I could write about fear all day long. My fear has been surfacing a little more since I lost my job last week. What am I going to do? Will the bills be paid? Will I have enough money to survive? So many questions and I have been searching for the answers. Then, I realized that there are no answers. As John Lennon said there are only solutions to the problems. My solution is that I will be okay. I will make it. I will find another job. I will continue to go through these moments of fear, these moments of panic. What I need to do is step back and know that God is in control. He will walk with me, not ahead, not behind, but *with* me. I have to exercise this faith with all my strength. As the Bible says, the size of a mustard seed. I gotta keep the faith. I realized today its okay to have fear. It's more than likely normal to be feeling fearful. It's when I allow the fear to overtake me that I know it's a problem. I am so amazed at where I am in life. I feel like my feet are planted on solid ground. There are curves and bumps along the road, but I am on the road, and that is what is important. I am still on the path.

Monday, November 12, 2012
Wreckage of My Past

I feel that since I have lost this job, the wreckage of my past is coming into play. I keep thinking about my decisions to drink instead of going to school. To drug instead of going into the military. To listen to negative responses from my mother when I wanted to make decisions about going away to school. I know there is no reason to look back, but, with what little formal training I have, I see how I have kept myself down all these years. I feel the pinch of it now.

I can do one of two things. I can continue to stay in this misery or do something about my lack of training. I just have to keep praying that God is going to do the right thing for me, that I just can't keep suffering like this financially. There is a world out there for me to enjoy and live in, and I deserve that living. I pray that I continue to keep the faith that everything is going to be okay and that I will stop looking at my past. But the Big Book says I should not regret my past or shut the door on it. So, I have to acknowledge it and move on, knowing that God is putting me through this for a reason. Stay strong. It will be okay.

Writer's Block

Okay, so I want to do some writing that I have neglected to do for the last several months. Well… almost a year. But I have writer's block and just can't seem to get motivated to get moving on this. I have so much to say, so much to get out, but I have come to this crossroads. I can't seem to put it down on paper. What do I need to do? I will just keep praying and asking God to direct me to what he will have me do with this matter.

I have decided that, with this particular problem and the problem of no job at the moment, I am going to turn it all over to God. I have also been reading about fasting, and how I can get closer to God that way. What I need to do is have faith. Faith without works is dead. I think that is where I am right now with my writing. I have little faith that what I need to put down on paper makes any difference. But it will make a difference to me. I just need to start, and I believe it will start flowing, come out, and I will be a better person for doing that. I need to have faith in me. Something that is a problem right now.

Sunday, November 18, 2012
Oh No, I am in Panic Mode

Out running errands last night and I realized, right in Walmart, that I was in panic mode. I saw an old school mate. Here I am, with mustache growing, and he is screaming my name, "Charlotte," from across the store.

I had already ditched down an aisle to avoid seeing one old friend. Now, I was going to encounter this guy face to face. I have not had this feeling in a long time. Do I have to explain? Or what will they think? Hating that they are still referring to me as "Charlotte" and using the pronouns "she" and "her." Do I just blurt out, "Hey, you are wrong: I am no longer Charlotte"? Or do I just let it go? This is where the rubber hits the road. I should not feel shame about who I am now, especially with people who I see only once every few years. What difference does it make?

I realized tonight, in a meeting, that I might have the same fear going to meetings. Since my transition, I don't talk as much as I used to. I want to think a lot of it has to do with just being calm and willing to listen. I don't want to think it's because I am hiding, trying to not be in the light. People will look. The new ones will wonder why some people are still referring to me as "she."

I don't know. Tonight, and last night, I really was dealing with my Gender Identity Disorder (GID). Guess some days are better than others.

Sunday, November 25, 2012
Sunday Morning

So, I start this new job next week and, once again, I will have to go through the explanation about why the name change when they do their background check, or maybe not. I pray that God will allow me to keep this job and I can have some longevity with it.

There is so much I want to do, and it all revolves around having money, like having the surgery and being able to travel to Dallas in March to finally meet a group of transmen of all ages. What a wonderful feeling that will be, to finally meet some of the men who I admire and would like to have as a mentor.

So, this Sunday morning has been quiet, a morning of getting things done. As I am at my computer looking out the window, I feel the warmth of the sun coming through the windowpane. It is soothing, and comforting. It's almost the same feeling I had the day I announced to myself, and to Jen, my questions about my gender. Once it was out, and I was able to speak those words, I felt the sunlight of the spirit wash over me. It was as if I was reborn.

I have been praying a lot lately and have recently started fasting once a week to get closer to God. It is really something that I am looking forward to doing, just building a better relationship with God, and getting stronger in my faith.

I guess I am growing up. I never would have dreamed that I would be fasting and praying and praising God the way that I do now. I am at peace with myself, my family, and with God. It is an amazing feeling to be at peace, to be able to match calamity with serenity. The promises throughout the Big Book are coming true for me. I am nowhere near where I want to be but, thank God, I have faith that I will get there.

Monday, November 26, 2012
More Stuff

So, I was at an AA meeting today and really started to feel isolated from everyone in the room. It was not a feeling of being scared or really any emotion at all. I just realized that there was no one in the room like me. I mean there was one other Black guy there but not a trans guy. Maybe, I need to stop thinking of myself as a trans guy and just look at myself as a man. But I have a hard time doing that sometimes. I know I am different, and that there are not any Black transmen in Charlottesville, other than me.

It was the same as when I was getting sober. I was the only Black butch lesbian, or even lesbian. I was accepted by everyone, but it is, and was, the truth that I was different. I try to keep my ego in check about that most of the time, but, really, it can be lonely. I don't know how to feel about continuing to hang out with the women or should I make relationships with straight guys? Will they accept me, knowing what I am? I have been very honest in AA about my journey.

I have to really pray about this and talk this over with other older trans guys. Sometimes, I really wish I lived somewhere else, a larger city where there are more people like me. I realized that more today than ever. I find myself really wanting more contact with transmen.

But, for now, I will just continue to be me.

Stuff

Preparing for next week, when I go out of town for this job, and hoping that I don't have to reveal too much about my personal life, I'm really feeling like I don't care if I have to or not. I am who I am.

This week, a young trans girl has been reported missing from Charlottesville. It has affected me because this girl and I have crossed paths. She met me at the booth during Charlottesville Pride. She talked at great length with me about her struggles and how all she wanted was to be on hormones to complete her life. I pray that she is safely returned to her family. I pray that wherever she is, that she is okay.

I went, last week, to the Transgender Day of Remembrance. I was so affected as the names of these young people were read, killed because of who they wanted to be.

I wonder, in this town, what people think of me? I so want to just be another face in the crowd, not go into a usual eating place and be called a woman because that is what they remember. I just want to be another face in the crowd, just your average guy, making it through life. Is that too much to ask?

I need to get back to writing more about my feelings and fears, get them down on paper. Sometimes just writing this out helps.

Tuesday, November 27, 2012
Why Do They Stare?

People who know me are beginning to stare at me like I am something from outer space. Could it be my own fear of what I am feeling and not that people are staring at all? I want to think that it's not me. I want to think that these people in AA are not staring at me. I have changed a little more in terms of a defined mustache. It makes me feel a little uneasy and, sometimes, I want to just shave it off and blend back into the woodwork.

I have moments when my GID comes out raging through, and I feel like, "Why the hell do I have to go through this?" It would have been so simple if I had been born a man. Am I crazy to be feeling like this? Am I crazy for doing this? Sometimes, I just wish it was a little easier.

Every time I go to the doctor and see someone different, I have to explain who I am and where I am headed in my life. Each time, it goes well, but it's the anxiety beforehand. I guess that makes sense. I find that writing more about my feelings this week has helped. I need to remind myself that the most important thing is to be completely honest about my fears when I write about it for two reasons, to be heard and to let the feelings out.

Wednesday, December 5, 2012
Passing

I have this new job and have been in North Carolina all week. It has been such a relief to be able to pass as male with no questions. Everyone knows me as a man, and I am accepted in the men's group just like one of the guys.

It is amazing what men will talk about. I have had the chance to hang out with them in the bar and get to know some of them. They talk about their wives and girlfriends and, yes, even talk freely about sex. It's just a free flow of conversation. Of course, it also gets a little more informative as they continue to drink and get a little freer with their conversation.

I found myself, at times, a little nervous that I might not be able to say the right thing or might do something that would dime me out. What I realized was that I just need to be myself, and everything will be okay.

Friday, December 14, 2012
Change In My Life

I feel like I am on the verge of having some big changes happen in my life. I have realized one thing. I am burned out in the career of sales. The fear I have is that it's all I know. But there has to be more that I can do with my life. I try to look at what makes me happy. I am basically very happy with my life, very happy with my transition, happy with my living situation. I am not happy with my finances. I would like to be making more money.

This job that I have now is, once again, one of those take-it-or-else-I-starve jobs. I was up against the wall. I know they say it's a lot easier to find a job when you have a job, and that is exactly what I am going to do, continue looking, praying that God's will is that I get a job with which I am content and feel like I am making a difference.

I never dreamed that my life would be so easy as it is right now. It has its ups and downs, but I am content with where I am. I never thought I would be content being single. I always needed to have someone in my life. I would have to be in love or in lust with someone. Right now, I am okay with me just being with me. I am loving me more every day.

As I look back, I see how miserable I was with myself. I could never have said, "I like me," "I am okay with where I am," or "Life is pretty good." What made the change? I think a lot of it has to do with the great therapy I got for about two years. I think some of it has to do with the meds that I take, and, finally, I think there is a mixture of my life sober having a more concrete feel to it.

Last week, I went to the training for this job in North Carolina. I had lots of time to think and pray, and it was good. I also watched people drink. I realized that it could have been me. It could have been me headed to the bar before heading to dinner. It could have been me the next day smelling like stale alcohol. But it was not. I was fresh and ready to tackle the day. I had this small lingering fear that I would not be able to retain information by studying. It was hard, but I was able to do it with very little problem.

I felt like it had been so long since I did the classroom thing that it was going to be difficult. I had to study hard, but I made it. One thing I realized was that I did not give myself enough credit for what I can do!

Monday, December 24, 2012
Christmas Eve

So, it's Christmas Eve. I am working today, so nothing special about today. But it seems to me that there is a special feeling in the air. For the first time, during the holidays, I feel very free. I am who I am these days, and I have learned to accept many things in my life. This is the time of year when people reflect back on who they are, what they have done, etc. I too find myself doing that. I find myself wanting to be in a better place than where I am now. I stop myself because to feel like this is such self-centered behavior. It's not about where I want to be but where I am at the moment and accepting that.

I have learned so much in the last few years. Over the last few days, I find myself thinking about Jen a lot and how broken I was when I came to her, how, through trust and faith, I left her a much better person, someone who was growing whole, someone who was willing to be teachable again. I thank God for that time with her and that time I had with God, how God has kept me through every situation I have encountered.

I realized that I don't write as much as I would like. I feel like I have a story in my heart and soul. But how can I express that to others if I am not taking the action needed to get it done? I have to make a pact with myself that I will write for at least 90 minutes every day. If I miss, I need to make up for that time. Can I do this? Yes, I can. It's called discipline, something that, many times, I lack.

I have to get my story out there. I have to be heard.

Wednesday, December 26, 2012
Peace

I find that every day I become more at peace about everything that is happening in my life. In AA, we have the 9 Step Promises. They tell us that we are going to know a new freedom and a new happiness, that we will not regret the past nor wish to shut the door on it. We will comprehend the word "serenity" and know peace. I am feeling that way right now. I have some fears, but I just keep having faith that God is going to see me through all of this. I have faith that I will be okay.

It's the same faith I had when I crossed over to the other side with my transition. It's the faith I have when I step out, every day, as Charley, the man, not worried about what people think or feel about me. I have faith that everything is going to be okay in my life. I know I have God on my side.

Saturday, December 29, 2012
Saturday Morning

It is something about Saturday mornings. I love to sleep in late, then wake up, and hear the silence. I feel at peace. I never felt this kind of peace before until I accepted who I am. Today, my serenity and peace are one. I have been thinking back to the day when I knew I needed to take the steps to become the man I was always supposed to be. I knew in my heart, a long time ago, that I was different.

AA was always telling me that I am *not* unique. But I knew deep down something was different with me. That I was hiding something deep inside. I thought it might have been about the abuse. But I have worked on that. I have come to accept what has happened. I am even at a level of forgiveness about that. What I have learned in my recovery is that I have to forgive in order to stay healthy. I have to be at peace about those things that shake my emotions, always accepting that its God's will, not mine.

So, this morning, I woke up thinking about the steps I took in order to accept my transition, the steps I took to start my transition, and the steps I am still taking in living my transition.

I am at peace. I used to worry about what friends and family were going to think, but I no longer have that deep-rooted fear. What I do have is a feeling of peace. I feel that this is what living is all about.

Sunday, December 30, 2012
It's All About Faith

As I approach a new year, I look back at the peaks and valleys and see that I would have never made it to where I am today without faith that God was, and still is, getting me through all of this. I see that, every day, I have more faith than I did the day before. Each day, I strive for something a little different. Some days, I fall short of the mark. Some mornings, I forget to pray but as the Big Book says, "Go back to it in due time." As this new year of 2013 approaches, I want to be able to continue to be the free man that I have become these last few months. I want to be able to continue to be proud of who I am and what I am becoming. I want to become the change I want the world to see. I have many goals that I want to set, but I want to take them in a realistic manner. Not set goals so big that I can't accomplish them and be disappointed. I want to take on my goals with truth and energy.

I want to be a man of God, a friend among friends, a worker among workers. I want to finally be happy in this world. I have come this far, and I will continue.

Tonight, I have a little fear about my job. What will it bring me? Where will I be with my employment status? I turn it all over to God. I say a prayer thanking God for seeing me through, asking God to enlarge my area and move on, trusting that God will take care of this. It is all about faith.

Chapter 10

2013

Live and Let Live.
Alcoholics Anonymous

Tuesday, January 1, 2013
New Years

So, it's 2013. Another year. This has certainly been a year of change and spiritual growth for me. I have learned to become teachable. I have embraced my emotional health and come out on the other side.

Today, I can say that, as I step into this new year, I am much better off than I was last year. I don't have the financial freedom that I want, but I have much growth in my emotional and mental state. I owe a lot of it to working with Jen, and I owe a lot of it to, day after day, staying sober. In AA, they say after five years of being sober, one gets their marbles back. After five, one learns how to play with them. I can say that for myself. I am learning to play well with others. That was one thing that Jen and I talked about a lot, that is, learning how to play well with others. Even wanting to play with others, period. That was something I never wanted, or knew how, to do.

Last night, I went out with a friend to dinner and a movie, and then, dessert after the movie. It was such a relaxing evening, an evening that was filled with laughter and healthy living. I am all about living a healthy emotional life these days

I remember what New Year's would be like before I got sober—sick and hungover, not sure what I did, or what I had said the night before, sad because I would be coming up on another year that had no hope or promise. I would feel like it was just another year for bad things to happen. I am so grateful that I don't live that way anymore. I am grateful that, today, I have choices and chances. I have the choice to serve a power greater than myself. I have the choice to love me just a little more and stay teachable. I have the choice to drink or not to drink. I have the choice to have a choice. As long as I continue to keep these choices, I have a chance at a good day. Living one day at a time.

Monday, January 7, 2013
Life On Life's Terms

Okay, so I have mentally been beating myself up a little over the last few days. My job is in jeopardy (again), and I feel like I just continue to go back to square one all the time. Is this a little pity party going on with me? During my high school and college years, I did a lot of drinking and drugging. I never thought that it was important to gain a skill. I just thought it was all about getting drunk and where the next drug was going to be found. Now, at 52, I am paying for it. I have no real skills and no college degree. It gets hard trying to find and hold on to a good job. I've lost 3 jobs in the last 3 years. Two were through no fault of my own, and the other was that the owner probably felt I needed to bring in more money. He didn't say that, just that the company was moving in another direction. I was just not going down the path with them. The job I have now is a failure waiting to happen. It's a product that nobody wants to buy.

As I write this, I see that a lot of this is no fault of my own. What *is* my responsibility is my lack of skills to obtain a different job. I am the last of a dying breed of salesmen, the kind that builds relationships, and then, they buy. In today's world, it's about grabbing the money and going. I was not trained as a salesman that way. So, here I go belly-aching about what I am not. The truth of the matter is that my past is kicking my ass right now. The one thing that I feel like I want to accomplish is finishing my novel. I can't even get focused enough to do that. I just want to sleep on the sofa all weekend and any chance I get after working. Am I depressed? As I write this, I don't feel depressed. I just feel like I need a kick in the ass to send me in the direction my life needs to go.

If I am lacking skills is there a way that I can get them now? I am hoping that there is. I pray that if this job folds and I can get some unemployment, then I can get some skills while unemployed and become a skilled worker in another field.

So, as I write, I begin to feel better. I feel like, "Okay, look at my life and change it." These jobs that are fly-by-night need to stop. I keep taking these out of desperation, but it's insanity, doing the same thing over and over again and expecting different results.

I was a little knocked down after not getting the State Farm job. It was something that would have been different, out of sales, and more customer service oriented. But God didn't see fit for me to have that. There is something else out there for me. Something big. I believe that, and I just have to keep focusing on that and waiting and preparing. Is it my novel? I have to get quiet and see where God leads me. Okay, so this all might sound confusing and going from one extreme to another. But it's just where I am for today, a little scattered, a little fearful, and a little on the pity pot.

I heard once it was okay to be on the pity pot every now and then, just remember to flush.

Tuesday, January 8, 2013
Faith

Something that I am learning through this whole ordeal about this job is my faith in God or a power greater than myself. I also have been a little hard on myself about my past again, looking at the things I should have done during my younger years. I should have finished school, acquired some office skills or some sort of skills. I could go on and on about what I should have done, but I know now that looking back will make no difference.

I was told once that the rearview mirror is the size that it is, and the front window is the size that it is, for a reason. We look at the smaller view from the rearview mirror and the whole picture from the front. I need to be looking ahead and seeing what is in store for me in front of me. Looking back just causes a whole lot of discomfort and discomfort is not where I want to be. Where I am today is trying to have a better walk with God.

I have been fasting from meat and sugar these last two days. With the meat, I have done okay. I have slipped with the sugar, with the hard candy I have in my candy dish. I need to pray that I can let that go. My prayers should not be for a job but for my relationship with God to get stronger and to have more faith in God.

When I pray, I have a comfort level that I can't describe. It is like something washes over me and says it's going to be okay. I don't think it will be easy, but it will be okay.

Wednesday, January 9, 2013
What About God?

Lately, I have been wondering if my life is always on alert because of God's approval of what I am doing. I know it is said that God makes no mistakes, and I am altering God's creation. It is something I have been struggling with. Why is it that, at 52, I don't have it all taken care of? I should be looking at retiring instead of looking for yet another career. I know I am just feeling a little sorry for myself this evening. This current job will more than likely end on Friday, and here I am, again, trying to figure out what to do with my life.

It's Humpty Dumpty. All the king's horses and all the king's men couldn't put him back together again. I feel like, sometimes, I am just coming apart. Always strapped for cash, struggling to be the man that I want to be. It's just a fucking struggle. When will the struggle end? I wait upon God's answer, but it seems like it never comes. When I lost the other job, I knew I had to find something before the unemployment ran out. It was a desperate move. Always in the desperate mode. When can I just sit back and be patient, looking for the right job that will finish out my career? I just want to enjoy life. When will I be able to just enjoy what life is giving me?

Not a good evening. God, please hear me. I know you are out there. I know that you will not let me fall, but God could you just allow me to take a deep breath and be okay?

Sunday, January 27, 2013
The Struggle

So, I have fucking lost yet another job. I just can't seem to find the right job that is stable so that I can settle in and be okay. It's going to be rough meeting the bills, but I just keep turning it over to God, along with the fear that goes with it. I go through the moment of fear, and I just stop, say a little prayer, and move on until the next wave of fear happens.

This is all so different for me. Usually, I am so wigged out that I can't function. All up in my head and really freaking out. What is different this time? Could it be that I am learning how to take these tools of living and apply them to my everyday living? Am I just not so emotionally attached since I have been on "T," that this is a different ride this time?

I know it sometimes feels like a struggle, but what the hell can I do, really? All I can do is apply for jobs, allow myself to feel the fear, move through it, and keep on going. What is the worst thing that could happen? I become homeless? At least, I would still have my life. I would still be sober, and I could still try to be a decent person.

What this time of not having a job is teaching me is that I need to be humble, let go of the pride, and ask for help. I don't have to be in the struggle unless I want. I can feel the pain and the fear and move on.

I want to go to that dark place where I look at the past and blame all my bad behavior back then for what life is like now. Leave that alone. Move on and get ready for the next ride.

Monday, January 28, 2013
2 Years

Two years are approaching since I made the decision about becoming a man. I can't believe that almost two years ago, I realized what had been missing in my life, that I was not truly happy because of the things lacking in my life. What was lacking? I made the decision to transition. I remember coming out to my therapist about this first. I just needed to say it out loud. It was such a freeing feeling. I felt the same way the day I walked into the rooms of AA and declared that I was an addict and that I was powerless over my life. Today, I am a free man. I am who I know I should have always been.

Two years of not being ashamed of who I am. Two years of being comfortable in my own skin.

Although there are other aspects of my life that are not in order, one thing is for sure, I know who I am and what I want to continue to become. That is, a good and decent African American man.

Tuesday, January 29, 2013
Just For Today

If AA has taught me anything, it is living in the moment, something I have been able to do for the last two days. Man, I have to admit that, for a few days, I was really in my head, fearing the worst about not having a job. But I just continued to pray to a power greater than me, that I choose to call God, and, well... I just don't have that level of anxiety that I had. I handled things these last few days that before I would have been over the top about because of everything else that was happening. I would have been out there blasting people for no reason. You know the damn cool thing is that I can see the change in me. I am becoming a really decent guy! Did making the transition do this for me? I will have to say feeling comfortable in my own skin makes a big difference.

So, just for today, I am okay.

Thursday, January 31, 2013
Another Day

Just got back from a meeting. Sometimes, I feel God in those rooms more so than others. Today, I felt very serene and was able to truly relax in the meeting, listening to people talk about unity. Before I got sober, I did not know what it was truly like to be a part of something. I look back over my life, and the one thing that I have done perfectly is stay sober. It amazes me that I have a hard time holding on to any job, lately, for any length of time. But I have held on to my sober life for almost seven years now. What a miracle! I don't think about drinking or drugging. When life is kicking me in the ass, I don't think about that default button of destroying myself.

Yesterday, I had to take a drug test for a potential job. What a relief that I did not have to worry about the results. I could walk into Labcorp with confidence, knowing that I had nothing to hide. It amazes me how much my life has changed. I recall a time when I was due for a really great job about eight years ago. They called and told me I had the job, but I needed to take a drug test. I was told where to go and I never went to take the test. I knew I would fail it. Today, I don't have that monkey on my back.

So, today is just another day to be kind to people, to love myself just a little bit more, and to take care of myself. During my quiet times,

I get in touch with my Higher Power and just be okay. Life is handing me some challenges, but I am handling life by staying sober.

Monday, February 4, 2013
Not A Part Of

I have been in AA now for almost seven years. I used to be connected to people, going out, and doing things. Then, I went into hiding after the breakup and concentrated on therapy. I went to very few meetings but was getting better emotionally because of the hard work in therapy.

After taking a break from therapy, I knew I needed to crank my meeting schedule back up. Which I have done. What I have found out is that, since my transition, I don't fit into any group socially anymore. Okay, is that my feeling about that? Let's take a look. I don't feel comfortable hanging around the women anymore, and I don't feel comfortable hanging with the guys. I just sort of go to the meeting, get my hour's worth of recovery, and move on. The fellowship is not there for me. Is that a problem? That is something that I need to ask myself.

Yesterday was Superbowl. I was hoping that I would get invited to go somewhere, but I did not. What really hurt was that I found out one of my friends was having a Super Bowl party and I was not invited. Now, I have no control over who he invites to his own home, but I did have him over twice to mine when I had Superbowl parties. I thought we were good enough friends that it would have happened. Did he just have guys and felt I was not one of the guys?

I was hurt when I found out he was having this party. It was just another stake in my heart that I feel like I am not a part of any group socially right now. I wish there were more trans guys locally here. But it is what it is, right now, with where I am.

What do I do to become accepted by men? It's tough because living here most of my life, men already know that I was once female. It's really funny that men accepted me more when I was a butch lesbian than they do now that I am a transman.

Once again is this my perspective?

It has gotten so bad that I don't even share in meetings a lot anymore because I am afraid someone is going to use the wrong pronoun with me and that people who didn't know me before are going to be confused. I'm not even sure that makes sense to anyone but me. But today is a day of getting this shit out.

So, here I am, afraid to raise my hand to say I will sponsor because who do I sponsor? Men? Women? What group am I really a part of?

The Struggle Without Fear

The 9th Step Promises tell me that, one day, I will live with little or no fear. I have struggled these past few weeks with fear of economic insecurity. But somewhere along the line, with a lot of prayer to a power greater than myself, I have lessened that fear. It does not consume me like it almost did a few weeks ago.

I am still without a job, still have little money, but I am content. How did that happen? I feel like I am just walking along this path. The scenery has not changed but my attitude has. I am more fit spiritually. I feel it. I have more confidence that everything is going to be okay.

Today, I am going to try to get back to writing my novel. It is something that has been blocking me for some time. The only way to overcome it is to start writing again. I have so much to say, so much to get down but, a lot of times, my fingers just can't hit the keyboard. I am ready to do everything else but settle down to the task.

Sometimes, I wonder if there might be a little depression going on. I don't know. I know it's not a deep depression if it is. Then, I think who wouldn't be a little depressed? I have no job, no money coming in, some bills are due, and, sometimes, I am just on the sofa staring into space.

I have to remind myself that I have to struggle without the fear. But what about the struggle without the struggle? Does that make sense? I have to stop the do-nothing attitude and do something productive every day. It's my promise today to myself. To do something. I can start by writing a blog every day. How about that?

Monday, February 11, 2013
Job

So, I started this new job today. No one knows about my past, and I am referred to as a guy by everyone. It's the perfect world of where I want to be. It was so comfortable today until it was time to go to the bathroom.

I just chose not to go until I got home. Couple of things I can see that I will need to do. One is to get a STP. I have been putting it off for some time. But it's something I am going to have to get. I didn't sweat it. I am okay. Lately, I guess I have been sort of used to not using public restrooms. It still frustrates me that I have to go through this. If only I was born male. But I deal with the hand that was dealt to me, and I am really proud of the man I am becoming.

Speaking of this job, I am thinking that it is easier for a man to get a job than a woman. In the past, when I lost jobs, it took a long time to get one, and almost no one would call me back for an interview. This time, I get tons of calls for interviews, and I got a job less than a month after being unemployed. Maybe it's the economy turning around. I want to think it's because I am male.

Either way, I am grateful to be back working. This morning and last night, I was feeling a little down about the job and how its yet another entry level position, but I don't have to stay there for the rest of my career. I still know what I want to be doing and that is finishing up my novel and getting it out for people to read. I have something to say, and I feel that it will help others who are walking this path.

I have to discipline myself to write every day. My plan is to get up early in the morning and write before going to work. Wish me luck on that!!

Friday, February 22, 2013
Being Outed

So, I started this new job. It pays very little money and is entry level for me. But it's a job. I just suck up my pride and do the task that is put before me. I realized about a day into the job that someone that I have known for a long time works there. He does not know about my transition, and I need to talk to him in private about it before he outs me to coworkers.

I have not had a chance to see him, and he didn't even know I was working with the company. I saw his name on the directory and have heard him talking while I was sort of hidden in a cubicle. Yesterday, he saw me and, in front of a bunch of guys, he said, "Hey, sweetie, what are you doing here?" I am not sure if anyone picked up on it, and I quickly told him to stop by my cubicle to see me. He didn't yesterday, but I am praying that we can meet up soon.

I have come up with things in my mind in terms of what I need to do. If he does not stop by today, I will seek out his cell number, give him a call, and talk to him then. If he leaks it out that I was once female, then so be it. I will just live with it.

I had a day or so of fear when I first found out that he was there, but I am living my life as I need, and want, to live it. It has no room for fear.

Saturday, February 23, 2013
Fear of being outed

I had this fear of being outed at work. I kept that fear with me for a couple of days, and then, I just let it go. I figured if it happened, it was going to happen. So, I continued to do my little avoiding with the guy that I knew from my neighborhood.

On Thursday, I saw him on the sales floor. He said "Hello" and called me "Sweetie" again. There were a few men around, but I don't think any of them picked up on the "sweetie" comment. I quickly told him where my cubicle was and asked him to please stop by to see me.

He stopped by the next day. As always, fear is not as big as I think it will be. I told him about my transition. He smiled, shook my hand, and said, "You know, I am cool with whatever you do."

March marks the 2nd anniversary of me coming out to my therapist. I am amazed at how I am still changing in looks, attitude, and action.

Monday, March 25, 2013
My First Tux

I am going to a formal event in April, and I got fitted today for my first tux ever. So many firsts are happening in my life since my transition. Going to this event will be the first formal affair I have ever attended. It is also the first time I have been fitted for a suit. I had a little anxiety when the woman was measuring me. What if she discovers I am different? What will she say? What does she think? It was very painless, and, I must say, I felt really at ease.

So, I now know my suit size and will be going out to buy my own suit in the future. This world has opened up so much, a world I never knew. In high school, I couldn't go to the prom in a tux. It was the 1970's, and I would have been laughed out of there. I stayed at home. Everyone else went to the prom, but I didn't. I don't remember if it bothered me or not. I just remember, the following Monday, not being part of the conversation about all that had happened. I didn't even know where the after parties were. I just stayed home that night. I do remember my mother asking me if I was upset. I would never have voiced it if I was.

I was different and that was all that it was. No one asked me to go, and so, I didn't go. I was not going to wear a dress, and I couldn't wear what I wanted. Life being a lesbian was pretty tough back then. I just didn't fit in anywhere. I don't even know if anyone missed me. No one asked.

Wednesday, March 27, 2013
Birth Certificate

My next step in my transition is changing my birth certificate. For some reason, it has been the hardest of the steps I have had to take. I'm not sure why I have a little anxiety about this. Why am I so uncertain about this? Everything else I have jumped right in and gotten it done, name change, starting "T," marker change. But this is making me hold off. I have to really look at this and see what is going on. Why am I holding back? I need to take this to the group. Maybe others are feeling the same way.

I printed out the form but that is as far as I have gotten. I need to take the next step. I need to remove the anxiety and push forward. Do this the same way that I did everything else.

I have to make a step toward freedom.

Saturday, March 30, 2013
Feeling Alone in AA

Lately, I have felt more alone in AA than ever before. I feel like being a Black man is keeping me away from people. My transition has isolated me a little from people. Once, I was always included in social events. Now, I am never asked. I go to a meeting, get my recovery, and go home. I don't have much conversation with people anymore and feel like I am just not a part of the group any longer.

I know this could all be in my head. But I see how each group of people have their own little clique, and I am just not "a part of." People I used to be around have disappeared and are a part of a new group.

I don't fit in with women, and I don't fit in with men. I don't raise my hand to sponsor because who am I supposed to sponsor? So, I just walk my recovery with me.

Support

Almost two years ago, I was given some information about transmen from Constance. She had found the information at a conference and mailed it to me to read. In the packet was information about Black Transmen Inc. It opened the door to my new life. I found this group on Facebook and joined. It has been one of the greatest things that ever happened. It's AA for my transition. There is never an experience that I am going through that someone else has not already been through. Just put it out there and someone speaks up and says, "Oh, yeah, I am going through this," or "I have gone through that."

I am so grateful to have this group.

Saturday, April 13, 2013
First Time

Lately, it's the little things that are happening in my life that make the biggest impact for me. Last week, I got into my first tux and went to a black-tie affair. I had wondered what it would feel like to be in a suit. Would it feel different? It felt just like I had put on a new layer of skin. It was such a great fit.

I had a little anxiety when they were measuring me for my tux. Touching me around my chest. What would happen if they discovered what I am. Then, I realized that I am me. I don't have to explain anything. I am Charley, and I am a proud trans man. Nothing more, nothing less.

It's amazing how my anxiety about being trans can come up on a moment's notice.

Monday, April 29, 2013
Life of a Black Man

Lately, I have noticed how women respond to me as a Black man. White women seem to be scared or they just ignore me. Black women very seldom even look my way. They ignore my presence too. Is this something that women do? I smile and try to be pleasant, but, a lot of times, I don't even get a response back from them. I have to wonder. I remember when I was much bigger than I am now. People would stare and ignore because it was like they were going to catch my fat. Some laughed, some even shook their heads. Men would not even look my way. Today, with a little less weight on me, I would have to say it's not about the weight. It's about the look. I am a Black man, and I am a threat. I have to remind myself of that when I am ignored in the rooms of AA by people who don't know me.

I am not a part of, just an extension. That's how I feel. But, for me, we are all there for one common goal—to stay sober. I think that, sometimes, their love and tolerance rule applies to only a few.

The other night, I heard a comment about a transwoman in the rooms. They called her a "he/she," and then, she was called an "it." There was laughter. I asked myself, *What are you calling me? What are they saying I am?* I had to let that go because its none of my business what they think of me.

Friday, May 3, 2013
Sometimes...

Sometimes, I forget about my gender change, and I wonder why someone is calling me a guy. A wave of embarrassment hits me, and I feel like I am going to be discovered. When I am around men, I wonder if I am man enough.

I was at work and was about to get up from my cubicle and grab a cup of coffee. I saw someone who knows me, and I went back into my cubicle. I knew this woman was going to call me by my other name and refer to me as female. I waited until she was gone. It's a fear that I can't describe when I think I am going to be outed at work.

Sometimes, I wish I had moved first before making my transition. Sometimes, I get angry because I just wish I was a man and none of this would have to be a worry. No binders, no trying to save money for surgery, life would be so much better at times.

Monday, May 6, 2013
Anniversary Month

Pretty soon, I will celebrate seven years of being clean and sober. As I look back over the past year, I am amazed at the things God has granted me. My transition is going okay. I finally have a job where I am doing well and am not being micromanaged. My sober life is good. I really don't have anything to complain about. On May 22, I will have seven years clean and sober, and five days later will be my birthday. I am so grateful that I came into the rooms of AA before my birthday. I would have had the possibility of not making it at the rate I was going. I was mixing pills and drinking more than I had ever before. I was feeling lost and all alone. Thank God, He led me to where He did. I am so grateful for my life right now. I still don't have a lot of money. I hold my breath that nothing major happens, but financially, all in all, I am pleased. This month, I am so grateful for where I am, compared to seven years ago.

Saturday, May 11, 2013
Next Step

I am preparing for my next step in my transition. I need to buy a STP. I find that I am having a lot of anxiety going to the men's bathroom. I have to use the stall because I don't have a STP. I am afraid someone will come in and hear or see me sitting down to pee. I know they say that most men go into the bathroom, do what they need to do, and get out of there. But what if I get caught? Why do I feel it's about a getting caught thing? I have found myself holding it until I get home, and I should not have to do that. With a STP, I could still use the stall but also could stand to pee. So, the next step is picking out and buying a STP, teaching myself how to use it, and throwing that anxiety out the window.

Friday, May 17, 2013
Family Gathering

Had my first family gathering at a funeral yesterday. I was a little nervous as I drove out to the church. How will I approach people? Will they see me as different? I felt that some people who know looked at me a little differently. Could that have been my perception?

As I was getting dressed, I realized that I no longer have to feel guilty for putting on men's clothing. I can wear what I want without fear of people thinking differently. Then, I realized that I didn't have to worry what people think of me. I felt a sense of comfort. For the first time in my life, I can be who I truly want to be.

I survived the event yesterday and never once worried about what people think. They still called me by my female name, at times, but that was okay too. These are not people I deal with every day.

Tuesday, May 21, 2013
Feeling Good

I realized yesterday that, even though I don't make the money I want to make, I am in the space where I want to be. I am feeling good about where my life is right now and how I handle things.

The 9th Step Promises say that I will not regret the past nor wish to shut the door on it. I will be able to handle things that used to baffle me.

That is so true. It does not promise that I am going to be free of everything, just that I will be able to handle things with a new pair of glasses. I sure do look at things differently now.

I am feeling more confident in who I am, and even though I still have my bouts of anxiety, they are fewer and less intense. What do I owe this all to? I owe it to being able to truly be who I am and being able to finally be free. I remember, before my transition, when I would have anxious moments about my dress. I was always afraid that people were going to make fun of me wearing men's clothing. Actually, men's clothing was the only thing I felt comfortable in. It's a crazy thought, but I was always thinking that people were saying things about my clothes. Today, to a certain degree, I don't care what people think. It's not my business what people think of me. I know that's easier said than done, but it's a motto I try to carry with me along my path.

Wednesday, May 22, 2013
7 Years

Today is seven years clean and sober. I can't believe that for seven years, now, I have not had a drink or drug. Each year gets just a little bit better in the process of dealing with emotional living. I am a sober man today. Today, I don't have everything I want, but I have everything I need. I am so grateful.

I would have never been able to embrace the life I have embraced if it were not for being a member of AA. AA saved my life. AA created the person I am today. Who is that person? I am just a little more honest, a little more self-assured about who I am. If I just stay on that path, things are bearable. Today, I am grateful for being the man I am. Sober, happy, and free.

Sunday, June 23, 2013
Checking In

It's been a while since I have written anything. It's like I have been in some sort of slump about putting words on paper. I have so much to say but don't know what or how to formulate it. Does that make any sense? My mother has been placed in a nursing facility for rehab, and it has rocked my world a little bit. Just knowing that she is there and seeing how helpless she is makes me realize that life never stays the same. It constantly changes.

I think the hardest part is that there I am looking totally like a man, and she is introducing me to the staff as her youngest daughter. What do I do? Do I correct her? Leave it alone? I choose to just leave it alone. She will never accept what and who I am now. Her mind would not comprehend it, nor would she want to accept it. She never truly accepted that I was a lesbian. She would never accept this.

She is one of those church-going people who believes that gays will all burn in hell. She would never present that to the outside world but, behind closed doors, and to me, she would express her feelings very openly.

I feel at peace with my mother. The steps of AA taught me about forgiveness, and I forgave and have made my amends for what I have done to her. I am free with that. I just don't talk a lot of substance stuff with her. We just do the same thing in the nursing home as we did at home. We just talk about surface things and leave the heavy-duty stuff alone.

So, tonight, I just check in with my writing, and I vow to write more.

Monday, July 8, 2013
Stages Of Life
These last few weeks, watching my mother as she continues to get older, I think about the stages of life. I think about how she did the best she could in raising three children with limited income and education. I watch as this woman, who was very smart and well-educated, despite her limitations, worked hard to provide for her family. Now, I watch as she just does not have the kick, like she used to, in order to get better. Is this her final stage in life? At 96, one would say "yes."

Last night, I was reminded by a good friend that death and our living is between us and God. She is right. The final say in when, how, and where we go is between the person and their higher power.

I cannot will my mother to get better. I cannot will her to get out of bed and go back to the way she was a month ago. That is between her and God. There is nothing I can say or do. I can be there for her, I can listen when she needs someone to listen, and I can be the daughter/son she can turn to for help. I have to learn that I need to stop being willful in this, wanting her to get better for my own selfish needs, and just accept that if she gets better, she gets better.

I look at my own stages in life, being the little girl that I never wanted to be, going through the stage of drinking and drugging, going through the stage of being a butch lesbian, and now, being what I always should have been—a transman. Today, I am comfortable in this stage of life. There is more I want but, in due time, that will happen. I am free to be who I want to be, and that is what I have striven for all my life. Today, I can take a deep breath and just as I can't be willful of my mother's health, I cannot be willful of my own stage in life. Today, we both are where our Higher Power wants us to be.

Friday, August 23, 2013
Fear

Something as simple as wanting to let my beard and mustache grow gives me a little fear in the pit of my stomach. What will people think who know me as a woman? How do I explain if one of them asks? Will my family think I have gone crazy? Will it confuse my 96-year-old mother who, already in her bouts of confusion, does not know who I am. What do I do?

This is when I wish for two things: that I was born a man, and that I did not live in this area. It would be so simple to be in a city away from the people I grew up with. Then, I could be who I truly am. Am I being a sellout by trying to be something I am not? What about honesty that all I want to be is who I am supposed to be?

I need to get feedback from others. I am sure I am not the only one going through this. I am not alone in this, nor am I unique.

Thursday, August 29, 2013
Just Stuff

I've got a lot of stuff going on in my head. I am feeling pretty good about myself this week. I'm feeling confident. But, man, that feeling of wanting to hide when I see people from my past can come on so quickly.

I see people from my past at work, and I find myself hiding. Like, today, I saw a few old friends from the past, and I would not go up and speak to them. First, I have not shaved in a few days, so I had the beard thing going on. Second, I just don't want them to out me at work. I know I need to step up and not worry about that, but it's something that I fight with daily. What if I get caught at work, and people find out that I was once a girl named Charlotte?

I see now that it might be some help to go find another therapist to throw this stuff at. A different perspective. But then, there is the problem of finding someone who deals with trans issues. I don't know. It's a lot. I thought I had dealt with it with the name change and telling some people. It's down to the nitty gritty now, and it's a little scary.

Thursday, September 19, 2013
2 Years

Last Friday was two years of being on "T" for me. In March, it will be three years since coming out as trans. I have had it fairly easy compared to what some people have had to deal with. I still have my family, who ignores my transition. Ignoring is easier than accepting. But that's okay. I am who I am. I pretty much came out as trans over the weekend by being interviewed by the local paper. That too was God doing for me what I could not do for myself. It was decent and in order. That is how God wants me to live my life, to live it as a good and decent man.

When I got to work on Monday, I had some people who looked at me funny. Was it my imagination or was it true? Then, I got a call that my pay was being cut, and I was the only one being affected by this. Last month, I was the best thing going, bringing in money for the company. This week, they are struggling and not meeting their goals. Which is it with me? But, you know, I took it all in stride. Was again the decent and in-order man that I am trying to be. I accepted it, but I don't have to work there for the rest of my life. So, I have started actively looking for a new job. I will do what God directs me to do. Stay in prayer over this and just do the next right thing.

Two years and it's bringing a lot of different changes. Who would have believed, two years ago, that I would be giving myself injections? Who would have believed, two years ago, that I would be speaking out about our local Pride? Two years ago, who would have believed that I would be so content with life?

Sunday, October 13, 2013
Two Steps Forward, Three Backwards

So, I have been laid off again. This time, I did not see it coming. I was performing well, meeting targets. So, what was the problem this time? They couldn't really explain, except that they are doing a reduction, and I am one of the people they were sending out the door.

So, here I go again, having to find a job, along with fear that I am not going to meet my bills, fear I will lose stuff. Just normal fear and panic. But I just keep praying. When fear creeps up, I just stop and pray. I don't know anything else to do. I am taking action. My resumé is up-to-date, and I am sending them out.

I have faith that God is not going to let me down. I have to do the next right thing. I have to just keep taking action. Faith without works is dead. I am much stronger than during my last lay off. I am more centered and grounded. I am going to take the off-time to also write more and just take care of me. I am not afraid for the moment.

Monday, November 4, 2013
Here I am

So, here I am with no job, money running low, and I have writer's block. Can't seem to get motivated enough to continue writing. I have about another 100 pages to go, and I think I will be finished. Why is it that I can't buckle down and write? There is so much in my head that needs to go on paper, so much of my past that I need to write about. I pray that I am going to start moving in the direction of writing and soon. I have so many excuses, so much idle time on my hands. I think I am a lot more depressed about this job situation than I am letting on. I am so grateful for the meds I am on that will not allow me to get any more depressed than I already am. It helps that I have someone to talk to. My good friend supports me in every endeavor I am doing.

Pretty much, my day is filled with minor things to do around the house. I basically sit and stare at the computer screen for hours. What am I to do?

Sunday, November 17, 2013
Changes

As I see more and more changes with my body, the more I feel like hiding. I have been growing a mustache, and I feel so open and raw about it. There are times that I want to just shave it off so that people, who don't know about my transition, don't think I am some sort of freak. Why should I care? I am living my life, being who I am comfortable being. These are the things that I carry around with me. I need to talk to someone about them, to express my fears and feelings. I wish I lived in a town where no one knows me, where I am just another person. Is this normal? Why should I care what people think? I am who I am.

Tonight, I was in the grocery store. I saw someone I knew from many years ago. I went down the next aisle to keep from speaking to her. I felt so raw, so ashamed of who I am. Am I being a fake? Is this normal for where I am in my transition?

I am comfortable being a man, but uncomfortable being a man in front of people who know me. I worry they are going to think I am some sort of freak, sick. Just the way I was treated when I was a little girl trying to fit in, being laughed at and bullied by friends. I was always treated like a freak. I was even called one. So, when I see someone that has no idea about what I am doing, I feel that rawness, the same rawness I felt as a child at the big tree near the merry-go-round. Am I that child again?

Tuesday, November 19, 2013
Feeling Grateful

You know, at the moment, I am unemployed. Money is really tight. But I still have a lot to be grateful for. I am grateful that I don't find it necessary to take a drink or a drug today after seven and a half years, that it's not my automatic go to, like it used to be, that drama and ego inflation is not a part of my life today. Today, I try to remain humble and know that it's not about me.

Tonight, I am going to pray for this job and know that it's okay to ask God to send it to me. Tonight, before I go to bed, I will have done the best I could at living as a decent human being, just for today. Tonight, I am okay.

Wednesday, November 27, 2013
The Gathering

Little things make such a difference to me at this time in my life. I will be gathering with the family on Thursday, and it will be the first time I am sporting a mustache. I feel a little awkward about it. I even considered shaving it off. But I finally realized that if I am going to truly be a transman, I need to not be afraid. Being afraid of what people will think of me has been the driving force of my life. I have to let go of that fear and just keep moving in the direction I want my life to go. I have to become the man I want to be, without any reservations.

For years, I lived my life in the shadows, afraid to express who I am and who I wanted to love, for fear of what people would think. Today, I am proud of who I am. I am a decent, loving, Black man of trans experience. I am someone who loves their life, who deeply loves the friends I have. I am proud to be a Black man.

Today, I will express who I am in whatever way I want. I will be loving, kind, and grateful for the life God has given me, knowing that God is by my side.

I am proud. I am a Black transman.

Thursday, November 28, 2013
Family Gatherings

So, today, I gather with my family. The pronouns will be different. I will not be looked at as Charley, but as Charlotte. Will I correct them or just let it slide? These are the questions that float constantly in my mind with friends and family. Amazingly though, my AA community accepts my changes and respects my wishes. Why is it that my family does not? Could it be that I need to distill it more for them? I don't know. I just wish I had been born a male. That way none of this would have to happen. I wouldn't have that fear-in-the-gut feeling every time I fill out an application or go on a job interview. I would not have to feel like I am a traitor. Most importantly, I would not have to feel like I am doing something wrong. It's a struggle with the transition. More so than just coming out as gay or lesbian.

Every day, I have some struggle about who I am. Will this get easier? Would it be better if I moved? I can't predict the future. I just have to learn to live in the present. For today, I am grateful to have a family to go to, that, later this evening, I will be spending time with a good friend and her family.

All is good. I am not going to let pronouns and a name change my course today.

Chapter 11

2014

Let go and let God.
Alcoholics Anonymous

Thursday, January 2, 2014
Loss of a Cousin

Yesterday, I lost a cousin. Growing up, we were always together. He rode with me every day to high school. We were always out and about and being the life of the party. We did a lot of drugs and drank a lot of alcohol together. He never stopped. I got sober. But he continued drinking. When I saw him on Christmas Day, he looked really bad. Should I have said something to him? He was not drunk on Christmas morning, always came to see us on Christmas morning, always happy to see us.

He is yet another Black male in our family who died at a young age. Besides my father and his two brothers, all the other males in our family never made it to retirement age. They die from drinking. This is the same thing with my cousin. His liver just said, "No more." His body said, "I can't take this." It could have been me. But I chose to get sober and clean, and to stay that way. I chose not to be one of those numbers in my family. Have I broken the chain? Or did I just step out of the circle?

January 2014
Another New Year

So, it's another new year. Everyone starts out with these New Year's resolutions. I am going to say that I am setting some new goals. I start a new job in a few days and will be back in sales. I realized that sales is really what I know in life, and it's a passion I have. A friend told me to find what I am passionate about and make it a job. So, goal number one is to do the best I can at this new job, be aggressive and honest about my work, be appreciative that I have a job.

Goal two. Okay, we all hear it—lose weight. I need to get on a healthy eating kick and stick to it.

Goal three. Live life. I am going to enjoy my life more, get out and do things that I have never done, have more fun in life, be more proactive with my work with Black Transmen.

Goal four. Write more! Write more here in my blog and, also, with my novel. I can say I want to write a novel, but if I don't continue writing, it will never become a novel. I have just had writer's block for the last two months. I need to see why I am not interested in getting back to this.

My last goal is to save money.

Okay, so these goals are not too hard, and they are within reach. I need to speak these out to a friend so that I can be held accountable.

Saturday, January 11, 2014
My Mother

My mother died yesterday. I don't know if I have the words to describe how this pain feels. Even though she was 97 years old, it's a shock. I really thought after she got sick this last time that she would be with us just a little bit longer. She died peacefully in her sleep at her home in the early morning hours. She leaves a generation of people that will live on. We are better people because of her. I watched my mother work long and hard hours to provide for her family. She always wanted the best for us and provided as best as she could.

I also watched my mother become a wonderful grandmother and, eventually, a great-grandmother. Although we never spoke about my transition, I felt that as her health began to fail, it was not important. It was not about me. It was about allowing my mother to live out her last years, about making her comfortable and providing for her as best as we could.

Next week, we will say our final goodbyes. She is at peace now. I just have to live the life my mother would have wanted, with grace and dignity.

Wednesday, February 26, 2014
Long Time

Been a while since I have felt like writing. I guess I am going through some depression. Missing my mother, finances, etc. I am trying to take it a day at a time, but I just have no energy. I get through what I need to but, all other times, I just hang out on the sofa and stare at the blank TV. Most times, I sleep. I wake up tired and go to bed tired. I have to get some help. I have a doctor's appointment tomorrow and will address all of this. I don't even have the energy to write or read. This all started right after my mother died. So, I know there is some of this going on.

I need to get back to praying and taking time to just meditate and get quiet. The quiet that I do have is not settled. I'm not sure how to explain it. It just is not a peaceful quiet. I sure hope I can connect with someone who I like and who can help me through this. I want to finish my book. I want to be a success at my job. I just want to get back to enjoying life.

Tuesday, March 4, 2014
Starting Therapy Again

So, it's time to get back on the sofa and start therapy. I have been battling a little depression. I want to address it before it gets out of hand. Man, this is different than in the past, when I would have been putting it off until I just *had* to do something. I see so much growth in my life. I know things are different. Is it because I am sober? Or is it my transition? Maybe it's a little bit of both. I think after working with Jen, I was afraid I would never connect with a therapist the way I did with her. I have come to realize that everyone is different. I have to accept that what Jen brought to the table for me is not what someone else will bring.

I encourage everyone who is in transition to get therapy and, if possible, continue for a long time. Things change in our lives. We have to be ready for the change. I had Jen when I first came out about my transition. I had Michael in my beginning stages of transition. I will use this new person for maintenance of my transition. I have so much to be thankful for right now in my life. Finances are not good but other parts of my life are great. I am feeling more secure in who I am. I am ready for the next stage in my life.

Wednesday, March 5, 2014
Tears

Last night, I cried. Normally, I would not make such a big deal out of this. I cried because I miss my mother. I cried because, for the first time, I felt alone. I felt like I just needed to be close to her. I have been missing my mother a lot these last few days. I just never thought about what it would be like once she was gone. There's a hole in my heart. In the past, I would fill that hole with drugs, alcohol, and even food. Today, I let the feelings flow, and that is okay. It's okay to just say I am sad and move through it. I am doing what I need to do to get by. If I cry tonight, that is okay too.

Tuesday, March 11, 2014
Just Want to Be a Guy

Life as a trans man is difficult. It really takes a lot of strength to come out and be who you truly are. Deep in my soul, I am so comfortable with who I am. I am comfortable being the man that I am becoming.

It's times like going to the doctor that are hard, having to take my shirt off and reveal my breasts. I want them gone. It takes so much to take that shirt off and then, the binder, exposing what I don't want to expose—women's parts.

I had to do that yesterday at the doctor's office. Just being exposed as a woman takes a lot out of me. I want to be a guy. They are setting up an appointment with a gynecologist (GYN) and I know that will be another moment. What will I look like in the waiting room at the GYN office? I don't want to be treated differently. I just want to be treated with respect.

One day, I won't have the breasts to worry about. That will be a great day. It will be a day that I will truly be free to express who I am. As for now, I just humble myself and keep on moving.

Thursday, March 13, 2014
My Past No Longer a Victim

So, next week, for my job, I have to meet with the man who 36 years ago raped me. I knew his first name but never knew his last name until today. He owns a lot of property here, and I will be asking for his business. I know he won't remember me now that I am male and have lost a lot of weight. I am sure if I were still a female, he might remember me.

How do I feel about this? I really don't have any feelings about it at all. I am no longer living in the space that I was 36 years ago. I am no longer a drunk or a drug addict. I took the role of victim away a long time ago. I am a survivor. I will admit when I saw his picture in my boss' office today, I cringed inside a little bit. For a moment, out came the feelings of being violated. But, just as quickly as they came, they went. I knew I was no longer that confused 17-year-old. I realized that when I got in that car, I knew what was going to happen. I knew that he was not buying the booze just to drink with me. I know these things because I have done a 4th step in my recovery—looking at my part, owning up to it, and moving on. Life, now, has a whole new different meaning for me. I will never forget what happened, but I will never live in it again.

Monday, March 17, 2014
Not Regretting the Past

I have been thinking a lot about my past. What if I had done this, or what if I had done that? In the end, it really does not matter what I have done before. It is what I am doing with it at this moment. I can be a victim of my past or I can be a survivor. Today, I choose to be a survivor. I choose to take my life and do something with it.

I have been feeling a little down lately and wondered why. I realize now it is possibly because of some medication issues. I really looked deep to find the source of why I am always so tired. This is called "taking care of myself." This is something that I would have never done in the past. I would have let things go until it was critical. I am going to a therapist for the first time because I want to, not because someone is making me or suggesting that I go. I'm going because I want to go. Big change.

The 9th Step Promises are coming true. I am amazed at where I am. These last few months have been a huge financial strain. Most of the time, I have very little money to live off after I pay bills. Being off for a month or so, really put me behind. I am now playing catch up and, most times, it seems like I will never catch up. But as the 9th Step Promises have told me, fear of economic insecurity will leave. I no longer have that fear. I have faith. I have faith that the God I serve will take care of me. It is true. I don't ever get an abundance, but I get just what I need to get by. Someday, my life will not be just getting by. Someday, it will be about making it and enjoying life. That means not having that financial cloud hanging over me. It will be okay. I will be okay.

Wednesday, March 19, 2014
Prayers

I have been more in tune with my Higher Power lately, just turning things over to my Higher Power more and more. I realized that I had no other choice. It was either drive myself crazy with anxiety or just pray and turn it over. Funny how things seem so huge and overwhelming until you take care of them and just move on.

I have been thinking a lot about my life and what it means and how content I am. I don't have a lot of money, I'm behind on some of my bills, but I am happy, joyous, and free. I am content. It's a good feeling.

Thursday, March 20, 2014
Finally Free....

Yesterday, I had an interview. It was one of the toughest interviews I have ever had. They put down everything I talked about, criticized my work history. I held my ground, but I left there feeling very low. Feeling like I had been a failure in my life. I quickly said a simple prayer of, "God have your way about this." I already have a job and it's not the end of the world if I don't get this one.

Just as I was talking about this with a friend, the email came in. I got the job! It's more money than I have ever made since my Value American days. It will allow me to not be so under the gun with money and bills. It will give me a financial freedom I have prayed for and wanted for years. And it is out of sales. I have prayed and asked God to get me out of sales. I just was not cut out for sales any longer, meeting quotas, asking people to buy things. I had just burned out from that. But God answered just in time. I think about that gospel song: "He May Not Come When You Want Him, But He's Right On Time."

Thank God, I never gave up looking for that right job. Thank God, He, in His time answered my prayers!

Book IV

What Happened?

We are not human beings sharing a spiritual journey,
but spiritual beings sharing a human journey.
Alcoholics Anonymous

Chapter 12

Constance
(An Interview)[12]

Keep coming back, it works if you work it.

Alcoholics Anonymous

INTERVIEWER: It's lovely to meet you.

CONSTANCE: Nice to meet you.

INTERVIEWER: So, whereabouts are you.

CONSTANCE: I'm in Princeton, New Jersey. I go to school here.

INTERVIEWER: What are you taking?

CONSTANCE: I'm in the Princeton Theological Seminary. I've just finished my first year.

---

[12] Interview by Margot Wilson, May 28 2021.

INTERVIEWER: Congratulations. Your exams went well?

CONSTANCE: Yes, they did. They went very well. It was stressful but everything went well.

INTERVIEWER: After many years at the university, I know exactly what you're talking about. One way or the other, no matter which side of the exam you're on, it is stressful.

CONSTANCE: It's stressful, yes. But I did really well. So, I'm happy.

INTERVIEWER: So, how many years is the program.

CONSTANCE: Three. It's a Presbyterian seminary, although I'm not Presbyterian. They take people from all faiths. But it started out as a Presbyterian seminary.

INTERVIEWER: Oh, that's interesting. I was raised Presbyterian. My aunt was the bursar at the Presbyterian seminary at the University of Toronto and my first job was in the library. So, look, we've got to a point of contact already, without Charley. I was very pleased that Charley suggested that I talk to you about that part of his life that you shared. I'm not sure how much he told you about my interview technique, which is pretty anthropological. Let's put it that way. I like to get to know people. I like people to tell me what they want me to hear. I do have some guideline suggestions about where we might go with this but I'm also happy just to sit quietly and listen to you talk, if that's comfortable for you.

CONSTANCE: Okay. Maybe get me started.

INTERVIEWER: Okay. I did ask Charley, "What should I ask Constance about?" And he suggested that two things were that time in his life when Charley was a butch lesbian, and the dark place that he went when he was about five years sober. I suspect that was just towards the end of your relationship with him. I'm happy to start with, "How did you meet?"

CONSTANCE: Okay. We met online. I had been in a long-term relationship, and with my daughters' prompting—I have three daughters—and they were like it's time for you to meet somebody and get out there. So, I was like, "Oh, I don't know. I don't want to do that." So, they helped me do a profile. Initially, I was a little anxious about it, so I really didn't think it was something I wanted to do. But they said, "We're going to help you write this and want to do a picture."

And so, they did the whole thing, posted it, and I got a lot of responses. But they didn't say much. I love the written word. And I guess, now, people don't. But I do. I love books. I like the written word. So, someone who can write and express themself, for me, is really different. And so, when I first got a response from Charley, that's what stuck out. And then, we just started writing. We just wrote back and forth for a long time. We could have talked on the phone, but we didn't choose to do that. So, it was a little while before we started talking on the phone. We just kind of went back and forth in writing. And we just kind of started from there.

We were both in Virginia, but he was probably about two or three hours from where I lived. So, although we were in the same state, we were a good distance away. Later on, we decided that we would get together. We met up and then, it was like the rest was history. Things went really well.

Then, we decided that, okay, we're going to be in a relationship, and, as it moved along, we decided that I would move. At that time, I was living in Chesapeake, Virginia. I would move from Chesapeake to where he lived in Charlottesville. We found a place and had some work done on it. So, I sold my house and all that.

He actually moved into the house prior to me. At the time, I had three dogs. So, I took the babies to the house, and they stayed with Charley for some weeks until I could wrap things up. I transferred with my job and went to live there. And so, a couple of days before Thanksgiving, I came to officially live at the house.

But that week, when I was going to move there, apparently, he found out that his company was going to be closing. It wasn't that they were going to be closing in a few days. It was like, "We're not going to be in business anymore, probably by the end of next week." And that was like, "What?" Because there was no warning. Everything had been fine. Business was going along as usual. So, nobody saw it coming. I think that was like an initial crack. But, you know, we were doing okay. Everything was fine with us.

This is November, and we're doing pretty good. So, I'm like, "No problem. I'm working. That's not going to be a problem. We're going to make it. Everything will be fine. The bills are going to be paid. It's not going to be a big thing."

But as it went on, I did have a concern because I'd been in relationships before with butch lesbians and they're very wed to their identity about their work and being able to be providers. What their work is, very much affects their value or their sense of value. And so, I was really concerned when that happened, but I figured, "Okay. Well, we'll just ride it out because he'll be okay. And I'm saying "he" because I'm so used to saying "he" now.

INTERVIEWER: I was just thinking that. It's difficult. Our language doesn't allow for the transition and the shift in language.

CONSTANCE: Yeah. It's different because, of course, I knew him as "she." But once he told me, it felt so natural to me because I always felt that. So, it wasn't like a big change to me. When he told me, he said, "Well, I want you to know that I've decided that I'm trans, and I'm in the process of transitioning." At that point, we hadn't talked for a long time, and I'll tell you about that. But I just said, "Okay. Well, you won't have far to go" because it was not, to me, a big leap.

As the time kept going on, it was the end of the year. It's November, and most places aren't doing a lot of hiring as it comes to the end of the year. And so, I was like, "Don't worry about it. A job will come. Don't worry about it." But I could see, as time was going on, he was getting more and more and more in his head. And I think because he was early in sobriety—five years is relatively early—he always had some anxiety. I didn't know why, but it just seemed like, even in the best of times, there was some unhappiness. And I didn't know what it was about or where it was going or what that meant. But it just seemed like there was something there. I knew that there had been troubles in childhood about identity and that kind of thing, and it had really been a struggle. And there still was some struggle with his family to accept him fully, 100%.

So, I knew that and that always has some impact on you. But I wasn't just 100% sure. But the longer that he didn't have a job, I think the more and more anxious he became. I could just see more and more and more cracking. And then, I guess, around the Super Bowl, around February or so, I broke my knee. I slipped on the ice in front of our house and my right leg shot up, my left leg went under, and I came down on my knee. It was still no big situation because I had disability with my job, and I had time. So, it wasn't that we weren't going to be okay. But that was very distressing for him. He continued applying for jobs and then thinking he got it and then he really didn't. It was very distressing. So, that continued, and I was really feeling some real concern, and he was just real upset sometimes and that kind of thing.

I think a lot of the stress came from, "Okay. Now, my knee is broken, so I can't do anything." I had surgery. After the surgery, for another three or four weeks, I was just in the recliner. So, I had to have helped to go to the bathroom. I couldn't even get water from myself. I'm on crutches. So, it was really a difficult time. I could still see this light kind of going on, and I could see he was just more and more and more anxious and unhappy and angry. It comes out for him as anger, just explosive at times. Angry.

And so, we move along. It's like mid-May, and I'm able to go back to work. I go back to work and I'm thinking, *Okay. Everything's going to settle when I go back to work*. But now, I think me going back to work and him being alone all day and still in the process of searching for a job… and you're in your head. Every time you don't hear something, or every time they say they're going to call you back and they don't, then, you're in your head. "I'm never going to get a job" and "You came here, and now I can't pull my weight." It was just all of that anxiety that was going on.

So, I asked, at that point, "Do you think it's something more that's going on, that's about your unhappiness, your anxiety? Something at the core seems unhappy." And so, he said, "No, no, no. It's nothing else. I'm just unhappy." So, I said, "Okay." But as time went on, it was anxiety about the job, but it was something else that was just basically unhappy.

I said to him, some months later, when he was just exploding. I can't even remember what he was exploding over. But he was just really exploding. At that point, I had become afraid for him because he was so unhappy. One day, I said, "You know, you have a lot that you can be contented about. I understand that you're unhappy about the work situation, but there's a lot of good things that are going on, and it doesn't seem that you can recognize any of that." I said, "I'm really concerned about you. I'm really concerned about what I'm seeing." And I said, "You just seem so unhappy. It's almost like you're on the edge unhappy. I'm just concerned that if we don't address this, you might harm yourself." I said, "Do you know why?" And so, he just looked at me and he said, "I am unhappy. I am. I'm so unhappy. I want to die. I'm so unhappy."

So, I knew then that this is way more. I don't know what it is. There's something. You're unhappy about the job situation and I get that, but there's something else and I don't know what it is. And he wasn't saying. But he did say to me that he was unhappy. He said, "I'm just on the edge, and I'm just so done." At that point, I insisted. I said, "I just cannot continue with seeing you this way. We have got to go to get some help, some counseling, and see what's going on. "

And so, we did. We went to counseling initially, and then, he stopped and said, "I'm not going back anymore." Then we restarted and we went back and we had a really good counselor, who was a woman, and she too was concerned. She said, "Maybe you and I should meet and work together, and then we can work on some couple things." But he couldn't eat, and he would withdraw. And so, eventually, what happened was that I just said, "I've had enough, if this is still going on." You know, this explosive anger and it was just becoming just miserable at home.

I don't know what happened. I mean, you didn't have to have anything particular happen and he could just fly off. I left to go to work one morning, and I left him and a friend of his, at the house and, by the time I had driven—my job was about an hour and five minutes away— by the time I got into the parking lot of the hospital, he called me. We had three dogs and a cat. His cat had been ill. Before I left home, I was like, "Okay, we need to go ahead and take her into the vet to see what's going on." And he was like, "I don't know. Every time we go to the vet, it's so expensive." And I was like, "Yeah, but we'll just have to work that out. We'll just have to work that out with the vet. Just take her in."

By the time I got to work and got into the parking lot, he was calling me, enraged. Just carrying on, angry on the phone. I didn't know why. And I was like, "Well, what is wrong?" So, he was very upset about the cat, and that I didn't understand about the situation and why he didn't want to take her. So, now I'm saying to take her. I'm like, "Okay. Well, don't take her." I didn't know. So as the day was going on, I kept getting these sporadic calls that were more and more and more angry. By the time it was time for me to go home from work, I didn't want to go home. So, I stayed at work a little longer, finished some things up. He was calling me, "What time are you leaving? What time are you coming home?" "Okay, I'm leaving now." So, he was like, "Okay." I was a little hesitant about going home because of this level of anger and, previously, we'd have some episodes where he was breaking things or throwing things. So, I was like, "I don't want to deal with that." So, I figured, *We'll give it a little time. By the time I get there, maybe things will be better.*

Well, by the time I got home, they weren't there. And then, it was, "What was going on?" And "Why were you late coming home?" And "I felt like you weren't going to come home. I was calling you and you didn't answer." "Well, you know I'm at work." And so, we were going back and forth, back and forth. So, I'm in the kitchen and I'm preparing dinner because we have to have dinner. But you're still all worked up. When he got really angry, his whole person changed. He just became, and looked, so different.

I had two German shepherds and I had a little mixed dog. but I had one German shepherd who was glued to me, was just everywhere I went. And so, I was at the counter, and he was in his normal place, sitting beside me, like up against my leg. I was chopping with the knife, and he is behind me, going on, going on, going on. The dog stood up. I guess I knew him so well that, when he stood up, I could feel that his body, up against my leg, felt weird. So, I looked down at him and he was staring. He didn't growl. He didn't say anything. They all loved Charley. So, I just thought that was odd. When I went to turn around to see what was happening, he was like advancing on me, advancing like something's wrong in your eyes advancing on me, which frightened me.

When I turned around, I still had the knife in my hand. Then, the dog moved in front of me. And then, his hair stood up and I felt like, "Oh! Wow! This is real." He feels like he needs to protect me. and I just said to him, "Stop." I said, "I want you to stop, and I want you to leave. I'm not going to be in this situation. I told you when I met you that I had previously, very, very, very early in my life, been in an abusive relationship with my oldest child's father." And I said, "I told you, then I would never go down that road again, not never, ever, ever. This is getting out of control. I want you to stop." So, he came forward a little more, and I said, "Stop."

So, I had the knife in my hand. It wasn't like, "I'm going to stab you," but it was that he looked at me, looked at the knife, and said, "Okay, I'm leaving." And he left. That, for me, was so frightening because I thought about how that could have gotten so, tragically, out of hand. That could have been horrible. It could have just been bad. And I said, "I am not going to be here in Charlottesville, away from my family, and, accidentally, get into a domestic violence thing or somebody get hurt or stabbed or..." The thought of it was just too much for me. I had previously said to him, "If this escalates or does not improve, I'm going to leave.

And so, he had said, "Okay. Okay." But I don't think he thought that I would because I know that he knew that I loved him. But I don't think that he thought that I really would go. I had really invested so much to move there, to move together, and all that. I think the thought was, "Well, she loves me. All this has happened. She's not really going to go anywhere. She's just gonna keep living with this and it'll be okay."

Well, I just couldn't do it. So, he was gone. He stayed gone maybe a day, a day and a half. And so, I, then, had gone back to the therapist because I was concerned, because I had heard him say he was already on the edge. I didn't know what was happening. The family hadn't heard from him. I was honestly afraid, at that point, that he would take his life. I was so concerned. So, I went to therapist, and I said, "I'm really concerned. I don't know if he's done something to himself. I'm not in in touch with him." And she said to me, "I hear that, and I am concerned for him as well, but I'm concerned for you. And I'm concerned for your safety." To hear someone else say that I was like, "Okay, I am too."

I guess, I waited for maybe three four days for things to calm some. When he finally did return, he was sitting on the porch and I came outside and I sat beside him and I said, "Do you remember when we had the conversation and I said that if things didn't improve that I was going to leave?" He said "Yeah." I said, "Well, I think they have gone to a place that I was frightened. I have never been frightened of you, or frightened in this relationship before, but I was frightened the other day." Where it could have gone could have been tragic for no reason. And I said, "I'm leaving." And so, he said, "Oh, okay. Really?" And I was like, "Yeah." And I guess the way I said it, it was just like "I'm leaving."

So, I don't think he believed me. By that time, he was living in the basement. There was a basement and a second level. So, I was living on the upper level, and he was living on the lower. And I think he kept thinking that, *Like before, she's gonna turn. It's going to get better.*

And I just wouldn't engage. I just was trying to get myself together, get my feet on the ground. Now, I have to find another place to live, get in line to move again. I had to pull those things together to be able to do that. And so, what I told myself that I was going to do was just walk quiet until I could leave, and that's what I did. And I just don't think he believed it. He didn't want to go back to therapy. He just kept saying, "Well, everything's gonna be okay. We can work this out. Now, I've found a job and things are going to be okay. Look, everything's gonna be better." I was just quiet, like, "Okay, we'll see."

I think he knew it was real. I had been looking for a place to live and I said, "If I'm gonna leave, I'm not gonna keep commuting an hour more to work. I'm going to move around the corner from my job if possible." So, I was looking around for a place near where I was working. One day, I got off work and I just drove around in the surrounding neighborhoods, and I stumbled upon this little house that had a "For Rent" sign. I rented the house. So, I knew I had a place to live, and I was saving boxes at work. I got so many boxes I had to bring some home, so I pulled up in the yard with the boxes in the car, and he was standing on the porch. I backed up to the house because I was going to unload these boxes, and he was like, "Hi!" Because now, as time has gone on, "She'll be okay. She ain't saying nothing. She must be really quiet." And I was like "Hi." And I opened the car and it's full of boxes, it's just full.

And I was taking the boxes out of the car, and he's coming down the steps, "What you gonna do with all those boxes?" I just turned around and looked at him and, at that moment, I could see that he knew. "Oh, my God! She is really leaving. She is out. Oh, my goodness." So, he said, "Are you really going?" I never said anything. I just started carrying boxes in the house because I was not going to have any disagreement. I'm getting out of here. I'm not saying anything. Because I knew how it could escalate.

We had about a month or so before I moved. He did everything he could to get me to stay but, I guess, at that point, my trust was fractured. And I was afraid. I knew that I couldn't say, "Oh, you're going to control it." Because he didn't appear to have any control over that. And the one thing I didn't want to do either is being in a place where a person I loved killed themselves. I knew that that would just be more than I could handle, and I knew I couldn't be a witness to that. I just couldn't. And I really felt, in my heart, that that's where it was going. Even with the way things were then, I felt we were just on the edge of the next thing, and I didn't feel like, whatever that was, had been resolved enough that he was okay.

So, I did leave, and we didn't talk. I want to say we didn't talk for probably two years. I wouldn't have conversations. I blocked him on everything I could. We just needed to move on.

Let me just say that when we had conversation again, he sent me a message and asked, "Can we talk?" At that point, I was okay. I felt like I could talk. And so, he called me, and we started talking. His first thing was that he apologized. He said, "You were right. I needed to be in counseling. I needed to do some real work, and I've been hesitant about doing the work. I didn't want to do it, but I found a counselor to help me that I picked for myself that I really like. And I've been working with her."

I said, "Well, that's great. I'm glad to hear that. You sound better." And he was telling me the positive things. He got a job that he really likes. And so, he's moving along. And he said, "There's another thing that I wanted to tell you before I really tell anybody else." And I was like, "Okay." So, he said, "Well, working with a therapist, I've come to the understanding that I'm trans and that, more than the lesbian issue, has been at the core of my not feeling who I was, not being able to connect..."

Because he always struggled to connect with the lesbian community. It was always like, "I just don't fit in. There are other butch lesbians, but I just don't quite mix with them." And who he actually mixed better with was gay men, and so he always said, "I just get along with them so well." And he really did. And they really liked him. So, it was like, "Oh, you're one of them." I always said that, early on, when I met him, maybe when we first met in person, in the first one or two hours we were together, I said to him, "Has anybody ever said to you that your energy, your self, is masculine?" He just looked at me. I know that butch lesbian women will tell you, "I don't want to be a man. That is not me." And usually, they may be offended. But he wasn't. He just looked at me and he was like, "No." And I said, "Does that bother you?" And he said, "No." And I always said, "Your energy is so masculine. It feels masculine." Which is different. Because I had been in relationships with men prior to coming out and dating butch women. To me, the difference was as clear as night and day. It was a totally different kind of energy. And he just was like, "Oh, well. Okay." I don't know if it was that, if it was always there. I think it was always in the head. But what does that look like? "Oh, I don't have any experience with that."

So, when we talked, when he told me that he was transitioning, that's why I said, "Well, there's not far for you to go." He said, "Well, I'm on hormones already." At that point, he was already on hormones. So, I said, "You're already taking it?" And he said, "Yeah. I'm learning to give it to myself." So, I said, "Wow! To me, then, you really want to do this." For him to inject himself was a big thing. So, he said, "No, I'm going to learn how to do it and I'm going to inject myself." And I said, "Are you okay with that?" Because it was a struggle with him with his identity, and fully living as a butch woman, and then, really, pressing that with his family to honor that and even respect him in that way. He always struggled with pressing, "No. This is who I am, and you're going to honor who I am. Or we won't be able to have a relationship because you're not going to be able to say things to me that are insulting or treat me other than who I am."

So now, I said, "Okay, this is a big truth. What do you think about that? Are you going to be able to do that?" So, he said, "That's what I'm working on in therapy. But this is a big thing. I know this is who I am. I'm comfortable that this is who I am. And whatever I have to do, or whoever has to be cut off, that's what's going to happen."

So, I could hear it in his voice, and I knew, "Oh. Okay. This is who you are." And so, I said to him, "So, I think this is the struggle that you were having when we were together." And he said, "Yeah." I said, "Did you know, when we were together?" And he said, "I knew I was not happy in that way, but I didn't have a name for it. I was afraid, and I certainly didn't want to tell you. I wasn't sure, so how could I tell you? And that's not who you got into relationship with. So, what was going to happen about that? And ultimately, that fear just blew up the relationship anyway."

And he said, "But you always knew that there was something else. I just couldn't identify or say what it was." So, I was like, "Yeah. That's very true." So, there was a lot of hurt and distrust there before that conversation. But once we started talking, I understood. I understood who that was, with all these things together, and why he was so different then, and why there was such a struggle. I understood. So, from then on, we just started talking again, chatting with one another, you know,

"How's it going? What are you doing?" And we just kind of walked through it and just kind of talked and became friends.

I went to a conference for my church, the MCC Church. This was some months later, and they usually have all these vendors and people who have information and all that. So, as I was walking through, there was an organization, Black Transmen, BTMI Incorporated. I'm like, "Oh, wow. I've never heard of them." So, I went up to the table and I was kind of chatting with the person who was there, and they said, "Take information." And I said, "Well, I'd like to take some. I have a friend that I'd like to send it to. So, I collected up everything they had and, when I got home, I put it in a big brown envelope and I called him and said, "Look, when I went to this conference, there was this organization called Black Transmen. Have you ever heard of it?" And he was like, "No. I never heard of it." And I said, "Well, they're there on the web. They said that they're on the web." But I got you a packet of information, and I'm going to drop it in the mail to you. And so, he said, "Okay. That's great. That'll be good."

So, I mailed it to him. But, in the meantime, he was looking for them on the internet, and he found their website. He made contact, and he got the information and, from there, he connected with other Black transmen. So, it helped him start to have a community. He's still involved with them now. He's on their board. I don't think it was an accident at all or coincidence that I was able to make that connection and provide that information, which really helped him connect to other transmen and start to have a community. Because where he was in Charlottesville, there was no prospect for a community for Black transmen at all or trans people. They were probably there, but they had no organization or connection. So, it was really good for him to be able to have an organization of other transmen who had been through the same experiences that he could talk to. That kind of thing. So, that really helped.

That's how we moved through that whole piece and became friends. So, we became really good friends, and I think we were always good friends even before we were in relationship. It just became fractured because of what happened in the relationship. But we forgave on both ends, and we became friends. And so, we still are friends now.

INTERVIEWER: That's a great story and you're a great storyteller. I hear what you say about the importance of communication and writing.

And how that was kind of the basis for your relationship. Just so much sensible advice for someone who couldn't take it at the time. But Charley did mention that you had sent that package of stuff. That was one of the first things he told me about you. That's just a wonderful story about caring.

So, let me just ask you a couple of follow up questions. You mentioned Charley's childhood identity struggle, that his family didn't accept it, or that he insisted that his family had to accept it. Is there anything that you would add about that childhood struggle.

CONSTANCE: Well, you know, he was very open, very early on, about knowing that "I am different. I know that I appear to be a girl on the outside, but I am not." And saying that from very early on. But when he was a child, that was unheard of. So, he felt like in his whole life, this quest to fit in, first of all, and for people to accept that, "Although I was born, and it says on my birth certificate that I'm a girl, I do not feel like that. I am not that. I want to dress like, look like, how I feel on the inside." And that was a struggle because, in little Charlottesville, all they knew was that if people were different, maybe they were gay. Maybe that. And certainly, we never want our child to be that. We're this rural black family, "Oh heck, no. We don't want our child to be that. And we don't know what to do with a child who wants to dress, who *is* dressing, as a boy, every opportunity he gets, and is not really caring that other people are seeing that."

And so, that was a struggle, even into adulthood, even to be accepted. "Yes, I am gay. No, that's not going to change. This is who I am." That continued to be a struggle, where, even when I met him, he was still trying to deal with being what he felt like and being fully accepted as the person that he was. And a lot of times, I think, in order to get along, to be part of the family circle, it seemed like he just didn't push it. But, at the same time, knowing you're not accepted, you're not 100% accepted. It's almost—it is—you're tolerated. "If that's what you're going to be, okay, but we're going to tolerate you, which is very damaging to your person, to your spirit, to your soul, to feel, in your own family situation, that that's how you're looked upon. And so, that was still there, still kind of going on.

And that's a big difference from then to who he is now. Because who he is now, when he had that discussion, that talk, to say. "Okay, look. Let me tell you what's different, what's happening, how this is going to look, this is what's going to happen," he was fully accepting that they can say or do whatever they want to do. "This is going forward. And that's just going to be how it is." So, like I said, by the time I was back in contact with him, he was already on hormones. So, whatever they're not okay with, he was okay with it. And I think he felt like, "This is life saving for me. So, whether they are on board or not, I'm saving my own life. This is who I am, and, if I have to live without family or their connection, then, I'm going to do that. But this is who I'm going to be."

And so, I think, not having had that connection as a kid, in some kind of way, now that he has identified, "This is who I am and I'm comfortable here," it has strengthened him because he's known not having that. He's known, "Something's just not right. I don't care how much you say I'm this, it's just not right. I'm not happy. Something's not going on." The difference that I've seen in him is that he's happy with who he is now, regardless of whatever surrounds that. He is happy, and he is okay with him. So, if that means, "I don't have connection or I do have connection, whatever. I'm going to forge ahead because I'm happy with me." So that's the difference that I see.

INTERVIEWER: That was one of my questions. Did Charley's transition make a difference in his personality or in his attitude toward the world in general.

CONSTANCE: Yeah, I think it's made a difference through his attitude to the world in general, I think it has just opened him up. It just opened him up to be the person that he is now, to have that sensitivity. He understands. He knows. He's been there. He knows what it's like when your family doesn't accept you. He knows what it's like to be alone in that and have no place to go. So, I think that has made him so compassionate about helping other Black transmen, because there's not a lot of resources out there at all for Black transmen.

And so, I think that's why he got into that. He found a connection that helped him, and he's just been paying it forward, from that, ever since. And as he's improved himself. He's been able to do more and more and more, even with his sobriety, in connection with that. He has become stronger as a person and opened up. Because I always used to say to him, "You really need to talk about your life and share your story and share your recovery. People would want to hear that." And I said to him, "I just believe that, one day, you're going to be in a position where you're going to be telling your story, where you're going to be lifesaving to somebody." I believe that. I used to say to him, "I think you should be an AA circuit speaker, because I went to an AA conference, and the people who spoke were okay. But I have heard him speak, and I've heard his story. I told him, "You need to tell your story. You need to say what has happened to you and where you've come from because your story is so compelling. And when you do, you need to be a circuit speaker."

And he would be like, "Oh no, I don't think I'm ever going to be able to do that." Because he wasn't accepting of himself. "How am I gonna stand up there and be this butch woman and they're not gonna like me. And what's going to happen? And what about my outside?"

But now, he's doing that. He is out there. He's talking. He's telling his story. He's sharing. Because he's okay with him. I didn't know that he would ever just get up and say, "I'm trans." He just gets up and says, "I'm trans and this is my story." And he just goes on, like, "Okay. Jump on board or not, like it or not. It is what it is." So, that has changed, and I think that has opened him up. His truth, living in his own truth and his own self, has made him selfless. It has made him able to pour himself out into others and to really be able to give back or to give to others who are struggling with their sobriety, struggling with their sexuality, who are struggling with whatever complications come with those issues. He has been able to do that.

So, it's just amazing. It's just been wonderful to see him do that, because I always believe that God doesn't pick the perfect vessel. He uses the imperfect. And then, He can make it perfect. And so, I think He's just made him in His self. He's made him who he supposed to be and let him honor that and live in that. And there's no other thing better than that for any of us. And I think that's why he's happy. He's good with his life and who he is now. He's not hiding. He's not hiding or denying or being afraid. He's not doing that. He's just not doing it.

INTERVIEWER: That's a very powerful statement of where you see Charley right now. That's amazing.

CONSTANCE: He's grown tremendously. He really has.

INTERVIEWER: And those of us who have made Charley's acquaintance, in various ways, are benefited by that.

CONSTANCE: You really are. Because you get to see him at his total best. And it improves. It continues to improve. He continues to grow. I see that. He continues to grow in different ways. He continues to grow more and more confident in himself, and who he is and how he presents to the world. And he's okay with that. So, that is really, really good for him.

And what was big for him with his family. There was animosity, there was a strained relationship. He loved his mother tremendously. She loved him. But there was this strained relationship because of that, because of not being accepted. "How I was treated as a child. How you continue to not accept me as who I am." And so, once he was able to say to his mother, which was a huge thing, to me, to be able to say to his mother, "I've said it to you before. Let me explain to you what it means that I am trans. I'm no longer Charlotte. My name is Charley. That's what I will be called. That's not what I want to be called. That's what I *will* be called because that's my name. And, although I was born female, I am transitioning and, I am now a male. And this is the process of what will happen. And this is how I will change. This is how I will change externally."

And so, once he was able to do that and say that and put that on the table as, "This is just who I am," it changed their relationship. And then, he was able, through learning how to repair those things, those hurts, those bad things that were happening, through therapy and through working with his sponsor in AA, he began to be able to forgive her. And be able to accept her, and she accepted him. So then, she was able to start calling him by his name and accepting who he was. And from there—which I was always moved by—when she became ill, he said, "I'm going to take care of her." So, he would set up time on the weekends, that would be his time. He would go out. He would cook for her. He would eat with her. Because he said to me, "I'm struggling because she doesn't eat, and she's not eating well." So, I said, "Well, you know, a lot of times with elderly people, they don't want to eat alone. They want company. You can make whatever, but they're not going to want to eat when they have to just sit there and eat by themselves." I said, "Set aside some time." She loved to cook. She was a wonderful cook. "Tell her what you're cooking. Involve her in what you're going to make. 'Look, what are we're going eat when I come over to your house this weekend?' And you cook for her, and then you sit down and eat with her. She'll eat." And she did. Everything he made, she loved it. And it was through that thing, where he was cooking for her, that was their time, they healed. And their relationship became something totally different.

So, by the time she died. He was so at peace. It was no, "Oh, I wish I'd said this, and this was always horrible." He was at peace. He had taken care of her. He had honored all her last wishes. They had spent valuable time together, where they talked, where they talked about some difficult things that were still there. And they just remade a relationship. They rebuilt their relationship. So, when his mother died, he wasn't distressed. He was greatly saddened, of course, because she died. But he wasn't in that place where you would be when you have all this unsettled and you're unhappy. "I wish I'd said this, and they didn't really love me." It was none of that. It was, "We did all we could together. We healed. We loved each other. She knew I loved her. I know she loved me." And he was able to live with that and walk on.

He found out his mother died when he had just gotten to work, and he got a call that his sister had gone over, and she had died in her sleep. And that's what she wanted. She wanted to die in her own house. So, she was there, peaceful. She had died, and evidently it hadn't been too long before she died because she was still very, very warm. So, they called him. He called me and told me that she had died, and I said, "Are you okay?" And he said, "Yeah, I'm okay. I knew it was coming. We had talked about it. I'm sad. I'm really sad that she's gone. But I'm okay." So, he left work, and, that afternoon, went to an AA meeting. I said, "You're going to an AA meeting?" And he was like, "Yeah, I just think I need to go to a meeting." And he went to an AA meeting. And he was fine. He was good. But had that not happened that would have been such a difficult thing to reconcile after she was gone. To have that time and be able to build that relationship, I think that only could have happened when he was okay with him. When he was good in himself, and he could open himself to that. Then, they were able to have that relationship, which is beautiful.

INTERVIEWER: That *is* beautiful. We've been on for over an hour now, and I'm taking a lot of your time. I so appreciate it. Is there anything that you can think of that you haven't told me or that I haven't asked you?

CONSTANCE: I just want to say I'm really proud of Charley. I'm proud of who he has become. I'm so proud of all of the accolades he has gotten and the acknowledgement of who he is in his personhood. I think some people transition and maybe they just live very quietly and you never know anything about them, and they may never want anything to be known about them. And so, I think that's extra special, that he has successfully moved into his truth. But then, for him to share that and open himself is amazing. You really have to open yourself, and there's backlash that sometimes comes with that. But to open yourself, I think that makes you a special person. Because you know what someone else is going through. Because you know how hard it can be, you make yourself open to that.

So, in closing, I just want to say that I am proud of him, and that selflessness that has evolved in him, his paying it forward constantly. And I'm always just really excited about the very next thing for him because things keep evolving and coming into his life. Richness just keeps coming into his life. And that's what happens. When it flows out of you, it will flow back to you. And it is flowing back to him in such a wonderful way that I'm just really proud of him. I'm proud to know him. I'm proud that we've been able to be friends and to support each other. And I'm very excited to see what happens the next time, because it's always something new and exciting happening for him.

Book V

What is it Like Now?

Fear is the opposite of faith.
Alcoholics Anonymous

Chapter 13

"Unfortunate"[13]
AA Guest Speaker 2021

Remember that alcoholism is incurable, progressive, and fatal.

Alcoholics Anonymous

There are such unfortunates. They are not at fault; they seem to have been born that way. They are naturally incapable of grasping and developing a manner of living which demands rigorous honesty.

AA Big Book, Chapter 5, "How it Works"

My name is Charley and I'm an alcoholic. My sobriety date is May 22, 2006. I have a sponsor, who has a sponsor, who has a sponsor. Tracy was there in my early days. We were both kind of knocking on the door

---

[13] May 5, 2021, open AA meeting, Charley as guest speaker, transcript (with permission) by Castle Carrington Accurate Transcription Services, April 2022.

at the same time. She was there in Charlottesville AA at the same time as me. She has watched me go through the trials and tribulations of staying sober in Charlottesville, Virginia.

I am an alcoholic, but drugs and mental illness are a part of my story. I used my first drug at the age of 8 when I drank two bottles of Black Bear wine on a dare from my cousins at a family picnic and my mother found me passed out. I had thrown up in the closet in my bedroom. I was thrown in the bathtub. I was not told that I was bad for what I did. I was not told anything. I remember the next day, my cousins and my brother telling me stuff that I did that I didn't know. So, at the age of eight, I blacked out, and I loved it.

So, I stayed dry from age eight to age twelve. I met a friend in Spanish class, and I can't speak a lick of Spanish today because we weren't there for Spanish, we were there because her father was a doctor, and she was able to get prescription pads and get pills. We were taking pain pills at the age of twelve and passing out in Spanish class. We figured out that we could drink beer and take these pills and get a better effect. Her name was Taylor. She was my best friend from middle school to high school. In the eleventh grade, Taylor decided to run away to Florida. She was drunk, running down a major highway in Orlando, and got hit by a Mac truck. That started a life of me knowing that I was not going to stay really closely connected to anyone. First of all, Taylor left without even telling me that she had run away from home. Then, she got hit by the truck and was killed.

Believe it or not, I was a really good athlete. I got a full scholarship for volleyball, shotput, and discus. I went and I spent one luxurious three months at Fern College, and I got kicked out because I had found the moonshiners in Roanoke, Virginia, and I was making and selling moonshine out of the dorm. So, I came home, and I didn't tell my parents anything on Thanksgiving weekend. When it was time to pack up and go back, I just announced that I wasn't going back. What I didn't realize was that my mother already had the letter that said that my ass was getting kicked out. She was just waiting for me to say it. By then, I was full-fledged. I couldn't hold a job. I was mixing pills and alcohol. I have, in my lifetime, probably spent 75—no exaggeration—75 psychiatric admissions. Seventy-five. I played crazy very well sometimes and, sometimes, I wasn't playing crazy at all.

But let me back up a bit. At seventeen, I tried to kill myself. I felt like I wasn't in the right body, even at seventeen. I'm a country kid and

I don't know anything. All I know is that, in my family, men who used to dress up as women were called all kinds of names I won't even mention. They were like the scum of the earth. But I was attracted to those women who we knew had something different about them. They were proud and they knew who they were. Unfortunately, a lot of Black transwomen, even today, even back then, were sex workers. They had to do what they had to do to survive. And so, there was this bad hotel or apartment place where a lot of the Black transwomen lived. But I knew nothing about transmen. I didn't even know what the name was. All I knew was that transwomen dressed up, they walked really great in high heeled shoes down Main Street and they went to the Silver Fox Club, and they would party hardy. And I loved to watch these women party.

So, at the age of seventeen, I was confused, and I made a real serious suicide attempt. I ended up in this private hospital. This psychologist or psychiatrist asked me to draw a figure of what I looked like, and I drew these stick figures. Because I drew these stick figures that looked like men, for the next eight weeks, I got ECT treatment. ECT is electro-shock therapy. So, I went into the hospital in October, and I did not get out until the spring of the year. Then, the big question was, was I going to graduate. Well, of course, I was going to graduate because I had all these scholarships waiting for me and people wanted me because I was a decent athlete. So, off I go and, of course, as I said, I got kicked out. And this just started a cycle for the next 30 years of I'd land decent jobs and I'd lose them. I'd land jobs and I'd lose them.

I remember one night it was my birthday and I had this party. There were close to 300 people there. I mean, when I partied, I partied. So, it was like the beer truck, the bartenders, the DJ, 300 people in this little town and we're just partying. I remember going off and sitting in this field at my house and looking back at everybody partying and realizing how alone I felt. How I did not want to drink anymore but I didn't know anything else. Because when you are brought up in this town, as an African American, it is expected for you to drink. You drink at funerals. You drink at birthday parties. You have birthday parties for three- and four-year-olds, but the adults got drunk after the kids had eaten the cake and gone home. Now, it is the adults' time. Everything I did had some connection with drinking and drugging. Everything. Like I said I was landing really great jobs, and I would just run before I knew I was going to be fired.

So now, fast-forward to that week. It's May and it's 2006. It's a Saturday and I decide to go to this women's meeting on Saturday morning. Before I transitioned, I was this big butch woman. I go into this meeting of all these White women, one Black woman, and I sat in the meeting. I'm really listening because they were reading how it works. I heard that word "unfortunate," and I had been told all my life that I was an unfortunate. I had been told by psychiatrists that the best thing I could do was to go on disability, hang out at the club house, catch the bus or drive or whatever, but hang out at the club house because you are mentally unstable. You are not going to get any better.

So, I hear this "unfortunate" thing that they read. What I also hear is that if I pick up this white chip, I'm not supposed to drink. And I knew that I had just one more drink in me. So, I didn't pick up a white chip. They had something called a group conscious. I'm too embarrassed now. I'd come into the meeting. I'd sat in the back and I'm too embarrassed, when they said the meeting is over but there is going to be this other meeting. I didn't want to get up. So, I stayed and listened to this group conscious meeting. The group conscious meeting was about this trans woman who had Asperger's. They wanted to kick her out of the women's meeting because she was using the women's bathroom and she was peeing on the seat. They wanted to kick her out and still it just wasn't registering with me about this whole trans thing. I was interested but, like, "It's not me." So, I didn't pick up a white chip and I overdosed three times that weekend.

The first time, I went to the emergency room with an overdose, but I didn't tell them I had overdosed. The doctor asked me, "What's wrong." I said, "My back's hurting." So, they do some x-rays, and he comes back, and he says, "You poor little puppy. You have kidney stones. You're trying to pass kidney stones. So, I'm going to give you this strainer and some oxycontin and you go home. You take the oxycontin for pain, and you keep the strainer and if you get the stones, you've passed them. If not, please come back because we're here for you."

That's exactly what I did the entire weekend. The clincher to it was that Sunday when I seized in front of my eighty-year-old mom. I had a seizure. I got up and I wiped the shit off my mouth, and I went back over to this little dingy, dark ass, apartment house where I was living, and I drank some more. Let me also tell you that I was 565 pounds. So, I couldn't even go downstairs in this apartment. I literally lived in the bedroom. People brought me shit. At this point, they had cut a door so that I could cut through my parents' house and get food. I never saw my living room. Never saw my dining room downstairs. Never used the kitchen. I couldn't get down there. Or I would drive around and go in and use that as a party spot.

So, I laid around. I had a job selling office products. So, I called out sick that week after this overdosing. By then I was losing weight. I had lost a lot of weight. I was really working on losing weight. I think it was because of a new drug that had been introduced. It was called "crack." It was making me lose weight. I would tell friends, "Oh, I've got the perfect diet plan for you. You just smoke crack and you're not going to eat." I'm just thinking this is the miracle drug for weight loss. Look at me, I've dropped 150 pounds smoking crack. I had the answer.

I laid around that weekend. I finally called a friend of mine who lived in Jersey who had told me, "You're a game player. I don't want to have nothing else to do with you." But she picked up the phone and she said, "I'm going to help you one more time. Then, after that, if you're not going to take the help that I'm trying to give you, don't call me anymore. Don't come see me. Don't call me. Nothing."

She kept me on the phone. It was a Wednesday. She said, "Do you know where Holy Comforter Church is?" And I was like, "How in the hell am I supposed to know where a damn Catholic church is in Charlottesville? I ain't Catholic." She was like, "It doesn't matter what you are. This is where they have meetings, in the basements of churches. It's at twelve o'clock on East Jefferson Street. Do you know where that is?" And she was in Jersey. I couldn't find it. I parked in a parking lot, and I had to walk about 11 blocks. It was hot as shit. I walk in and it's this old woman and five other White dudes. And I'm like, "This is the biggest bunch of losers that I've ever seen in my life." Then, there was this White girl who had cerebral palsy. The joke is, when it came time to give out the chips, I wanted a white chip. She's got this big box of chips and she's shaking so badly that she drops the chips all over the floor. She just looks at me and says, "Just pick up a white chip and congratulations."

What I heard that day again was that we are *not* unfortunate. I listened to the stories that they told. The girl who had dropped the chips was long gone, and I was standing there talking to this old White man and I said, "Will one of you be my sponsor?" Now, let me back up, that Saturday, I asked three White women at that meeting, "Can you tell me what sponsorship is about?" And they said to me, "We don't have anything to offer you. You see that girl over there? Talk to her. She's the Black woman." I'm thinking, "Fuck, she just picked up a white chip. How is she going to tell me what to do?" But they saw my colour and they didn't want to deal with me. They saw what I looked like, and they didn't want to deal with me. The guy said, "We can't sponsor you, but she can." And they called this woman over, who is still my sponsor today. We call her God's cousin. She's tough as shit. I've had her from day one, except for one time when she fired me because I was totally in love with this crazy redhead. She told me not to do it, but I did it anyway. That was a disaster.

She told me, "The answers to your recovery are the first 164 pages of this book." She handed me the book and she wrote down her phone number. I said, "Here's my number. You can call me tonight." She said, "Uh uh. I'm not calling you. I don't want what you have. You want what I have. You don't have anything. But the answers to what you need to know are in the first 164 pages." So, I was like, "Ok, bitch, I'm going to go back to work. I'm going to read all 164 pages. I'm going to make notes and I'm going to call you at nine o'clock because no White man who wrote a book in 1935 is going to be able to tell me how to stay sober. I know how to stay sober. Smoke crack. Then you don't drink."

So, I'm sitting there thinking, *If I smoke crack, I'm not going to drink. I don't drink when I smoke crack.* This is what I told this woman and she was like, "Well, that's real smart. Just burn your brains out with cocaine." So, I call her at nine o'clock and I had a series of questions and none of them made any sense at all. But she listened and she said, "What's your plan for tomorrow?" I was like, "What do you mean?" She said, "If you are going to work with me, before we end the call, every night, you are going to know where you're heading the next day for a meeting. Then, when you leave that meeting, you're going to know where your feet are heading for your next series of meetings. And so, that started my life in recovery.

On May 22, 2006, I said, "I'm done." I started going to meeting after meeting after meeting. The thing I didn't like was they were too friendly. I was like, "They are too damn friendly." They want hugs. They want to hold your hand. I don't want none of this shit because after 30 days, I'm going to be ok. I'm going to know how to smoke crack and drink successfully. I just need these 30 days to chill out. I'll take this chip and I'll keep it for 30 days." That was a Wednesday. That Thursday

James Brown was coming to town. I picked up the phone and I said, "Ma'am, tell you what. I'm not going to call you at nine o'clock tonight because I'm going down to the mall to listen to the Godfather. Do you know who the Godfather is?" She said, "Very well. I've heard that he's in town." I said, "More than likely, I'll have a couple of drinks. But I'm going to come back on Friday and I'm going to pick up another white chip. I'll see you then."

And she said, "What if the last 20 minutes is the last 20 minutes of your life?" I said, "What do you mean?" She said, "So, you've had just two days when you haven't had anything in your system. You are detoxing. You're not in good shape." This woman was a retired pediatrician, a retired doctor. She said, "Sometimes when people stop like that for a little while, then they go back, they go back really hard and that's what I think you will do. Your heart could give out. So, what if the last 20 minutes of your drinking down in that mall with the Godfather is going to be the last 20 minutes of your life?" So, I said, "What fucking meeting do you want me to go to? I'll go." She said, "Well, there's one on Hinton Avenue and Eighth."

So, I drive up and here are these White boys in pickup trucks, and they're outside kicking a Hacky Sack. I'm on the phone with her and I was like, "Oh, hell, no! Where are you sending me? These White boys are kicking a Hacky Sack and there are a lot of trees in this church yard. They'll have me hung in a noose and dead in 30 seconds." And all of a sudden, these guys rushed my truck.

There was this real tall one with weird eyebrows named Merv. Merv comes up to the truck and motions me to roll down the window. I just kind of cracked it. He says, "Are you new?" And I was like, "Yeah." And he was like, "How new?" I said, "I picked up my white chip yesterday." It was like Santa Claus coming to town. I couldn't understand why they were so happy. I get it today because we get happy when we see newcomers. And that's what they saw in me. I got out of the truck and now I'm two blocks from the Godfather. So, I've got a huge resentment because just as I got out of that truck, Godfather was getting set to get on the stage. And I was like, "I could have been down there with Godfather." But I kept playing in my head what she said, "What if the last 20 minutes is the last 20 minutes?"

I went in and this guy was telling his story. He was a huge manager for the ABC Stores and this dude stayed sober, selling alcohol. And then, because of his sobriety, moved through the ranks of the Virginia

State ABC and was like a huge manager. I was amazed that this guy could work in a liquor store and not drink but the other thing that amazed me was how quickly his life got better. And that's what I wanted. So, I would just go to meeting after meeting after meeting.

I remember they had a convention in Waynesboro, and I remember going with a woman, who I thought would be the love of my life. Both of us newly sober, she was crazy as shit. So, I go to this meeting and I'm standing in line, and I had an ice cream ticket and there was Tracy. Tracy was like, "I'm trying to get a ticket for ice cream." And I was like, "Oh, well, I've got an extra ticket. Here you go." It was my girlfriend's ticket, but I gave it to Tracy and that set her off. We got to fighting. The end result was that we got to throwing things and screaming in the Walmart down the street. I was like, "This is cute. I'm sober now and I'm going to get arrested for the first time in my life." Those were the craziness of sobriety but there were also good times.

Five years into being sober, I got suicidal again. My ex had moved in. We had gotten a house and it was bad. When I say bad, I mean I was depressed most of the time. I was suicidal some of the time. I was angry some of the time. I didn't want to be intimate with her. I didn't want her to touch me. Didn't want to touch her. Didn't know who I was. I came home one day from a meeting, from work, and there were cardboard boxes on the front porch. I walked in and I said, "What are these cardboard boxes for?" And she said, "I can't take this anymore. I just can't mentally take this anymore." And I'm like, "What's wrong? I remember that I had this little figurine that was broken. I said to her, "What happened to the figurine?" And she said, "You threw it at me." I was like, "What?" So, that made me realize that I was going through these blind rages just like I would go through blackouts.

Before I came in, every drink that I had, I used to blackout. It wasn't a social drink. I never went to a bar. I would go to the ABC Store. I would hit the bottom of the bottle, throw the top out the window, get a soda at the ghetto IGA because the sodas there were 45 cents, and, to chase it, that was fancy. The cup was even fancier. That's where I was. So, that's how I blacked out. At this point, now, I'm five years sober but I'm blacking out from rage and the love of my life, which is exactly what she was, is leaving me in a house that I can't afford.

So, I sit there and, within a month, watched her drive down the road in a U-Haul, and gone. And so, I went to the basement and just lay in the bed. People like Tracy would call me, my sponsor would call me. I wouldn't answer. I wouldn't go to meetings. I just knew I wasn't going to drink because I knew if I killed myself, I didn't want people in AA to think I killed myself because I was drunk. Because I had stayed sober for spite for so long. So many people in AA, I felt like didn't even think that I was going to stay sober. So, I'm five years sober. I woke up one morning and I knew I had to pay the light bill, or the lights were going to be cut off. I had this old couple who were renting the basement, so I decided to go to the pawn shop and buy a gun to end my life. I bought the gun and came home. I got these towels together and I was going to shoot myself in the kitchen. This was the day when they were supposed to bring up their part of the light bill. Hopefully, they would come in and find me. So, I'm getting everything prepared. This is where the power greater than myself, that I choose to call God, got involved.

We had this mailman, who was horrible. He would throw mail all over the place. And if we complained, he would say, "Walk down to your neighbor's house and get it. That's how you get to know your neighbor." The doorbell rings and I'm like, "You know what? I'm not even going to answer this doorbell. I'm going to wait until I think he's gone." And I see the shadow of him going down and I'm like, "What the hell is John doing?" So, I open the door and he's like, "I have a package for you." Now, normally, when he would do a package, he would just put a written card in the mailbox that says, "Come to the post office and get your package." He didn't even want to come to your house to bring you a package. But he brought this package. When I look at the package, there's my ex's handwriting and I'm like, "What the fuck is she trying to get money out of me for now?"

I opened it up and she had been to a conference where she had met Carter Brown. Carter Brown is the CEO of Black Transmen Incorporated, which is a national organization. There was all this information about this organization and why it was started. And I shook the envelope to see if there was anything else in it and on the counter fell his business card. I called him and he answered. And he says to this day, I normally don't answer my phone, but I answered that day because I didn't recognize this 434 area code. We talked and we talked, and, at the end, I said, "You know, Carter, today I was going to kill myself. I don't know who I am. I'm looking at this body and I don't recognize it. I don't know what to do with this body. I don't know what to do with what I'm feeling. This trans thing, I don't know what it is about. I'm a country guy. I don't know anything about this." So, he said, "I don't know a lot about recovery, but do you think it might help you if you go to a meeting? And call me after you go to the meeting."

So, I went to a meeting and in that meeting, I shared where I was at because I was taught that if I share something, I'm going to cut it in half. More than likely there will be somebody there who might not understand totally. So, people there didn't understand when I talked about that I didn't fit in my body. But they do know what it's like to be sober and thinking about killing themselves because they're sober. So, I came back from the meeting, and I called Carter again. This started a series of me, Carter, and Antoine talking. He started telling me about his dream of Black Transmen Inc. Then, we would get on this thing called OoVoo and we would talk on OoVoo. Then, at one point, he connected me with other Black transmen that were in recovery.

Then, I went to my therapist and admitted to my therapist what was going on. There was no help in Charlottesville for trans people. So, I would drive twice a month to these support groups, and I just kept staying sober. And I got more comfortable in my skin. I am so glad of the program of recovery because I did not rush my transition. I took my time because I wanted to grow and know. Because I'm a schemer. I know how to scheme shit. So, was this a scheme I was trying to do? What was the angle? It wasn't an angle. It was who I was truly supposed to be, and it happened in the way that it should. It happened because I needed to get sober first to recognize who I was. I needed to get sober first to get comfortable in my own skin.

And so, here I am today. In a few weeks, I'll be fifteen years sober. I have people that I sponsor. A year ago, we started hearing about all the unrest with George Floyd and Breonna Taylor, and, most importantly, Tony McDade. And we saw, as Black transmen, especially with our national organization, that Tony McDade slipped through our fingers. Because if we had been where we really needed to be, the day Tony went to jail, somebody would have been in that courtroom with him who was trans. The day that Tony got out of jail, and said, "I have a problem with drugs and alcohol, somebody trans should have been there to walk him to a meeting, to do something for him. So, Tony slipped through our fingers. We were having problems in Charlottesville with people in meetings not wanting people of color to talk about what was going on in our world. They would tell young people, early in their sobriety, that they were stepping out of the traditions, the principles, for personalities.

So, I got a call from this young girl who said, "This is what's going on. What do you think we need to do?" And I said, "I've always heard that if we have a resentment, a coffee pot, and a meeting, start one on your own. Create your own space. So, we created Diversity in Recovery. We went hard at first and we struggled hard and we're struggling now, but we're still here. It is a space where people can feel safe. It's a place where you can go on a Sunday morning and Wednesday evening, and you can talk about being trans. Even today, I struggle sometimes thinking, *Do I really need to be this out in my transition, or should I just hide and just be the Black man?* I struggle with that back and forth. And I found the answer to that is, I have to do what this program taught me to do. The twelfth step in any recovery program says, "If you have had a spiritual awakening as a result of these steps, you carry the message to the next sick and suffering alcoholic." So, I have to do that. I don't know whose life I'm going to touch in the same way that those people in that basement and my friend, Sherrie, touched mine.

Sherrie told me that day that she walked me through that door at Holy Comforter, I don't want to talk to you again for three weeks. You are threatening my sobriety. I didn't know what that meant at that point, but I do now. I believe it was my first or second year, Sherrie came with a friend of hers and watched me pick up my medallion. We went out to dinner.

Last April, on the 23rd, Mo called me and said, "She's gone." I said, "What do you mean, she's gone?" He said, "Sherrie, she's gone. I took her to the New York hospital. She was having trouble breathing. She had a high fever. They came back out and they told me she had COVID, that they were going to put her on life support." He said, "She never made it an hour on life support." But this person was the reason that I knew about Alcoholics Anonymous. From New Jersey. You see this is the amazing thing about this program. We knew each other for years. Finally, she recognized what I was all about. She said, "You need help." Then, those words that she told me, "I can't talk to you any more right now because you're threatening my sobriety," that was tough love. I remember being so angry. I called her up and I was so angry about what my ex had done. And Sherrie said, "Do you see the love that she still has for you? She might not be in love with you but the love that she has for you. She took time to pack up a package and sent it to you because she knew, before you knew, what you needed. And that saved you by meeting Carter Brown.

Today, all I know is to help people. All I know is that I spend a lot of hours doing a lot of stuff and, at the end of the day, I'm just like, "How did I do this? How did I do all that I did at the end of the day?" But the Book tells us that if we work our program, we will stop spending energy foolishly. We will be able to pretty much conquer anything that we want with a sober attitude.

My life is unreal. I've got a book that's being published about my life. I just got an award for being an outstanding Virginian. And I'm sitting here thinking, *What did I do outstanding?* This is somebody who was convinced that the weight loss plan that I needed to stay on was smoking crack. Out selling stuff to pregnant women, I had young boys out there selling dope for me. I was tricking, lying, mistreating my parents.

The beauty of this is that at age four or five, I went to my mother and said, "Uncle Willy is doing stuff to me that I don't think he should be doing." My mother was in the kitchen, and she turned to me. She said, "You're just going to have to suck this up because somebody has to be here. I have to go to work to put food on the table." And I hated this woman, passionately. The love that I had for my sponsor taught me how to love my mother. So, the last four or five years of my mother's life, we were best friends. We would spend Sundays together. We would talk every day. She died after a beautiful, beautiful life at the age of 97.

It was because of this program that I had to do that dreaded fourth step. I had no part, as a four- or five-year-old child, in what that man did to me. But what I had to realize was that I was now 50 some years old, doing this fourth step, and I was no longer a victim. I was a survivor. And that's a big difference. Because if I lived in victimhood, I was surely going to go back out to drink. I had to stop being the victim and grow up. I survived that shit. There's nothing that I can do now to him. Just make sure that if anybody else goes through this, my hand is out there to them.

So, I'm going to end with I don't even know how Savanah and I connected. But I remember that I started reading this stuff about what this woman was doing. I reached out to another trans woman, and I said, "You guys need to connect because this woman is going to go places." Savannah said, "We need to have a recovery meeting." I was all confused all day long. I'm sending the wrong link. I'm calling Savannah and I was like, "Savannah, you got me down for May 15th. It's not May 3rd." It was amazing how, as trans people, we do what we need to do to help each other. This series of month-long events that she's having, somebody is going to get help. This series of everything that she's doing, this is what it is all about. It takes one vessel to create leadership.

So, my vessel was Sherrie, who is no longer with us. Because that was the first glimpse of AA that I saw. I wish today that there was no COVID because Sherrie would see me pick up 15 years. But I can tell you that her spirit is still with me because she taught me the true meaning of service. Don't ever say "no" when somebody says, "Can you help me and talk to me about that."

I thought my heart was going to be broken when Tracy left and moved to Pennsylvania because that was my Ride or Die chick right here. Tracy, which is the way the program is, rode with me the night that I went and got my first vial of testosterone. Because I pretty much did that whole journey by myself. I didn't have a partner. I didn't have a lot of support in Charlottesville. People didn't' know anything about this. She jumped in that car with me, and we went down and got that vial, and then, we went to Red Lobster to celebrate like we'd picked up a bottle of cognac or something. We were as happy as we could be. It was just like, "I got this shit now. It's time to put the juice in the veins." That's what we do. We're there for each other.

So, I am going to end with, "Savannah, thank you so much for creating this platform. I think I'm back on May 15th to do it again. Thanks, Vanessa, for reading. I'll turn it back over to Savannah.

Chapter 14

Into the Fourth Dimension[14]
AA Birthday Meeting 2021

Go to meetings when you want to, and go to meetings when you don't want to.

Alcoholics Anonymous

I was rocketed into the fourth dimension of existence—the spiritual—when the dimensions of my physical, mental, and emotional states (the three dimensions within which we humans live, experience, and struggle) came into harmony and balance with each other, at the moment of my total surrender and my complete abandonment to God. With my physical, mental, and emotional states in harmony, I was at a level of peace. I did consciously surrender to the belief that "God is everything," because if that weren't so, then He was nothing; He had no meaning or purpose in my life.

---

[14] AA meeting, Charley's 15th Birthday Meeting, May 28, 2021, transcript (with permission) by Castle Carrington Accurate Transcription Services, April 2022.

I became aware that a quantum shift had occurred within myself and, I now understand, that, in that moment, I was rocketed into a fourth dimension, which I never considered.

Now, through maintaining daily conscious contact with that power greater than myself, God (and I consciously work at making that contact), I continue to live in it. This, for me, was a huge transformation.

Today I can live in a place where I know I am not the center and can reach within for a source of power and peace that I always had denied, suppressed, and intellectually fought against for many years. From this source, particularly where I make a conscious effort, I receive the ability to live in peace and harmony within me, knowing that I have the ability to live with both the good times and bad times that life continuously presents to me.

I can make good choices. As crazy as it seems, I now can appreciate that when three dimensions, through hard work and the help of God, came into harmony, I was able to surrender my need for control to God, and entered into a 4th dimension of existence.

I exist today in a place where my spiritual wellbeing and conscious contact must come first; and a wonderful place it is.

Charley, April 2022

It was May 22, 2006, in the basement of Holy Comforter Church that I met Frank. And for 16 years God has said that I don't have to come back in and pick up a white chip. And that, right there, is a complete miracle. I am very fortunate to call myself a member of Alcoholics Anonymous. Years ago, I would not have been able to say that. I would hear people say that they were grateful for being an alcoholic and I thought that they were just crazy as hell. How can you be grateful to stop drinking?

I have to admit to you, it worked for a while. The drinking worked. It gave me the courage. It gave me what I thought was strength. I could be something that I couldn't be when I didn't have drugs and alcohol in my system. And so, my story is a little bit about outside issues with mental health. My story is a little bit about a path I chose to take—it will be 10 years this September and I'll share a little bit about that—but in a general way, that's what I'd been taught. I was raised in Alcoholics Anonymous by people like Frank and Sarah Beth. How to be a productive human being. I didn't know how to do that when I first came in the doors. I was very angry. I hated you because of the color of your skin. I hated you because of the status that you might have. I hated that you might have a couple of commas in your bank account. I hated you just to hate you. Because I hated myself.

And so, I will share with you that I think a lot of my drinking had to do with two parts. A lot of my drinking had to do with as a child of four or five, I endured things that no child should ever have to endure. And so, I learned how to completely disassociate myself from the world. And it wasn't until I told my father one day that this family member was doing things to me. And all I knew was that I never saw that family member taken care of. And so, my father saved me, but I had this hatred for my mother because I felt like she was the one who put me in harm's way because she didn't have anywhere else to put me. I was a bad kid. She was a cook in a home, and I had broken something in the home, and I couldn't go with her anymore. So, I was boot-kicked off to this evil, evil man. That's the only way that I can describe him. He did things to his daughter and, more than likely, my mother, who was raised by her grandparents. So, that would have been her uncle. I'm almost certain that circle didn't break until I talked to my father.

I struggled with my gender all my life. I know that we are allergic to alcohol. I was definitely allergic to it because I came from a family of nothing but drunks. When I go to put flowers on my parents' grave, the majority of my family in that cemetery never made it to retirement. They died from alcoholism. And so, once again, I've been someone who has broken that chain of addiction.

I came in 15 years ago as one gender and about 5 years into my sobriety, I was like—I didn't really do this, but I like to say this sometimes—"I'm going to really "f" with their minds. I'm going to switch myself all up, and I'm going to confuse these people. They're going to reject me, and they're going to kick me out." And all you did was continue to love me. So, you see what you did, in the beginning, was that you loved me until I could love myself. I hated myself. I hated looking in the mirror. I hated everything that I did. I wasn't a success at anything. Even coming in sober.

I remember something my sponsor, who I still have now, told me. I was at her house, one day, and my phone was just buzzing. I'm about two weeks into this program and the phone was just buzzing, bootleggers, drug dealers. And she said, "You've got to get rid of that phone." I told her, "I can't be a loser and go to 7/11 and buy one of those phones that you get 10 minutes on." Well, for about a year, I was one of those losers who have to go to 7/11 to put minutes on their phone because what I realized was, as much as I was trying to make it, I didn't want to do what you told me to do. Underhandedly, I did what you told me to do. I was slowly becoming teachable.

And I have to share this story because it's just classic. They started announcing that they were going to go rafting down the James River. Sarah Beth kind of put me in her back pocket and just dragged me everywhere. She said, "You're going rafting with us down this river." And I was like, "I am *not* going rafting with you White people down a river. This is *Deliverance*. No way! No way!" I was trying to figure out—I was sitting in a meeting—what's the best way to hide from her. How can I hide from her, and she won't find me? Then the lightbulb clicked. I'll just go to an AA meeting. She can't find me in an AA meeting. So, I'm just going to go to the Rock Church and I'm going to sit in the back. It's a huge crowd and she'll never guess that I was at the AA meeting. So, I was on the walk that comes down to the church door and I looked up and there she is. And I'm like, "Damn! I can't even hide in an AA meeting without her coming after me."

So, she comes in, and she just beckons to me like some kind of sergeant, like, "Tag. You're it. Let's go." So, I get my big ass up, and I go with her. You can imagine that was a pretty interesting sight, with my big ass in an innertube, floating down a river with a bunch of White girls. And so, I look over to my right and there's this crew and they're just partying. And I'm like, "Why don't we just kind of paddle on over that way." I don't know how Sarah Beth keeps all this stuff in these pants that she wears but she comes over with a rope and a knife. And I'm like, "Ok. Here we go. They're going to show their true colours now." And she proceeds to take this rope and ties it around my ankle and the other end of the rope is tied around her ankle so that she could drag me down the river and I wouldn't go over to where the people were drinking.

And I share that story in that this is how we roll in AA. We look after each other. What she was trying to do was to show me that there are other things that I can do to enjoy life, that I didn't have to drink. And that I had to be willing to do things that were different. I had to be willing to float down this damn river.

I have been back on that river since. But, you know, I floated down the river with them and I learned something that day, once we got all the way down to the other end, when they were trying to pull my big ass out of the innertube because I'm wet and I'm stuck and they're trying to pull me out and get me up. And it's like six of them trying to pull me out of this innertube. People truly wanted to be around me. And I didn't have that when I was out on the street. They wanted one thing and one thing only from me. Either I had the drugs, or I had the alcohol. I had the money. When all of that ran out, they didn't want to be around me anymore. In AA, you all just wanted to see what that twelve step says: how to get a spiritual awakening and help the next sick and suffering alcoholic. And trust me, I was a sick and suffering alcoholic

About nine days into the program, I'm sitting at the Martha Jefferson Center, and someone asked me to read The Promises. I held The Promises and voices were beating in my head so badly. I wasn't sure who was talking or what was going on and, at nine days sober, I was having an extreme mental breakdown. I needed medication. I needed medication to help me get straight. So, I called my sponsor and I said, "Something is going on. I'm not sleeping. I'm not eating. I'm hearing voices. I'm anxiety ridden. I can't go to work." And my sponsor's response was, "I don't know how to help you but let me make a few phone calls because I'm here for your recovery. I'm not a psychiatrist. But I can help you find somebody who can help you."

I heard that a lot of people in AA didn't believe in medication, but I needed it. Today, I take nothing, but I needed it at that time. And so, what we did was I worked with my sponsor on my steps, and I went to a shrink to work on what was going on with me. And I peeled a lot of stuff for many years sitting in that office talking to that woman who was experienced with working with alcoholics.

I struggled with my fourth step and, once again, my sidekick, Sarah Beth, my sponsor, puts me in her house, locks the door and says that she's going to the noon meeting and when she comes back, let's see how far you've gotten on the fourth step. Where I was suffering with that fourth step was that I didn't know where to put my uncle, the very man who had done all of these horrible things. How could I put him down on the fourth step? What could have been my part? What I realized, in working the fourth step, was that I had absolutely nothing to do with what my uncle did to me. But I have everything to do with where I am today. So, I can be one of two things. I could continue to be the victim, or I could be a survivor. I got into survival mode. And so, today when I have to write down and do a fourth step and look at my part, this program has taught me to just be honest. That's the bottom line. Just be honest.

My life, today, is beyond my wildest dreams. There is a person sitting here, Margot, who is my publisher. Together, we are writing a book about me. Who in the hell would have thought, fifteen years ago, that someone would want to write about me? Why in the name of God would anyone want to know about me? I was a thug. I was nasty. I was racist. Why? It is because of sitting in these rooms with Alcoholics Anonymous. Not only did I sit in the rooms of Alcoholics Anonymous, I sat in the middle. I went to meeting after meeting after meeting.

Still, I can't ignore where I was at a year ago, last June. I was so confused about what was going on in the world, where I was seeing and hearing things that were going on with AA and I said, "'F' it. I'm not going to AA anymore. You don't want me in here because of the color of my skin." This is what I had conjured up in my head. So, I'm in Richmond and at Wawa getting a soda and the phone rang and it's Tracy and she says, "Do you have a minute? I've got some ideas I need to flow off you." And she said, "I'm only going to take ten minutes of your time." So, I pulled off and for the next ninety minutes to almost two hours, we talked about the state of the world and that you can't control what's going on. But we can control what we do in AA.

And she said, "If you will just come back to AA, come back to my 9 o'clock meeting and, if you don't like it, go. But if it's ok for you, stick around." And that, again, is what we do in AA. If you read the daily reflection for today, it pretty much talks about how we don't need to have our hand on the outside issues. We need to be able to see what's going on in this world, but we need to know that this is a special mix that we have right here. This is safety. This is comfort. If you feel like you're not safe, speak up. And there are people who will make sure that you feel safe in these spaces.

That's exactly what you all did with me. You made me feel safe. When I first came in, I came in on a Wednesday. The Saturday before, I said, "I'm going to check this thing out." So, I went to a meeting, and I got that if you picked up this white chip, that meant you can't drink anymore. So, I wouldn't pick it up because I knew I wasn't done. I knew in my heart that I was not done and knew that I wasn't going to pick up this chip and, a few days later, come back and pick up another one. I didn't want any more. So, I didn't pick one up and I remember approaching three women and asking them about sobriety, and they kind of blew me off and that was my excuse to just go. And I went really hard that weekend. That weekend, I overdosed four times. That fourth time was rescue squad. It was a bad gig. And I could hear them outside of the door talking about putting me somewhere like maybe upstairs on the psych ward. And it was like, "I ain't going upstairs." And I was yanking out the IV and rolling down the hall and gone. Just gone. And I suffered that entire weekend.

A friend of mine who lived in Jersey had said that she just wanted to come down and pick me up and bring me to her house. She had about 25 years sobriety at the time. So, I called her that Wednesday morning and I said to Sherrie, "I think I'm done. I don't know where else to go. I don't have any friends. I don't even know what's going on in my head. One minute, I think I'm female. The next minute, I think I'm a man." She said, "You don't need to know about any of that right now. All you need to know if that you need to find a meeting."

That was 15 years ago, and we didn't have access to the internet. But she called me back about 11 o'clock and she said, "Do you know where Holy Comfort is?" And I was like, "I don't know where no damn Catholic church is. I barely know where a Baptist church is. Why do you think I'm gonna know where a Catholic church is?" And she said, "It's on Jefferson Street." I said, "I know where that is."

I couldn't find a place to park so I parked in the parking deck. It's hot and I walk in and there's maybe six or seven of them. There's Frank and Kirby and the guy who used to wear that funky blue cap, Max. And so, I'm sitting there and I'm like, "These are some losers to be sitting here at lunch time in a dingy basement, praying with each other." I mean, they are holding hands and praying. Good Lord! How much more of a loser could they be? But when I realized how it works, the word that came out to me was "unfortunate." I had been called an unfortunate for so many years. Doctors said I was unfortunate. They said the best thing I could do is get on disability, hang out at the clubhouse, and take Thorazine. That's the best we can give you right now. This is going to be your life. This is what your life is going to be. I remember a guy telling me that like five years before I came into the program, and I was like, "That's just not me. I think there is more to me. I just don't know how to find it."

And that day, when they said to surrender, I said, "Wait a minute." So, I remember walking up to Frank and Kirby, and I said, "Hey, dudes, I need a sponsor." And they were like, "No, no, no, no, no. We can't sponsor you." I was like, "Here we go again." They were like, "Men can't sponsor women. You are going to go with her." And I'm like, "She's crazy as shit. She's holding a rosary and reading the Big Book and rocking. What are you trying to do here?" So, I went up to her and I said, "I need a sponsor." And she was like, "We can discuss sponsorship. I can be your temporary sponsor." I was like, "Here, I'll give you my phone number." And she was like, "I don't want your number. Here's mine and, if you are serious, you call me tonight at nine o'clock and the answers to your recovery are the first 164 pages."

So, I remember walking back to my car and I was like, "That bitch is going to get it because I'm going to go back to work. I'm going to read all 164 pages. I'm going to make notes and I'm gonna prove to you that this book is a crock of shit, and I'm going to have questions for you." And so, when I called her that night at 9 o'clock, I had about 30 questions that I was just firing off at her. And she said, "Are you done?" Then she said, "Right now, you know nothing about recovery. But we can walk this road together and learn about recovery with each other. So, I just want you to keep reading."

So, for the first nine or ten months, I read the first 164 pages. I would fall asleep. I would wake up. I would finish the 164 pages. She told me to go to a meeting a day. So, I'd go to a meeting.

That Wednesday, I picked up a white chip. That Thursday, James Brown was in town. So, I pick up the phone and I call her. At that point, I didn't know if I should call her Gloria, Miss Gloria. I just said, "Ma'am, I don't think I'm going to be at the meeting tonight." And she said, "Why not?" I said, "Well, Godfather is in town." And she said, "I heard that." I said, "My friends are down on Godfather. I've got to see Godfather before either he or I die. So, I'll tell you what. I'll probably drink, but I'll come back and pick up a white chip tomorrow because I'll probably only be down there for maybe 40-45 minutes." She said, "What if those 40-45 minutes are the last drink you ever take?" I said, "What do you mean?" She said, "What if you have a drink and that drink, that last drink, right there, kills you?" She said, "Well, let's make it a little more glorious. You have a stroke because you are mixing all kinds of stuff. You have a stroke, and now, people are going to be praying that you either die or you come out of it. Because that's where alcohol can take you. You don't know when that drink is going to be your last."

So, I said, "Where's a meeting?" And she said, "There's one on Hinton Avenue." So, I pull my truck up on Hinton Avenue and there's Merv and that gang, and they're out there kicking a Hacky Sack and I said to her on the phone, "Oh, hell no. You got these boys out here kicking a Hacky Sack and you want me to go to this meeting?" She said, "We go to any lengths to stay sober." And I went to the meeting, and they welcomed me with open arms. They didn't know a thing about me. They were so giddy that I was 24 hours sober. That's all they were concerned about. That I stayed that one hour and be sober. And then, after that, they took me to somewhere where we had coffee and we had dinner. And I just couldn't get it, what this was all about. I understand it today.

So, five years into my sobriety, what I thought was a solid relationship, but wasn't because I was so angry, I mean I wasn't physically abusive, but I was emotionally abusive. I was verbally abusive. I was throwing things. I just wasn't a lovely person, and she took a hike. And that forced me to be with me. And then, I realized, "I'm waking up every morning sober. Each one of you wake up every morning and your body is comfortable. You might not like a few pounds that you have on or you're getting grey. But you're comfortable with who you were born to be. I wasn't like that. I couldn't tap into that this is who I was.

I knew I had to pay the light bill that day or buy a gun. When I woke up, I said, "That's the two things. I'm not going to drink because I'm not going to kill myself and everybody in AA says, "He killed himself because of drinking." So, I went to the pawn shop, and I bought the gun, and I came back home, and I put pillows and towels down and I was standing in my kitchen. This is dramatic, but it's true. I'm standing in the kitchen, and I had the gun, and the doorbell rang. I thought, "Ah, shit."

So, I put the gun down. I go to the door and there's a mailman. Now, this lazy sucker would never bring a package to my door. He would either throw it in 29 or try to stuff it in the mailbox. But for some reason, my higher power, who I choose to call God, had him walk that package up the steps and ring the doorbell. I opened the door, and he said, "Next time, order a smaller package."

So, I came back in and opened the package, and it was from my ex. She had been to a conference where she had met a gentleman named Carter Brown, who was forming the first national Black transman Incorporated.[15] It was all these pamphlets and all this information. When I shook the envelope, Carter's card fell out. So, I called. And Carter will tell you today that he rarely answers his phone. But he answered that day. So, we talked a little bit, and, at the very end, I said to him, "You know, I was thinking about killing myself today because I'm just not comfortable in my body." He said, "I don't know anything about AA but didn't you tell me you are in recovery?" And I was like, "Yeah." And he said, "Well, okay. What time is it?" And I said, "It's five o'clock." And he said, "When is the next meeting? Maybe you need to go to a meeting." So, I went to the 5:30 meeting. The next day, the gun went back, and I paid my light bill.

I was so worried. I wasn't worried about my family accepting me. I was worried about what my family would think of me if I transitioned. I was afraid they were going to reject me. I was afraid I was going to get kicked out. So, he doesn't know this, but the first person I went to talk to in AA was Frank. I called Frank, and I told him what was going on. And Frank said, "You need to tell your story and I'll be sitting there right beside you. You need to share with the people in AA what you're doing, and I want you to see what happens." Then, he said, "If something bad happens, you know I've got your back." And that's exactly what I did because you know what? There are some people in AA who suggest, and there are some people who are just going to tell your ass, "Do it and shut up and get it done." And that's what Frank does with me. "Shut up. Get it done. I don't want to hear any slack from you. Just do it. If you don't like what it is, I'm more than happy to hear what you've got to say but more than likely it isn't going to be right. So, just do what I tell you to do, and it will be ok." And I respect that. So, I told my story, and, in September, I will have been 10 years since I transitioned.

I've had an incredible year. I was named OUTStanding Virginian by Equality Virginia this year. I am now the National Program Director for Black Transmen Incorporated, and I've helped save a lot of lives. I

---

[15] https://blacktransmen.org/.

sponsor three guys. My life is rich. My life is full. But I cannot ride on yesterday's successes for today and the only reason I'm where I am today is because of Alcoholics Anonymous. The only reason I'm sitting here today—it wasn't Carter's card falling out—it was Carter telling me, "Aren't you in AA? Maybe you need to go to a meeting." As much as I didn't share anything about that at that meeting because I was scared to death, I was safe. I was safe because I was hearing that language.

You know, we talk about the language in the heart, and I listened to that language in the heart. I tell you, in the wild, kick-ass group of Sober AF, there are no holds barred. You come in there. It's hardcore recovery. It's life. It's love. And I love that group. But I tell you what has really, really spiraled me into a good space in these last couple of weeks is going back to those stomping grounds of Sober AF.

That's where I would sit at noon, and I shook. I tried to get into rehab. They wouldn't take me. So, I just came in and I detoxed right in these rooms. I remember that I was shaking so badly one day that Frank got up and told me to go sit in the padded chair. I was in one of the metal chairs and I was shaking, and it was making noise. And he just gently told me to go sit in the padded chair because it would be less noisy. And David, God bless his soul, would pull me aside and tell me, "You need to get some B12 shots. That's what we did back in the day." "Okay. I'll do that." I did everything that you guys told me, but I did it undercover because I didn't want you to think that I was listening to you. But I *was* listening. So, today, I don't even play that game anymore because that was a little drama game going on. And I wanted you to think I was this badass. "I hate you. I don't want to be around you." That's just not me today.

The one thing that's been a blessing, a positive, during the pandemic is Zoom. But I'm just craving to sit in a room with my people. I'm craving that. When we hold hands, and we say that prayer. That very thing that I thought was cult-like, when everybody was holding hands, is the most strength-giving thing. Now, I'll admit. What does Tracy call it? Cacophony. I'm like, "This shit drives me crazy." But I do it. I do it because I'm a member of AA. I don't know where my life would be without me being in this room right now. This is a program beyond my wildest dreams.

Today, I'm in a house. Today, I'm driving a car. Today, I manage 21 people who society would not normally want to give jobs to, who have mental and physical disabilities. I'm well-respected. A friend of mine wants to write my freaking story. It's unbelievable.

I was sitting at my desk today and I just started crying and I couldn't figure out what was going on. It wasn't tears of sadness. It was like it is right now. I get so filled with the goodness that this program and my higher power, that I choose to call God, has given me. I don't know how many do-overs I've got, but He saved me in the kitchen that day. He saved me when I was laying on that gurney with me ripping IVs off. He saved me five years ago. Sherrie, the person I told you walked me that day into the Holy Comforter, her boyfriend called me last April. And all he said was, "She's gone." And I said, "What are you talking about?" He said, "Sherrie, she's gone. I took her to the hospital because she was having problems breathing and she wasn't feeling well. They came back out and told me they were putting her on a ventilator." In less than 24 hours all this went down, and she died from this dreadful pandemic disease. But as much as that saddens, you know, we are all put on this earth as vessels, for one reason or another. And that was the vessel that got me into this program. I would never have come into AA had it not been for Sherrie walking me into that meeting. And I know all of us have done those miraculous things with other people. That's just how we roll. We don't stop there. We just keep doing it.

So, what is my day like? I get up in the morning and I read the daily reflection and I pray to God. A year ago, I would get in my car, and I would say, "God, please just don't have the police pull me over because they are going to see me as a Black man." And I prayed that prayer for about six or seven months. But then, one day, I realized, "What kind of God do I think I have?" I don't need to worry about having to go to a meeting. Excuse my language but if my Black ass just does what I'm supposed to do, don't speed, keep a driver's license, do what I have to do, my odds are a little bit greater. I still have to remind myself of what society sees me as, right now. Sometimes, among the people in my society, I'm the only Big Book that they see. So, I have to walk that walk. I have to show people that you don't have to be afraid to be coming to this program if you look different. That's what the daily reflection talked about today. We are all different. But we all have one common thing that we want. And that is to stay sober.

Frank, I think I'm done. I want to thank you guys for being here and being with me today.

Chapter 15

Sometimes I Wonder...

Live for today. Yesterday's history. Tomorrow's a mystery.
Alcoholics Anonymous

Today I am a little angry. I have to pretend all the time that I am a man. Wearing two binders. T shirt, two binders, t shirt and then my shirt. Why do I have to do this? Am I being punished because I am trying to make myself something that I am not?

Last night, I had this great dream. I was all boy. No breasts, a penis, and my name. It was so real; I woke up and realized it was just a dream. It's shit like this that makes me want to take a drink and just say fuck it. Fuck being sober, fuck trying to live this whatever normal life is. This is too much work.

I think this downward spiral is for many reasons. At my job I just get by, behind in bills, and just got denied for having top surgery. When I read the letter, I pretended that it didn't matter. I pretended that just because I have breasts doesn't mean that I cannot be a man.

But what fucking man do you see who has breast as big as mine? There are days that I know people are staring. Some days, it just can't be hidden. I fucking have the body of a woman. A body that has curves, parts of my body soft. Sometimes, I want to take the knife and just start cutting. Starting with the breasts. Cutting away at the hips.

How can someone be truly happy dealing with this? I make sure I don't even look in the mirror in the mornings. I just don't like what I see. I see a fake. I see someone who is stuck. When something is stuck, you pull and pull until its unstuck. But what if there is nothing to grab hold of to pull this body out of this deep dark hole?

Yeah, I am sure I probably need to go back to therapy. I am just not ready. No need to waste anyone's time or mine. I don't know how to explain. I don't know what the answer is. I guess the best thing I can do today is put on the mask, wrap my body in these layers of material, and move forward.

What happens when I can't move forward any longer? What happens when I just don't have it to give, to live any longer? I have been here before, and I have come out of it. I have gone through worst shit than this. But what happens when I just don't have it to pull this stuck body and mind out of the tube of despair?

Charley, 2018

Sometimes, I wonder what life would have been like if things had been different. What it would have been like to be born as a boy. Would I have had the fighting spirit I have now? Would I have been in 12 step recovery? Would I be married with a wife and some kids and even grandkids by now? Would all of the wonderful people have been in my life? I ponder these questions a lot. Sometimes, I have an answer. Sometimes, I wonder why does it matter? "I am where I am today. I am where I am today." I say that phrase over and over again.

Am I satisfied with my life? Yes, but there are still some missing pieces. Love, particularly. I miss being in love. I miss the excitement of dating. I also miss being able to sit down and just have a drink. But I am strong enough in my sobriety to play the tape back. Nothing about my drinking and drugging days were productive. So, I can't say that I believe that it would be better. All I know is, at this time, almost 16 years without a drug or a drink, that my life is tremendously better. I can honestly say that it's a fleeting notion. As they say, my disease is playing tricks on me. I write this because I have to remind myself that I am human and, sometimes, this stuff comes to mind. But back to the being in love part. I know that, now, with all the work I have done on myself, I will, or would, make someone a great partner. But here is where the fear part comes in. Have I walked this path alone for so long that I no longer know how to be in a relationship? I enjoy my life but what would it look like if I was sharing it with someone else?

Being an advocate for trans people here in Virginia can sometimes be too much. It's like an ask that just never stops. At times like these, I think that I just want to be a regular man, living a regular life. I guess that is the Gemini in me. When life slows down, I get bored and feel like I am not helping anyone, that someone out there needs my help. I just can't imagine someone living life the way I had to in the beginning days, especially the loneliness. Eleven years ago, I had very few successes. I was just trying to survive. I had no drive, no ambition. And, as I have always said, I had no voice. I wanted to. I would see others and think I should do that too. I wanted so badly to go to events, but I didn't want to go alone and be alone. I tried going to a few things, only to end up at the table or in the room, never engaging. I often wondered why people didn't want to be around me.

I realized now that I didn't want to be around myself. How could I expect anyone else to want to be a part of my life when I didn't even want that life for myself. Now, when I see Black transmen, or people in recovery, in that wallpaper mode, just pressed against the wall of the world, I can relate. I have been there. I know what it's all about.

And so, looking at how things are for me today, I find myself complaining that too many people want my time. It is amazing to me that, sometimes, I am still not satisfied with what I have, who I am, and what I have to offer. I guess it's true. We are always a work in progress. I will continue to learn until I take my last breath.

Returning to relationships and the falling-in-love thing, I have tried to meet several women. Is my standard too high? Am I expecting too much? I know that, in the beginning, when I knew I should not have been out in the dating scene, I honestly thought there would be a replica of Constance, waiting. It was then that I realized that I was expecting everyone to be someone else. Instead, I needed to see what they could bring to the table. So, I stepped aside and admitted that I was not ready yet, especially not if I was still expecting someone to be someone else. I realized that I had two options. One was to settle for someone just for the sake of being with someone. Or I could do the work. I am so grateful that my recovery program has taught me about action. Take the action. I just kept hearing my two sponsors and the other solids in the room of AA saying, "Dive into service." So, I jumped into service.

But my service in AA felt one-sided. I must be honest. Charlottesville AA saved my life, but I got tired of seeing people who don't look like me in many of the boxes that I check. I wanted to find just one other sober trans person in the room. Someone who knew what it was like to go to sleep satisfied with life, my body, and my spirit but to wake up afraid to look at your body, afraid for my hands to even touch my body. Why? Because my body didn't match my face, my feelings, my self.

Here I am, mustache, beard, pronouns matching. But, underneath, were breasts. Many mornings, just the act of taking a shower was too much. How the hell do I wrap the 12 steps into that? How, in a general way, do I say that I thought about drinking and killing myself this morning because I touched my breasts? How could I explain that one to either one of my sponsors? Truly, I am over 14 years sober, and I still have bouts of this kind of thinking. Perhaps, I could talk to another transman about this. But, in my mind, I am Charley. I am the elder now. They look up to me to have the answers. I can't let the world see me like this. I often wonder is this how other people who represent the movement feel? Who do I turn to? Not any of my ally friends. I can't turn to my young brothers. But why not? Am I not human first and Charley, the one who can help us, second?

So, what do I do? I do what I do best. I Clark Kent it. Suit up and keep moving. This requires me to become even more teachable and willing to ask for help in order to learn this. Just because I am Charley does not mean I don't hurt. I hope someday when I can have top surgery, maybe I won't feel like this. Maybe, one day, I won't have to hide these layers of flesh.

Every morning, when I get dressed, I put on a t-shirt, then 3 binders, another t-shirt, and then, my shirt. Just so I feel like I won't get discovered. When it's hot outside, I develop rashes and my body burns with sweat. But this is the life I must live right now. I have lived this way for 10 years. Sometimes, I feel like a fraud, pretending to have a body that I don't really have.

Most mornings, I pray for two things. First, that as I travel, I can survive as being perceived as a Black man. These days, being a Black Man is open season, not only when racist people are concerned but with law enforcement as well. I just obey the law and pray that I don't get caught. My second morning prayer is, "Please let me not get sick to the point that a rescue unit is called. If they open my shirt, I am discovered."

I also pray to be as good of a human being as I possibly can be. Then, during my drive to work, I pray for others. What a difference my prayer life has become. Now, I pray for others and, as AA has taught me, I don't throw out those Santa Claus prayers any longer. You know, "Please let me find lots of money. Please let me find the perfect girlfriend. Please let me be happy." Those prayers are only for my benefit. To me prayers should be for others. "Please let me help others as others have helped me along the way." Prayers for me to be of service as best as I am able, to help the next person.

I remember that when I first started really praying and paying attention to prayer was during my first year in AA. My sponsor would say prayers for others, and I would think, *But who is praying for me?* Today, I realize that I am alive because of prayers from others. I can't imagine everything I put my parents and family through, the prayers they must have been saying to save me.

Now, don't get me wrong. I am not a Bible-thumping religious nut. I believe in something greater than me and that is what I call God. I believe that something is happening in my life that was out of my control. But I also believe that, as I was taught in recovery, I must act. If I want something, God is not going to throw it down from the sky. I must work for it. Looking back, even during my darkest hours, I wanted life. I worked for it and now look at me. I have a life beyond my wildest dreams. Life has taken on a new meaning for me. I have opportunities because I just didn't sit back and wait. I worked. Am I proud of where I am. Yes! Do I know that something bigger than me brought me here? Yes! But I also believe that angels are put in my path. Along the way, I entertained these angels. Today, I see that each angel in my life, even if they are now gone, served a purpose for me, although at times, I was too self-absorbed in pity to see the works of something bigger.

I was never a big believer in AA, especially when I walked through the door on that long-ago Wednesday at noon. I just knew that my friend, Sherrie, from Jersey, told me that there is a meeting and that I needed to go to it. What I never envisioned was that this program of recovery was going to give me a life that I had never had. I hear many people in AA talk about being given their life back. I didn't have one. I only had existence. But deep down, I knew I was more than just a soul existing here. I was here for a purpose.

My sister talks about how I was a sickly child. So, I guess I was fighting even then. I was fighting to be here. I guess that power greater than me, that I choose to call God had a plan for me. I fought even from birth. On May 27, 1960, in the back seat of the 1956 Chevy Bel Air, I decided I was ready to face this world no matter what I did against it, or it did against me. So, I was born in that back seat on Jefferson Park Ave at the Charlottesville city limits sign. My mother, who was also a fighter, held herself up in the back seat so as not to smother me. If my mother fought so hard to keep me, then it seemed like it was my duty to fight to stay here, something I took for granted many times. Previously, I never really valued my life until I was faced with fighting to value my very existence. How do I see it now? Look at what the people I have helped would have missed if that bullet had worked, or the pills that I took had done what I was expecting them to do, or if that last drink had truly been my last.

But here I am, ready to experience what life has to offer. Today, I love me. I am 15 years sober as the clock strikes midnight January 2022. I sponsor men who want what I have—to stay sober. I have created groups that save lives. People want to hear what I have to say. 2021 was an incredible year. The awards and accolades I have received have been mind-blowing. But as humbling as they are, I must continue to remind myself, "Charley, this is just you. You are not special. There is nothing special you are doing." I am just doing what I would have wanted someone to do for me.

Every year, on New Year's Eve, I would question, "Why am I alone again this year?" And the hamster wheel starts. My hamster wheel is not very well oiled, and it makes a lot of noise. Each year, I would become this horrible victim. "I am alone, I am a loser." No matter how many people would be in my world, I would go straight to that life of hate. Each year, I would go into my living room and cry. I would always tell myself, "It will not be like this next year." But as the year winds down to an end, here I am, sad, playing the victim, and surprised that I am here, yet again, for another year. Alone, lonely, and feeling desperate. When will I realize that this is my choice? But is it?

Something I realized in the last several years is this fear of rejection, this fear that if I ask, I will be told, "No." I remember after AA meetings when we were meeting in person, the anxiety would creep up as soon as we finished the prayer to close out the meeting. Will the group start making plans to eat together? Do some type of outside AA fellowship? Will I be asked? So, I did what I do best, I ran out of the door. No after the meeting conversations for me.

But 2021 was different. It's amazing how, in what seems like a blink of an eye, my life changed. AA tells me that my whole outlook will change. Things that sent me into a spiral will no longer be the case. When did this growth happen? When did I become a confident man? A man that can look in the mirror and be okay.

It's funny but until about 2 years ago, when I thought about myself, I still thought in terms of the pronouns "she" and "her." I can't explain it and maybe other transmen experienced this too. But it would be like a slip of the tongue or thought. I would be in my head thinking about something or talking to myself—I tend to do that a lot! I would call myself "Charley," but I would think in terms of "her." It was not until after my top surgery that I felt whole, and the slipping of my own pronouns stopped.

I remember that when I was first transitioning, I hated to have to go to funerals. I could grow a little peach fuzz on the mustache or beard area but would have to shave it off just so I felt like no one would be looking at me. One day, I remember having to go to Greenwood for a family funeral. I went to work, got off, and then, was heading to the funeral directly from work. Then, I remembered, "Damn. I didn't shave and haven't for weeks." I stopped frozen in my tracks, then headed to my car to take the ride. "No time to go home. Must pay my respects." It was at that moment that I realized, "Who am I transitioning for?" If I am expecting the world to accept me and I get angry when they don't, who am I to judge them? I can't even accept myself.

I could now see what dysphoria is about. I was struggling with that because my body as I wanted it was not a match for what I saw in the mirror. How I hated looking at my body before the surgery. Here I am running all over the place, speaking, connecting, telling guys how to live their authentic life. Yet, I was feeling like a fake. I couldn't accept my body as a male, but I was so tired of the routine—shower, t-shirt, 2 binders, t-shirt, and then, a dress shirt. And I was still living in fear. Fear of being found out. What if I get sick and I need to be attended to by EMT's? I prayed every morning that, for that day, I would never need to open my shirt. It was an exhausting life to live. Summers were the worse, the heat rashes, the sweat running down my back, the fear of someone looking at my bulging chest and wondering. Oh, how I hated the wondering in people. I got so tired of folding my arms in front of me all the time. When would this stop?

Then, on March 25, 2021, it happened. I met the man who would change my life. Dr. J. T. Stranix not only created the chest I longed to have, but he also created the confident man that had been engulfed in all those layers of breast tissue. As he crafted my body, he also crafted the man. I remember waking up from the surgery in my hospital room.

My first thought was, *Nothing feels different.* I was so scared to touch the bandages. I was also convinced that something must have gone wrong. It's just the way the universe always was for me. Something was always going to go wrong. But I could feel the flatness of my chest, even through the bandages. It was at that moment that I realized that life as I knew it was going to be different. Just removing 11 pounds of flesh was the momentum I needed to take yet another step into my new world.

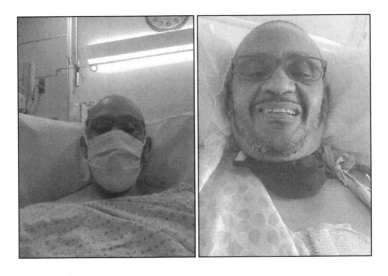

Now, it's May 11, and I am taking an online training course to become certified as a Transgender 101 trainer. My car is in the shop because a headlight needs to be replaced. Throughout the day, I have been pretty much cut off from social media. I remember we had a break, and so, I hopped on social media. The buzzing from my local family and friends was all about there being no gas in Charlottesville, how it was expected to last for weeks. My beautiful projecting mind starts, "Oh no! What happens if I get my car back, but I can't get any gas?" I am spinning in my head, "How do I get to work? How to find gas. I need my car." The mechanic calls and the car is ready. Back to class, the trainer announces that we have finished early for the day. I rush down and ask my brother to take me to get my car. But in my mind, I think, *Wait, I have to go back upstairs and do the routine. T-shirt, binder, t-shirt, shirt.* As I rush down the hallway and up the stairs, it hits me. I never have to do that again. I remember pulling off the old shirt and pulling a freshly laundered t-shirt over my head. I can still smell the freshness of the shirt as it goes over my head. The next moment is a moment I will never forget in my life. It is the first time that I felt the cotton fall directly upon my skin. The softness and how it feels is like a beautiful wave. I remember rubbing my hand down the front of the shirt. Flat, smooth, manly, human, acceptance. Just like they said in the Big Book, I had arrived. Never again would I have to worry about the bulge, the looks, the wonder, the fear. Oh yeah! I got the gas. I passed the class. Life was different.

Finally, its New Year's Eve again. I know my life is different. I prepare all day for a night to just be with me. I could have gone to an event but chose to stay safe from COVID and stay home. I yearn all day for this night of quiet reflection. As I move through my day, it strikes me like a slap. I was in the grocery store just picking up some fun food to snack on, and I realized that I was having my own personal "welcome to the new year" party. I had to smile. Years past that I can't even think about, I would be drunk and not even knowing if it was already New Year's or not. Then, New Year's without a partner and I would be devastated. What was different about tonight? What was different about me? I have grown into a comfortable space of being. As the Big Book says, I have arrived! I have arrived at being at peace. I have arrived at knowing that I don't need the approval of someone else's love to complete me. I love myself and I am complete. Not only am I complete, but I am also grateful. Reflecting back on my year, the awards, the recognitions, people honestly wanting to be with me, guys I was talking to about recovery, mentees, young guys who truly listen to me speak about my path of becoming a Black man with a trans experience. I was so grateful on December 31, 2021!

On January 1st, I grabbed the *Daily Progress*.[16] On the front page, there I am, telling my story. Suddenly, there was this rush of fear. What have I done? I realized that what I had done was possibly help someone else who reads my story. I realized that my life and everything that has happened is for someone else. I believe everything I went through in life has made me stronger, but it also can help heal someone else. I mean really isn't that what Jesus was all about? I am not a Bible thumper, but, these days, I try to live the way a good man should. A good man like my daddy. That is why I bear his name. I will never fill his shoes, but I can walk in them. Jesus just wanted people to love each other. I believe there are other Jesuses in this world. Just moving through life wanting the best for everyone, at least, that's my take on the man in the Bible, the one people strive to be like. Like my daddy, strong, but loving, who had his flaws but was a good man.

Through the course of the last year, this life has been incredible. The one thing I keep telling myself is, "Don't let the ego get in your way. Just keep moving and helping. Share your world and allow others to be a part of it." I owe all of this to my recovery. I never thought I would see almost 16 years sober. I'd never even thought about life at 61. I should have been dead that day I got the package from Constance, but other plans were in place. I guess it's true that one can never expect what curves life will throw at you. I certainly didn't expect any of this.

I decided a few days ago, with a kind and loving heart, to leave Black Transmen Inc. For 10 years, that organization and Carter's love gave me a purpose. For 10 years, I too gave my heart, my sweat, and sometimes tears. I lost a job because I represented BTMI. But I gained being a good man. I gained a voice. I gained respect within my community of trans people, allies, recovery, and in my family. It was more than just working for the organization for 10 years. It was a labor of love. It was a hard decision to leave, but it's one that I needed to make because I love me. I want to see the next chapter of my life. What will life be like just going to spaces as Charley? Helping because I'm just Charley? Just seeing how I am, go out, and continue to tell my story.

---

[16] https://www.dailyadvent.com/news/c106e3a90e98fff8fc12008f597bdb9d-Burton-works-to-make-transitions-easier.

One of my favorite movies—and I have many—is *Ferris Bueller's Day Off*. He skips school to show his friends what it's like to just have a day of enjoyment. "Life moves fast," he says, "Every now and then, you gotta stop and look around and enjoy the moment." This is my time; this is my story, and this is my moment.

Chapter 16

Becoming the Man I Want to Be[17]

***The road to sobriety is a simple journey for confused
people with a complicated disease.***

Alcoholics Anonymous

*It was like a moment that just came from out of
nowhere. I had to run out quickly to grab something from
the store. I had been attending a class on Zoom. I got up
from the computer and hurried to catch my ride. As I got
into the car I realized, I didn't have to run and put on a
binder. I was wearing just a t-shirt and shorts. This was
my new life. No binder, no hiding, this was different, and
I like it.*

*As I was riding in the car, I felt my chest, flat, tight.
I wanted to rip off my shirt and feel my skin. I was now*

---

[17] Transcript from "Becoming the Man I want to Be": Charley's Gender-Confirmation Surgery, a video and blog about Charley's top surgery at University of Virginia Health Center, https://blog.uvahealth.com/2021/06/24/charleys-gender-confirmation-surgery/.

feeling like I was connecting to the right body. I am not completely whole but getting there. I have arrived!

I don't know why it took that moment in time to realize the impact of my surgery. I have found myself many times in the shower as the water is cascading down my skin. I no longer have to hold up a breast and wash underneath. I am no longer looking in the mirror seeing this manly face and looking down and seeing those big breasts that remind me that, at one point, I was a woman.

It's like a half and half feeling. Here is this face, this mental attitude, these mannerisms that are all male. But underneath a t shirt, two binders, and another t shirt are remnants of my female life.

I don't ever want to erase who I was. I lived over 30 years as a butch lesbian and, for that time, it served me well. I don't want to ever forget the little boy moments I had. But as I evolve, I am now a transman. I say transman because I am proud to be that. I am proud to let people know that as a transman I have walked a journey.

Charley, May 2021

CHARLEY: I'm Charley Burton. I'm a native of Charlottesville, Virginia. There's a picture of me as a little kid, and you can't tell that I wasn't a little boy. I always knew. My body just didn't match my mind. And I pushed that in for the next 30, 40 years until I became 50 years of age and started my journey.

REAGAN THOMPSON: When I first met Charley, he was pretty frustrated. He had hit a lot of barriers getting appropriate transgender care and had given up on our system.

CHARLEY: And so, when I go to the hospital, there's this level of anxiety that builds up in me every time. But I've been lucky because I've had a Reagan Thompson in my corner. She truly wants to know, what can she do as a medical professional to make my life better?

REAGAN THOMPSON: I think it's super important to listen to your patients and try to figure out what they're angry at.

CHARLEY: She has seen me at my lowest. And she now sees me where I'm at today.
Today's the day that I have my top surgery. Top surgery is the removal of the breasts. It's another stage in my transition. So, I'm a little nervous today. Nervous and excited.

JT STRANIX, MD: It's impossible not to like Charley when you meet him. We talk about what the goals are for surgery. His, in particular, were to have a chest that was congruent with his male identity.

NURSE: And can you tell me what Dr. Stranix is going to do? And Dr. Sopata?

CHARLEY: Yeah, we're doing a double mastectomy.

NURSE: OK.

CHARLEY: The top surgery.

NURSE: Yup.

CHARLEY: And total hysterectomy.

CARRIE SOPATA, MD: Trans patients should feel comfortable coming to any location in UVA and knowing that they're going to get the right care and the best care.

CHARLEY: There was this one nurse. One night, she came in and she just wanted to know so the next person that comes on her floor that has had top surgery or is trans, what could she do better? And she asked some of the most beautiful, poignant questions. It was just total respect.

JT STRANIX, MD: In my mind, a successful gender-affirming surgery is one that makes a patient feel more comfortable with their gender identity and really improves their overall well-being.

CHARLEY: The first day that I was able to take the ACE bandages off, I saw the chest that I've always wanted, and it was... I'm getting emotional now. It was just 10 times more than what I thought it would be.

REAGAN THOMPSON: And now Charley is a very happy person with very few complaints and has a desire to fix a system that is driving him to be more involved in the transgender community.

CHARLEY: I'm becoming the man that I want to be. I am confident in who I am, and I never thought I'd ever be there.

Blog Discussion

The day I received the call from plastic surgeon JT Stranix's office, I really was not sure I was hearing the employee, Destiny, correctly. "You have been approved and let us set up your surgery date."

I have wanted this for about six years. Three years prior, I was denied. I watched everyone else in my circle of trans brothers getting their surgery dates, showing their results. I did not want to go into the "Why me?" mode. I just continued to do the work I needed to do to help others.

I had resigned myself to the fact that gender-confirmation surgery—a hysterectomy and a double mastectomy—would never be a part of my transition. I lacked confidence without the surgery, although I knew how to fake it until I could make it.

I had always wanted to have my surgery close to home. I had wanted my surgery to be at UVA. When I heard that my previous doctor was no longer there, it brought on some anxiety. But then, my nurse practitioner, Reagan Thompson, informed me that there was a new surgeon performing top surgery.

I had to go through so much with my insurance. First, I was told they did not cover. Then, I was told that they did. I kept getting bounced around.

Taking Care of Me

I made sure I had up-to-date tests and a mammogram. It is important to me to take care of my health. For so many years, I had not. It was important to me that, if there was a slim chance of getting this surgery, I was healthy enough to have it.

Going for a mammogram, looking the way I looked, was a challenge. It is COVID, and I had to go to these appointments alone. I found that strength and courage to do everything I needed to do. I was so close to being able to feel my authentic self. Every week, I would slay one more dragon closer to that March 25 surgery date.

Am I Doing the Right Thing?

About 2 weeks before my surgery, I started having doubts. What if it is botched, and I will not have the chest I expected to have? I am not a small guy. Can this doctor do the right thing? But I liked Dr. Stranix's style, and I felt comfortable. I trusted Reagan's recommendation.

What would it feel like to not have breasts? Would it be what I wanted? I am removing a piece of my body that I have had for 60 years. Will I ever date again, and would someone want me with these battle scars? So much going on.

I felt like I could not talk to anyone about this. So, I just did what I did best: stuffed it in.

Every appointment I had went so smoothly. For the first time in my journey, there were no potholes that I was hitting, forcing me to take a different route.

Two Surgeries

I had two surgeries at the same time. The hysterectomy and the top surgery. Somehow, I never had anxiety about the two of them. I knew how important the top surgery was, even with moments of doubt. This was to complete and save my life. It was not for vanity reasons. It was to live.

Again, there could not have been a better person to have besides gynecologist Carrie Sopata, MD. The first appointment: again, lots of anxiety, anger, and fear. Here I must go to the third floor of the women's OB-GYN clinic. If there was ever a reason to be grateful for COVID and mask wearing, it was when I would go to that clinic. I could hide the beard and mustache. Still, I was sure there would be questions.

All on my own, I mustered the strength to go every time. I was not fearful of the nursing staff or doctor. But I wish I'd had someone to just be my cheerleading team. COVID made my whole experience very lonely.

Surgery Day

March 25. The day that would change my life. I have had so many milestone "change my life" days:

- May 22, 2006: When I gave up my life of addiction and surrendered to the program of AA
- September 13, 2011: When I took my first testosterone shot (T shot)
- March 25, 2021: The day I would take my next step in being my authentic self

Again, with COVID, my sister dropped me off at the door. But what a relief to have UVA video producer Nate Braeuer there. Someone I had created trust with. Everything moved so quickly and so well, I cannot remember a lot. I just knew in a few hours, life would be different. Lots of questions and different people. Each person made me feel valued. I knew I was in good hands.

Recovery

I remember waking up and feeling my chest. It was done. Even through the pain and bandages, I knew that life from now on would be different.

My overnight stay could not have been any better. I was afraid. But the nurses turned out to be kind, caring, and nonjudgmental. I remember sleeping a lot. But I also remember the great conversations I had with those nurses about my life and what this surgery meant to me. I felt valued. I felt like a human being, something that was lacking for so long.

LGBTQ Healthcare

Most LGBTQ people experience healthcare discrimination.

There was one slight problem: I was told that I would be provided a compression vest that I would need to wear. The staff thought I had my own. Seems small, but the miscommunication was a big deal when it comes to recovery.

3 Months Out

I am now 3 months out. I had an opening of a wound that I must pack twice a day. I still need to have a hernia repair. My chest looks great, but the big hernia in the middle sort of lessened my feeling totally great. But it will get repaired. The wound is healing.

My feeling about myself and my life is so different. Almost like the day I got my first "T" shot.

This was when I finally realized what this was all about: I am at my desk taking a class. I need to run out quickly during my hour break. I grab my keys and stop in my bedroom, thinking I need to pull my shirt off and put on my binder. I realized I do not have to wear a binder any longer. I can just walk out of the house.

Most mornings, I must smile. I take my shower, dry off, and put my shirt on. My skin feels the softness of the fabric. How it falls over my head and onto my chest. It is then that I know, deep in my soul—I did the right thing, and my life is where it needs to be today.

Thank you, Reagan Thompson, Dr. Sopata, and Dr. Stranix for being the vessel steering my ship in the right direction.

Chapter 17

Morehouse

If it's God's will, I will.
Alcoholics Anonymous

If anyone would have told me at 61, I would be back in school, I would have never believed it. But here I am.

This is how this happened. I am speaking on Zoom at an event. I mention that I have some regrets in my life but was grateful for where I am today. In the chat, someone asked, "What are your regrets?"

I was able to name them.

1. I have yet to fall in love again
2. I never finished school
3. I had gotten sober earlier
4. I had transitioned earlier in life.

Later, in the private chat, someone wrote, "You can do something with two items on your list. You will fall in love again, just wait and see. The right person will come along. You can always finish school. A degree does not have an age limit." Then, they typed, "Oh, and by the way, Morehouse is taking transmen now. I could see you as a Morehouse Man."

That statement stayed with me for a few months. Finally, one day, I opened the Morehouse website and googled "Morehouse and transmen." They were right. Next, I applied. Each step was a little more disappointing. The most devastating part was when I had to get my transcript for high school and college. They were horrible. I talked to the admissions counselor and told her why the transcripts looked the way they did. In AA, they tell us to hold nothing back. Pocket that pride and go for the truth. I did just that.

So, here I am today. I just finished my first semester at Morehouse with all A's. It was hard and, frankly, there were words I have never read in my life. It took me longer because I had to take time to look up words. But, like everything else, I just kept it moving. I know I have the intelligence, but I just was never exposed because I chose to drink instead. At the time, a life of drinking and drugging seemed a lot more important than academics.

Now, I am signing up for the summer semester. I am a Morehouse Man. I have been asked to be an Online Ambassador to help others become Morehouse Men too. I was voted by my online class as Morehouse Man of the week. I don't know what it is. All I know is that I love enriching my mind. I love the idea of being on a new path. In 2020, Morehouse College started accepting transmen. In the Fall of 2021, they created their online program. Again, I feel like I am a part of history. I am the student who is learning and walking a new path.

It is amazing to be online with a group of Black men. I remember my first night. I was in my head trying to figure out who was trans and who might know that I am. As soon as the thought came to mind, I intentionally stopped the hamster wheel. Why does it matter who knows that I am trans or who else might be trans in the class? I am in an all-Black male school. I transitioned to become a man. It does not matter. All that matters is that I am in a space and in a school that Martin Luther King attended and so many other great minds. I am a part of a HBCU (Historically Black Colleges and Universities) and this is a whole new part of my life.

Afterword

The Last Word

If you don't have a Higher Power, borrow mine.
Alcoholics Anonymous

I always have been one for the last word. In April, I made a hard decision to walk away from an 11-year relationship with Black Transmen Inc. (BTMI). This organization was my lifeline for years. It was the first organization that I became involved in for the trans community. I learned a great deal about myself and how I could contribute to the community from that relationship. I found my space.

Although my departure was not what I might hope for, it showed me that I am truly walking in the steps of healthy behaviors. The last 11 years was about the passion of an organization that can help many Black transmen. And it helped me. But as with anything in life, we are always striving for better.

I am now the man I always was hoping to become. I have the fire of the tongue, like my mother, and the work ethic of being fair and just, like my father. I like to think that they would have been proud of me.

As I leave BTMI behind, my hopes are that someday people will understand that it was never about what was not being done, Rather, it was all about what I have done and now can offer to my local community.

Not too long ago, I spent an evening with some young trans brothers in Virginia. I watched as they gathered and interacted with laughter in the room. I watched as one young man came in, who I had met previously at a restaurant. I encouraged the young man, who is the facilitator of the group, to invite him. When he showed up, that was when I realized that I need to do the work in my own back yard.

I see these young men wanting to create spaces for themselves and others, but they just don't have the funding to do so. It is my hope that by putting myself in venues with Charley Speaks,[18] I can paint the picture of the need for more safe spaces. That's the beauty of helping community. One organization does not need to have the monopoly for all trans people. We need to work together.

So, my final words are, "Reach out." Reach out to us. Help us create more spaces. As I get older, it will become important that I pass the torch. It is my duty to do so. It is also my duty to teach and uplift my community. I will never stop following my passion just because I need to change direction. It simply means that I see that more is needed, more work to be done, in different spaces.

I will continue to serve until I take my last breath.

Want to hear Charley speak in person or via Zoom for your company or organization?

Reach out to him at
www.charleyspeaks.com

---

[18] https://www.charleyspeaks.com/.

Acknowledgements

Shout Out

Count your blessings.
Share your happiness.
Alcoholics Anonymous

There are so many people to thank.

First and foremost, Charlie and Leona Burton. Simple country folk who taught their children to strive for better. My mother taught us the new foods that she would bring or cook, food that she had cooked in White people's homes and the ideas that she learned from them and wanted to pass on to us. Whether we wanted to eat or know about this different culture, she made us. I wish I had respected these two people when I was younger. I was always disappointed that they were not younger, like my other friend's parents. But today, I have taken every lesson, every word and action, and clung to them. I am so grateful that they were cooks and janitors. They were the best cooks and janitors anyone could have had. And they also commanded the respect of a community. When my parents died, there were many people at their funeral. Very few were there for any of their children. They were there because those two people made a difference in so many people's lives.

I wish they could have seen that. But I know that they both are orchestrating every bit of this. I am their symphony and they have directed a masterpiece.

To my sister, Carolyn. There is no amount of love I can explain that I have for her, and she has for me. She never gave up on me. She loved me unconditionally back then in the same way as she does now. Now, she is the matriarch of our family. I am so grateful that I am teachable and can ask for her advice and honor it.

To my brother-in-law, Curtis. I had not transitioned when my father was alive. I looked at Curtis and saw how I wanted to create a home, how I wanted to be a man of men. It totally amazes me how this old-school guy says my proper name and almost always gets my pronouns right. Even if he still calls me "honey," from time to time. I remember how I would dress up in his Army uniform and how he taught me the love of Al Green, Wilson Pickett, and the Queen of Soul, Aretha Franklin. I didn't know there was any other kind of music for years. The little kid riding in the back seat of his fast cars, going to baseball games, life didn't get any better.

To my brother, Charles. I cherish our childhood. You were the best coach a kid could have. You coached me to be an athlete despite my size. Rock baseball with a plastic bat was the highlight of our summers. We would play for hours. You playing with me distracted me from all the bad shit that was going on in my mind. Those rock baseball games saved my life. How I missed them when you discovered cars and girls.

To my nieces, Adrienne, Megan. I saw a different side of my mother being with the two of you. She was a wonderful grandmother who loved her grandchildren enough to cut herself off from family and friends just to be there for you. She was the type of grandmother I would have wanted. I think she kept life in her by having you two around. We discovered that "Beans and Cornbread" was her favorite song, and she would cut a step in the kitchen to it.

To Gayle. I don't have words to say how much you have been a force in my life. I came out to you as being trans and you took the task of telling your mother. With you, Adrienne, and Megan, we flew kites, had sleigh rides, I was able to live a childhood with you all. But mostly, Gayle, you are my rock. You have always believed in me. You even taught Willie the proper pronouns and right name!

There are three great nieces that I am watching grow up as little women. But most of all, I am watching my brother be a wonderful grandfather and how he communicates with those three girls. I see that grandkids are special to grandparents. I see it in how he loves and lives for those three.

To Jamari. I am saving the best for last. She is my biggest cheerleader. Watching this woman handle difficulties in life and keep striving is amazing. As a wife and mother, holding down a career, you are amazing. Two years ago, I got a note from Jamari thanking me for a gift for her son. In her note, she said she would never have to explain to her children who I used to be. They will just know that this is their Uncle Charley. I cherish that note and will always keep it near me. When Jamari told us she would be naming her daughter after my mother, I knew that she would come into this world fighting. Despite all her hardships, she is a beautiful soul. We all know that my mother is in her spirit. She is special, just like her great, great grandmother was. In your son, I can see me as the little boy I always wanted to be.

To Constance. You had to be in this book. You were an important part of my life during a time when I wish I could have erased many things. I know I made my amends to you years ago. But I am sorry that our relationship ended the way that it did. I am honored that our friendship is now far better than it perhaps could have been otherwise. I remember when, on Saturday April 6, 2013, you told me at the Equality VA dinner that, one day, they would be honoring me. I didn't believe you at the time. I could barely speak to people, let alone do anything for my state. But you were right. You sending that package about BTMI was nothing but pure love. I owe my life to you, Constance. We have taught one another the art of forgiveness.

To Constance's daughter, Mani. You will never know what it means for you to call me "Dad." Good stuff.

To my AA community. Thank you for loving me until I could love myself. I never expected that I would still be around. But here I am. 16 years sober, and I still remember that first day that I walked through the doors and realized that there could be a better life. You have accepted me with all my flaws and anger. You all definitely showed me that you would love me until I could love myself.

To my sponsor, Gloria. Thank you for showing me how to love and be sober. How did two people from entirely different worlds build a relationship of trust, then love? Your love for me when you told me you just couldn't handle the destructive relationship I had gotten into in early sobriety and walked away. Your walking away showed me how much your cared about your recovery and that I needed to do the same. You definitely loved me until I could love myself.

To my second sponsor, Frank. You were there from day one. You have seen the raw, the growing, and the person, as the Big Book promises, who is now in the 4th dimension. We still need to take that picture to show the world that people, despite their differences, can still love one another.

There are several organizations that, if you wish to donate to, please do.

Equality Virginia does wonderful work.[19] They sponsored the first trans conference that I went to. It changed my life. Even though I didn't see many who looked like me, I did see many members of my tribe. I will keep coming back. I am proud to be a part of the board that supports and helps our trans community. Give if you can.

WorkSource is my place of employment.[20] My team consists of people with disabilities, who suit up and show up for work every day. We are a family. This job has taught me to love people who are different. Just like I want people to love me. I have an amazing team, and I am forever grateful to be a part of this wonderful local organization that empowers people with disabilities. Give with a loving heart.

PFLAG Blue Ridge[21] is another important organization that promotes, supports, educates, and advocates on behalf of lesbian, gay, bisexual, and transgender persons, their friends, parents, families, and allies.

Consider donating to Black Pride RVA,[22] which is the first Black Pride created in 2018. The mission of Black Pride RVA is to educate, embrace, and celebrate the unique lived experiences of the Black LGBTQ

---

[19] www.equalityvirginia.org.
[20] www.worksourceva.org.
[21] https://www.pflagblueridge.org/.
[22] https://ugrcrva.org/.

community. I am privileged to have received the 2021 Root Award from this excellent organization.

To Jamison Green. Yours was the first book I read about being trans. Today, I call you, my friend. It was on the panel with you at the Moving Trans History Forward conference in British Columbia that I met this wonderful woman named Margot Wilson. Every week, we weave and created a beautiful tapestry of friendship. I am forever grateful that you are now a part of my life.

To Jude Patton. Meeting Margot, contributing to the TRANScestors series, and now, writing this book would never have happened except for you. Thank you for believing I had a story to tell.

There are angels that entered my life for a season and for a reason. Reagan Thompson was one. Reagan saw me at my rawest moments and took me under her wing and led me to a life I never thought I deserved or would have. She believed in me through my anger, depression, challenges, and changes.

If I can say one thing to my trans Brothers, it would be to get all the medical help you can get. Build a relationship with your NP or GP. I did and it led me to the life I am living right now. Love yourself and the love of your body will come.

To Jen Leyton the first person I voiced my gender questioning to. I wish you were around to see this. You were a wonderful therapist for me. You drove the car until I could slide behind the wheel and drive myself. Oh, the beautiful sights I see now. The windshield is clear, and the world looks beautiful!

AA Serenity Prayer[23]

These simple words ring clear through the hearts and minds of Alcoholics Anonymous members across the world:

God, grant me the

SERENITY

to accept the things I cannot change, the

COURAGE

to change the things I can, and the

WISDOM

to know the difference.

This often-used AA prayer is an excerpt from a longer prayer commonly attributed to Reinhold Niebuhr. Although its origins are a bit unclear, its impacts are not. The Serenity Prayer serves as a focal point for the very spirit of AA, anchoring its members to its quintessential teachings about surrender and acceptance.

The Full Serenity Prayer

God grant me the serenity
To accept the things I cannot change;
Courage to change the things I can;
And wisdom to know the difference.
Living one day at a time;
Enjoying one moment at a time;
Accepting hardships as the pathway to peace;
Taking, as He did, this sinful world
As it is, not as I would have it;
Trusting that He will make things right
If I surrender to His will;
So that I may be reasonably happy in this life
And supremely happy with Him
Forever and ever in the next.
Amen.

---

[23] Excerpted from https://www.hazeldenbettyford.org/articles/the-serenity-prayer.

Other Publications from Castle Carrington Publishing Group

Life Stories Available from TransGender Publishing
Publishing Transgender Life Stories and Non-fiction
https://transgenderpublishing.ca/

The Transgender Compendium: Medical, Psychological, Social and Legal Aspects of Gender Diversity (2022)
Diane Saunders
With Contributions from Joanna Clark and Jude Patton
We all know what LGBTQ stands for, but how many of us know that the "T" in LGBTQ stands for "transgender"? What does "transgender" mean? How many people fall under that "umbrella" term, which, over the years, has come to encompass more than just one aspect of gender?

The Transgender Compendium discusses gender as a part of who we are, how we perceive ourselves, and how others perceive us. But gender is not necessarily set in stone. It is inherent in our makeup as human individuals, but not everyone perceives themselves as male or female. Human diversity is truly amazing, and *The Transgender Compendium* takes you on a journey that explores the many aspects of what it means to be transgender.

The Transgender Compendium delves into these subjects and, in doing so, reviews the legal, medical, and social research, the diagnostic criteria in the medical, psychiatric, psychological, and sociological literature, and the legal landscape regarding the civil rights of transgender people. *The Transgender Compendium* also provides information on the LGBTQ community more generally and reviews the professional resources available to help others understand the transgender experience along with the treatment options available. Come along and enjoy the ride. (https://transgenderpublishing.ca/transgender-compendium/)

Inspired: A Guide to Becoming Your True and Authentic Self (2021)
Stella Paris

Inspired is about being your true and authentic self, of overcoming challenge, embracing change, and becoming all that you can be—not in spite of change but *because* of it. We have all been through a momentous period with Covid and lockdowns, and many of us have struggled with issues around mental health, negotiating our changed world, and questioning life's purpose.

Now, as the world slowly comes to a new normal, with old freedoms regained, many in a new form that require an altered way of thinking about the familiar, I believe that transgender people can inspire non-transgender people to embrace change and understand that thinking about things in a new way is OK. It's healthy and can lead to greater satisfaction with life. The lesson to be learned here is the importance of being one's authentic self. (https://transgenderpublishing.ca/inspired/)

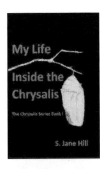

My Life Inside the Chrysalis (2021)
The Chrysalis Series Book I
S. Jane Hill

My Life Inside the Chrysalis is an autobiography about what moulded me from birth to transition to the present. It is a sometimes brutal, often philosophical, story of my life and that which moulded me into the true self I am today...the strong woman that I have become. (https://transgenderpublishing.ca/my-life-inside-the-chrysalis/)

S. Jane Hill
Mr Winky Goes to Melbourne (2022)
The Chrysalis Series Book II

Mr Winky Goes to Melbourne, the second book in the *Chrysalis* series, begins where *My Life Inside the Chrysalis* ends. Detailing what has occurred since, *Mr Winky* uses flashbacks to reflect on the time when the author first met her (then) alter ego and culminates in the lead up to and experiences during and after gender reassignment surgery. (https://transgenderpublishing.ca/mr-winky-goes-to-melbourne/)

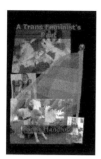

A Trans Feminist's Past (2021)
Forest Handford

Forest Handford was brought up male, but never felt comfortable with that gender. As early as preschool, it was clear that she had interests and habits that were considered feminine. While Forest has supportive parents, they didn't have the knowledge to alert them that she was transgender, a word that wasn't even widely known until long after Forest was an adult.

What little information Forest found about being trans was misleading and harmful. It took cosplaying her favorite Dr. Who character, Clara Oswald, in 2018 for her to find acceptance in feminine clothes. Forest soon discovered that she met the definition of transgender. For a short time, Forest considered herself genderfluid because she didn't believe transition was possible due to misinformation she had been taught to believe. A non-binary friend of Forest's mentioned that their therapist had recommended that they try hormone replacement therapy (HRT). Curious why a therapist would make such a recommendation, Forest did some research that revealed that not only was transition possible for her but that trying a small dose of HRT was a safe way to determine if it could help with her gender dysphoria.

Forest's transition began when trans rights were under attack in her state of residence (Massachusetts). In 2018, Forest knew multiple trans folk who were fired due to their gender identity. Forest had to balance her trans rights advocacy against her safety as a frequent business traveler to Egypt, where being LGBT comes with a 10-year prison sentence.

Forest's memoir covers details of her life and the historical context in which it has been lived. Many of the stories in this book reveal the challenges of being feminine. While those challenges were painful, and some aspects of transitioning during her midlife were difficult, she values the views she has had on both sides of male privilege. She uses this rare perspective as an analogy for her understanding of white privilege.

While many trans stories exist, Forest's perspectives as an Eagle Scout, as somebody who lived in Egypt, and someone who transitioned while in a management position, bring new dimensions to the space, further illustrating that there is no single trans narrative. (https://transgenderpublishing.ca/a-trans-feminists-past/)

Triple Trans: One Woman's Journey to Freedom (2021)
Rose Barkhimer

For me, *Triple Trans* means:

Transgender, the knowledge that one has been born with the incorrect physical body,

Transverse myelitis, a neurological affliction that was a catalyst in my decision to change gender and,

Transition, the process of change.

It is my hope that *Triple Trans* finds its way to at least one individual who is wrestling with the conundrum that is gender dysphoria and that my story helps them to understand their own journey. I also hope that my story will explain to the general public the experiences of one transgender individual and demonstrate that, despite our differences, we are all human beings struggling with life's journey. (https://transgenderpublishing.ca/triple-trans-one-womans-journey-to-freedom/).

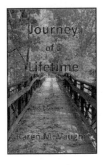

Journey of a Lifetime (2021)
Karen M. Vaughn

For all of her life, Karen has struggled with gender dysphoria and her true identity. Frightened, confused, and tired of living a lie, she embarks on a journey—one that will change her life, her marriage, and the world she thought she knew. This is her story of coming to terms with who she really is, her struggles to find her way, and the life-altering changes that came along with her journey. (https://transgenderpublishing.ca/journey-of-a-lifetime/)

Before My Warranty Runs Out: Human, Transgender and Environmental Rights Advocate (2021)
Joanna (Sister Mary Elizabeth) Clark and Margot Wilson

Joanna (Sister Mary Elizabeth) Clark is an elder trans woman and advocate. During the 1980s and 1990s she was an LGBTQ+ activist and speaker. She was the first person to serve as a man in the US navy and as a woman in the US army. Later, as Sister Mary Elizabeth, she was the driving force behind the AIDS Education and Global Information System (AEGIS) database. These days, her focus is primarily on environmental activism. *Before My Warranty Runs Out* is a personal narrative that recounts Joanna's life experiences. (https://transgenderpublishing.ca/before-my-warranty-runs-out/)

TRANScestors: Navigating LGBTQ+ Aging, Illness and End of Life Decisions (2020)
Volume I: Generations of Hope
Edited by Jude Patton and Margot Wilson

This volume (and the ones that follow) have been in the works for some time. What finally emerges after many months of assiduous advertising, recruiting, editing, and organizing is a volume of intimate, nuanced, and heartfelt stories that reflect the wide diversity in the ways in which trans, non-binary, and Two-Spirit people have come to recognize, signify, embody, and celebrate their difference as their authentic selves. Moreover, with an increasing emphasis on the experiences of trans youth, elders constitute a routinely overlooked, disregarded, and/or silenced segment of the community. In response, this volume documents the myriad ways in which trans elders are coming to terms with the real-life challenges of aging, illness, and end of life decision-making.

TRANScestors is planned as a series of edited volumes that address the issues of LGBTQ+ aging, illness, and end of life decision-making and will be published by TransGender Publishing. Additional volumes include: Volume II: Generations of Change, Volume III: Generations of Pride, and Volume III: Generations of Challenge. (https://transgenderpublishing.ca/life-trips/)

TRANScestors: Navigating LGBTQ+ Aging, Illness and End of Life Decisions (2020)
Volume II: Generations of Change
Edited by Jude Patton and Margot Wilson

Generations of Change is the second volume in the TRANScestors series. These stories are, by turn, heartfelt, revealing, inspiring, sad, joyful, humorous, irreverent, and incredibly varied. And yet, strong, common themes of courage, persistence, honesty, resilience, and authenticity emerge clearly through the detailed recounting of the individual lives lived. Each author details those specific circumstances that have led them to the places and situations in which they find themselves today. On the whole, these are places of comfort, confidence, revelation, and affirmation. The wide range of attitudes, expressions, and worldviews held by the LGBTQ+ elders presented here challenge us all to carefully consider and adjust our perspectives on our own aging processes and, ultimately, on finding our own places in the world.
(https://transgenderpublishing.ca/live-trips-vol-ii-generations-of-change/)

We are God's Children Too (2020)
Rona Matlow

At the heart of Jewish experience is narrative. Around the dinner table, we tell stories of our families, recalling the quality of a grandmother's cooking, the kindness (or stinginess) of a particular uncle, the ways in which traditions have developed and shifted in our families. In synagogues and Jewish schools, we read the Torah, which is filled with stories of our religious patriarchs and matriarchs. And then there are the stories of Diaspora–the history of Jewish communities existing in exile for over two millennia. There are family stories and history books dedicated to our many wanderings. All of these stories help Jewish people connect to their heritage and lineage. What of the queer Jew? Even as more and more Jewish communities emphasize inclusivity and find a place for queer congregants, Jewish stories do not. The Bible offers no queer lessons, leaving queer Jews split in two; a Jewish heritage and a queer present. Enter Rabbah Rona Matlow, with hir queer *midrashim*. *Midrashim* are stories which approach Biblical texts from new perspectives, often exploring areas of confusion or possible contradiction within the Bible. Unlike Torah, they are not presented as factual, but as possibilities. Fictions which might yet be possible alternate histories. *Midrashim* bridge gaps. Rona's queer *midrashim* bridge the gap between the contemporary queer Jew and the (seemingly cisgender and straight) Bible, offering a way for us to see ourselves in our Jewish tradition. (https://transgenderpublishing.ca/we-are-gods-children-too/)

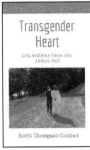

Transgender Heart: Life Stories from the Inside Out (2020)
Bodhi Thompson Gardner

Transgender Heart is a collection of short stories that trace the heart-journey of a small farm kid, youth, and adult, from rural Saskatchewan, across the binary landscapes of life. A deeply grateful soul emerges, while exploring all the hidden nuances of the people, places, and things that held them together. Hidden comforts are revealed from the inside out, an inner harvesting of an authentic self. Their true self searching for somewhere to belong, finds love, acceptance, and authentic connection in the most intriguing and unusual spaces. Black hockey skates not only enrich their game but authenticate their heart. Spaces of unconditional love come from four-legged wild beasts, two-legged mentors, matriarchs, warriors, and elders. An RCMP officer who saw their struggle and offered a hand instead of handcuffs, gifts of nature, and family support abound: however, the biggest surprise of all is their most cherished treasure, the one thing that kept them alive for over 50 years. Transgender Heart highlights the courage and tenacity of the human spirit to rise up!
(https://transgenderpublishing.ca/transgender-heart/)

QdQh: Queen of Diamonds, Queen of Hearts, The Life and Journey of Michelle Nastasis, the First Known Transgender Professional Poker Player (2020)
Michelle Nastasis

QdQh: Queen of Diamonds, Queen of Hearts is the life story of Michelle Nastasis, the First Known Transgender Professional Poker Player.™ Michelle is courageous whether going head-to-head with the best poker players in the world, speaking out on television for LGBTQ+ rights, or marching in parades to celebrate being transgender. She is calm, cool, collected, and absolutely fearless. Possessed of fierce intelligence, Michelle is a beacon for younger transgender people. She shoots straight from the hip. She's blunt, loud, sarcastic, and occasionally irreverent. So, sit back and enjoy the ride.
(https://transgenderpublishing.ca/misunderstood/)

Dancing the Dialectic: True Tales of a Transgender Trailblazer, Second Edition (2020)
Rupert Raj

Rupert Raj is a trailblazing, Eurasian-Canadian, trans activist, and former psychotherapist, who transitioned from female to male in 1971 as a transsexual teenager. Dancing the dialectic between gender dysphoria and gender euphoria, cynical despair and realistic hope, righteous rage and loving kindness, this Gender Worker tells us all about his lifelong fight for the rights of transgender, intersex, and two-spirit people—and his later-life role as a Rainbow Warrior working to free Mother Earth's enslaved animals. (https://transgenderpublishing.ca/dancing-the-dialectic-true-tales-of-a-transgender-trailblazer-second-edition/)

Glimmerings: Trans Elders Tell Their Stories (2019)
Margot Wilson and Aaron Devor (editors)

Tell us your story. A story about growing up before the age of global communication, at a time when the Internet and worldwide connectivity were still visions of the future; when inflexible, dichotomous categories of male and female, men and women, existed; when heterosexuality was the only sanctioned form of romantic attraction or sexual conduct; and when any expression of interest outside of these strict prescriptions was severely censured. Tell us your story about living in a time when those whose preferences, perspectives, and behaviours contravened the prevailing paradigms and prohibitions, when you had to negotiate dark, prejudicial places where fear, shame, guilt, despair, isolation, and a little bit of hope. Contributing authors include: Stephanie Castle, Joanna Clark, Ms. Bob Davis, Dallas Denny, Jamison Green, Ariadne Kane, Corey Keith, Lili, Ty Nolan, Jude Patton, Virginia Prince, Rupert Raj, Gayle Roberts, Susanna Valenti, and Dawn Angela Wensley. (https://transgenderpublishing.ca/glimmerings-recognition-authenticity-and-gender-variance/)

My Untrue Past: The Coming of Age of a Trans Man (2019)
Alex Bakker

Born the youngest daughter in a small-town family in the Netherlands, Alex Bakker underwent gender reaffirming transition when he was twenty-eight years old. A new beginning, in the right body, he literally put everything that reminded him of his old life into boxes, never to be opened again. More than fifteen years later, he has finally gathered the courage to face his past. In *My Untrue Past*, Alex goes in search of the painful truth.

What does it mean to be betrayed by your body, to be immensely jealous of boys, and to decide that everything needs to be different? (https://transgenderpublishing.ca/my-untrue-past-available-now/)

Girl in the Dream: Stephanie (Sydney) Castle Heal, a Transgender Life (2018)
Margot E. Wilson

Girl in the Dream is the life story of Stephanie (Sydney) Castle Heal, an advocate, activist and elder in the Canadian transgender community. The outcome of an almost four-year collaboration of storytelling, recording, analysis, and writing, *Girl in the Dream* is a first-person narrative that depicts in intimate detail Stephanie's transgender journey. An enthusiastic and accomplished *raconteuse*, Stephanie tells her story with the verve, passion, and expressiveness of a veteran storyteller. (https://transgenderpublishing.ca/girl-in-the-dream/)

Feelings: A Transsexual's Explanation of a Baffling Condition, Second Edition (2018)
Stephanie Castle
Edited and Introduction by Margot E. Wilson

Feelings is written in a style that reveals Stephanie Castle as a woman of great confidence, conviction and humour. It reflects her attitudes toward life in general and transgender issues in particular, and definitively emulates the intricacies of her personality and character. *Feelings* provides a very personal view into one transgender woman's journey, a metamorphosis that is as vital, authentic and significant today as it was when she wrote it. A complementary volume to *Girl in the Dream*, *Feelings* provides a comprehensive and in-depth view into the nature of the transgender experience based on the intimate, challenging, and often poignant experiences and perspectives of one singularly remarkable woman. (https://transgenderpublishing.ca/feelings/)

Trans Fiction Available from Stephanie Castle Publications
Publishing Transgender Fiction
https://stephaniecastle.ca/new-releases/

Tips (2021)
Newly Chronicles: Volume I
H.W. Coyle

College is a time of discovery, when students find out just what sort of people they are. This is especially true for Andy Newly, a freshman who embarks on a unique journey of self-discovery, one that defies convention and brings into question the most basic aspect of his being. It begins as a bet made between student waiters over who makes more tips, males or females. To determine this, they agree to a rather unorthodox experiment. Though feigning reluctance, Andy accepts the challenge of taking on the role of female waitress as part of the bet.

The original purpose is forgotten as Andy finds that his female persona is more than an act, causing him to question his gender identity. His behavior while Amanda—the name he has given his female persona—does not escape the notice of his friends. Along with Andy, they conclude that their experiment is having unintended consequences. Rather than stopping, Andy uses the opportunity to determine who he really is and where he belongs on the gender continuum. In the process he discovers that there is a vast difference between sex and gender. This already bewildering situation becomes even more complicated when a male college student becomes smitten with Amanda. (https://stephaniecastle.ca/tips/)

A Different Kind of Courage (2022)
Newly Chronicles: Volume II
H. W. Coyle

How does a person go about rebuilding a life that they willingly tried to throw away? For Andrew Newly, this journey begins by realizing it will take a different kind of courage. His efforts begin by returning to where he and a group of friends bought into a crazy bet that changed his life forever. Together with those friends, he struggles to gather up the frayed threads of his life and begin the daunting task of building a new one for himself, this time as a girl named Amanda. Amanda finds that she must not only find a way of dealing with problems that are as confusing to her as they are complex, she must also come to terms with a past that seems to have no place in her new life. This difficult journey is complicated by Amanda's friendship with Tina Anderson, the daughter of an entrepreneur who has accumulated a fair number of enemies who prove to be as much of a threat to Amanda as they are to the Andersons, causing her to draw upon a past that she is trying to put behind her. (https://stephaniecastle.ca/a-different-kind-of-courage/)

Inconvenient Truths (2022)
Newly Chronicles: volume III
H.W. Coyle

Living on the edge with nothing but a safety net woven from lies to keep you from tumbling headlong into disaster and disgrace is as dangerous as it is demanding. For Amanda Newly, it is an inconvenient fact of life, one she must deal with every day.

Amanda is a unique college student. Bright and intelligent, she manages to maintain a GPA of 4.0 in a discipline where most of her fellow students are simply happy to survive. To the casual observer, Amanda presents the very image of a young woman who is on the verge of making all her dreams come true. The only thing holding Amanda back from achieving this elusive goal is a past that is totally out of sync with her image as a vibrant young coed, for the girl everyone knows as Amanda started life as Andrew Justin Newly.

In many ways Amanda is still very male, an inconvenient truth she must hide behind a veil of lies from all but a select circle of friends as she struggles to reconcile her past with her future. One aspect of Amanda's past that threatens to destroy her chances is not of her own making. Tina Anderson, the daughter of a wealthy entrepreneur and one of Amanda's dearest friends lives under a constant threat of kidnapping, a danger that Amanda once foiled and, as a result, leaves her vulnerable to retribution from those seeking to bring harm to the Andersons.

The journey Amanda Newly makes toward a new beginning is one that is as difficult as it is contentious. For Amanda must step outside the accepted norms, which define who and what we are, in order to discover not only what is right for her, but to build a new life for herself. (https://stephaniecastle.ca/inconvenient-truths/)

A Lion in Waiting (2021)
H.W. Coyle

While serving as an observer with the British Expeditionary Force in 1940, Ian Wylie survives a massacre of prisoners. In its aftermath, he resolves to find a way of sitting out the rest of the war, safe from both the Germans and his responsibilities. At first, he finds sanctuary on a small farm owned by a teacher, Andrea Morel, who harbours him until an incident leaves her no choice but to send Ian away. With no wish to return to England and the war, Ian assumes the identity of Andrea's sister, Diane Lambert, and accepts an offer to teach at a Catholic girls' school in Normandy. His efforts to turn his back on the war are frustrated by a local businessman who enlists Ian's aid in passing intelligence on German activities in Normandy to the Allies as well as by a group of schoolgirls who take it upon themselves to fight for the liberation of France. (https://stephaniecastle.ca/a-lion-in-waiting/)

The Legend of Alfhildr (2020)
HW. Coyle and Jennifer Ellis

For generations, a legend spoke of a young Viking girl who led a Saxon-Dane army against a usurper. The story was passed from storyteller to storyteller, who freely embellished the feats of Alfhildr as they sought to entertain and enthrall their audiences in the great halls of their lords and masters. Some claimed she had been raised by a wolf, others that she was a witch. The truth was vastly different.

But before she became a legend, Alfhildr was a flesh and blood person with a family, a past, and a secret. With the passing of time, all but the legend was lost from living memory until an archeologist stumble upon something he has not been expecting. Bit by bit, Professor Bannon and his students come to realize that the legend once thought to be little more than a myth could be grounded in history. He also begins to suspect one of the students participating in the dig has a secret that links her to both the discoveries they are making and the legend.
(https://stephaniecastle.ca/legend-of-alfhildr/)

Flipping (2020)
It cost him nothing, but it cost her everything.
Forest J. Handford

Born on a space station, Samir Zeka was raised Muslim, observes a Halal diet, fasts during Ramadan, and prays 5 times every day. An introvert, he mostly stuck to his work, his home, his family, and his church community, until the day he decided to push beyond his comfort zone and attend a party that would forever change his life. Intending to look his best for the party, Samir searched his neural link "mesh" for random looks until he came across one that suited him. After some fine-tuning, he "flipped" to the persona of Samantha, a late 30s East Asian, cat-eared woman with shoulder-length purple hair. At the party, Samantha meets Anna, someone who will change Samantha's perceptions of herself and transform both of their lives.
(https://stephaniecastle.ca/flipping/)

The Elysian Project: A Story of Betrayal and Payback (2019)
D. Axt

The Elysian Project is an expertly written, fast paced action thriller with a twist. It follows US marine scout sniper, Brent Chandler, his surviving teammate, Lyle, and his adopted father (the Gunny), as they go after those responsible for betraying Brent's sniper team during a military operation in Haditha, Iraq. Chandler's betrayal didn't just change the lives of his U.S. Marine sniper team forever. It set him on a path of unimaginable discovery. His quest for the truth and revenge quickly goes awry, drawing the attention of billionaire Stanley

Tivador and the DOJ-FBI cabal he controls. The chase is on, from northern Minnesota's Superior National Forest to the Canary Islands. With help from the Gunny, his crotchety, retired Marine father, and Staiski, his friend and former sniper teammate, Chandler uncovers a terrorist plot of carnage inconceivable in magnitude and in lives lost. With seconds remaining, they risk everything to stop The Elysian Project. (https://stephaniecastle.ca/the-elysian-project/)

Partnership: A Novel about Friendship, Love, Family and Gender Transition (2019)
Stephanie Castle
Edited and preface by Margot Wilson

What happens when a lawyer, the son of a prominent Vancouver family, and a baker, the son of a devoted Catholic family who moved from Italy to Montreal following WWII, team up while going through gender reassignment? This humorous, yet serious, depiction of two families coping with gender dysphoria and the challenges of keeping family relationships intact addresses both legal and religious issues. The depiction and commentary on a range of human personalities in the hands of the author are both perceptive and entertaining. The underlying accuracy of this fictional story depends on the author's personal experience as a transgender woman and as a counselor in the transgender community in Vancouver. (https://stephaniecastle.ca/partnership/)

Far Side of the Moon: A Novel about the Life of a Trans Child (2019)
Stephanie Castle
Edited and preface by Margot Wilson

In Far Side of the Moon, Marjorie Burton and her husband, Jack, demonstrate all the attributes needed to help their child, Jenna, through a successful male to female gender transition. For children raised in an era when the condition of gender dysphoria was unknown, when anything unusual or unexplained was written off as a sexual aberration, it is small wonder that children, like the author, kept their feelings hidden out of shame and fear. Fortunately, that is not what happens with Jenna. (https://stephaniecastle.ca/far-side-of-the-moon-a-novel-about-the-life-of-a-trans-child/)

Available now from Perceptions Press
Publishing innovative, avant-garde (and occasionally provocative) transgender fiction and non-fiction
https://perceptionspress.ca/

Trans Deus (2020)
Paul Van Der Spiegel
The Queer Testament Book 1

In the beginning was the Verb,
the Verb was with God, the Verb was God.
In her was life,
that life was the light for all people.
The Verb was made trans woman.
and she lived amongst us, full of grace and truth.
Her light shone in the darkness,
and the consumer-military-technocracy
comprehended it not.
We cast our votes on TV remotes,
crucified her live on Channel Five. (https://perceptionspress.ca/trans-deus/)

7 Minutes (2021)
Paul Van Der Spiegel
The Queer Testament Book 2

At the point of death,
lost to all we've known,
adrift from those we've loved,
what stories do we tell
ourselves?

7 Minutes is the story of a death—charting the progress from cardiac arrest, the brain's release of its massive reserve of endorphins, through the unravelling of personality, memory, and identity as the brain's consciousness-generating areas are hit by a tidal wave of opioid neuropeptides that are simultaneously being starved of oxygen.

Self-told narratives unfold and are re-contextualised, fears awaken, desires awaken, time is warped and regresses as the mind is trapped inside a dead husk, unable to communicate, lost to those it has loved and been loved by.

Those who have experienced so-called 'near death' experiences have described bright lights, meeting loved ones: but no-one has returned from behind that light to describe the process of dying. And so, we are left with either a gospel of redemption and condemnation, or its opposite, a gospel of cosmic resignation and the final extinction of personality. One day, perhaps not too far away, we shall know—or, then again, perhaps not.

7 Minutes is the collage of stories and half-truths that our protagonists' collapsing neural networks narrate as the brain asphyxiates—light and dark, fact and fiction, actuality and narrative—until the final arrival at the truth of an earthly existence. *7 Minutes* is a head fuck. But after you've read it, I hope you can celebrate being alive. (https://perceptionspress.ca/7-minutes/)

Parably Not (2021)
Paul Van Der Spiegel
The Queer Testament Book 3

Parably Not is Book 3 of the *Will2Love Series*.

William Blake wrote in the preface to *Jerusalem The Emanation of the Giant Albion* of his desire to "speak to future generations by a Sublime Allegory." One could also argue that the miracles and the parables of Christ are metaphors, and one of the errors of the religion that bears their name is trampling sublime allegory beneath the heel of process and doctrine.

If *Trans Deus* is Mark, if *7 Minutes* is Matthew, then *Parably Not* is Lucy with the dynamic of "Q Source" thrown in for good measure. "Q" is not a ridiculous conspiracy theory cooked up to delude and obfuscate a population. "Q" is the theory proposed by biblical scholars to account for the shared content in Matthew and Luke, the oral "sayings of Jesus" tradition that is absent in Mark's account. We can only speculate on who Quelle was, but it wouldn't surprise me if they were a woman, or a group of women—a female gospel airbrushed from history by the patriarchy that followed. As someone who passionately believes in inclusion and diversity, it was not too much of a leap to make my Q Source a queer source.

Having written two "text only" books, I wanted to emulate the Prophet of Hercules Road and illuminate these recontextualised parables, continuing the process I had pioneered as a child, cutting up my mum's copies of *Woman's Own* and pasting the chosen pages into my scrapbook.

"We were worried about you for a while," my dad told me as a teenager, as he recollected my enthusiasm for *Woman's Weekly*, sparkly tights, and walking about in my mum's heels, carrying her handbag. I said nothing.

"Poetry fetter'd, fetters the human race," Blake wrote. He's right. But there are plenty of other things that fetter the human race, too.

Our job as sub-creators is to unfetter, to explore, to challenge, to remake. I offer you *Parably Not*, as it is intended: scrapbook literature, unfinished, scruffy, feral, confused, uncertain; ready to be woven into new allegory. (https://perceptionspress.ca/parably-not/)

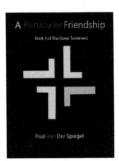

A Particular Friendship (2021)
Paul Van Der Spiegel
The Queer Testament, Book 4

Tom Morton is a Roman Catholic priest who is devoted to his church in northern England, to his parishioners, and to his calling. When the man he fell in love with twenty-five years ago comes back into his life, Tom finds himself on a collision course with a powerful bishop, a man determined to pin the blame for the Church's sexual abuse crisis on its closeted gay clergy. (https://perceptionspress.ca/a-particular-friendship/)

Demon of Want (2020)
Freja Ki Gray

Izumi Yamakawa, a directionless twenty-something, is a part-time employee of the Oh Joy Toy Store. When she witnesses her manager die in a horrific merchandising accident, she discovers that he was a member of a Japanese demon hunting organization and had been eyeing her for recruitment due to her family lineage. Now Izumi, along with her trans girlfriend Maria, and a boisterous sword-for-hire, Rhea, get caught up investigating the various monsters and demons running the Oh Joy Toy company. Demon of Want is an eclectic blend of tongue in cheek urban fantasy, over the top violence, and gratuitous sex. (https://perceptionspress.ca/demon-of-want/)

Can't Her Bury Tales: A Transfeminine
Coloring Book (2020)
Iona Isabella Rivera

Hail weary traveler! Come closer! I don't bite…hard. You lookit poorly, come take a sit by the fire. Rest and grab yourself some stew I got cookin. Tell me, what brings ya my way? Adventure? Hearsay? Curiosity or plain ol' boredom? Well, no matter whence you came, I surely have a story that will peak your delight.

Perhaps a tale of a terrible tragedy? Or a catty, Communist comedy? How about some lore on fallin in love? Or a heroic tale of harrowing a horrible governorship? Or be you one that pines over Power? Maybe a familiar fable of family? Oh! Pardon my rambling. Come tell me your tale, traveler. What colors will you paint with me? Tell, was your way hard, rocky and steep? Show me. Perchance our stories crossed at some point. After all, we have more in common than our differences tell. (https://perceptionspress.ca/cant-her-bury-tales/)

Available now from All Genders Press
Publishing LGBTQ+fiction and non-fiction
https://allgenderspress.ca/

The Gospel According to a Witch (2022)
Diana Bishop

The 200 angels who procreated with human women and fathered the Nephilim were cast out of Heaven. Their Nephilim children were ordered by God to be destroyed because of their destructive and corruptive behavior on Earth, but not before they fathered children of their own. These children of Nephilim came to be the witches, vampires, and werewolves of lore. It was generally believed by these supernatural beings that God disapproved of them, although they were three-fourths human and were left untouched by the purge. Lena's parents were such Nephilim offspring. They suffered under the same assumption until they met Jesus when he was physically among humankind. They became a part of his discipleship and Lena was born in his presence. They, and, in turn, Lena, were charged by Jesus with the mission of spreading the message among the Nephilim decedents that they were loved by God and were welcome in Heaven upon their death, contingent on the life they had lived. *The Gospel of a Witch* is a part of Lena's story as she endeavors to complete her mission. (https://allgenderspress.ca/the-gospel-of-a-witch/)

Rise of the Magical Three (2021)
House of Phoenix Chronicles, Book 1
Wilhelm Ostir

Raised by a mysterious grandmother and believing their parents to be dead, Roslynn and her older identical twin brothers, Oliver and Ethan, had only read of magical beings and creatures. But, transitioning into young adulthood, the three embark on an incredible journey as they are introduced to the riddles of their family's past that will forever change who they are and are yet to become.

As the three siblings discover the ways of the magical arts, they quickly learn that they are not alone in their quest. Finding help when and where they least expect, the three develop friendships, confront the darkness, work together to save their family from an ancient curse, and learn of a mysterious and ancient bloodline that will forever shape the fabric of time and love.

Their fight becomes more significant than even they had anticipated and forces them to make decisions about whether they can effectively save the world, the multiple realms, and magic as they know it. Learning that magic is driven by passion, knowledge, bloodline, and time, will they be the ones to save time, or will they become mere echoes of time? (https://allgenderspress.ca/echoes-of-time/)

Available now from Castle Carrington Publishing
You have a story. Let us help you tell it.
https://castlecarringtonpublishing.ca/

My Dog Rigby: Just Like Me (2021)
Jan Olsson

My Dog Rigby, Just Like Me explores how we react to our dogs, and what this ultimately reveals to us about the way we treat others.

The approach we use to train and connect with our dogs can provide us with insights about how we can enhance our relationships with our partner, children, extended family members, friends, and co-workers.

My Dog Rigby shares personal short stories that everyone can relate to, focusing on themes shared by dogs and their owners, such as anxiety, capacity, aggression, trust, self-regulation, and patterning within the brain. While also giving practical training tips and advice, this book attempts to reveal who we are, who our dogs are, and the ways we are similar. (https://castlecarringtonpublishing.ca/my-dog-rigby/)

Pushing the Boundaries!
How to Get More Out of Life (2021)
Peter Jennings

Pushing The Boundaries! How To Get More Out Of Make Life features profiles of 32 people from around the world (many of whom are well-known and featuring many Canadians) who reveal how they triumph in life. We're talking people who have overcome uneasiness about taking risks, like daredevil Nik Wallenda; doctor-of-change, Patch Adams; intersex supermodel, Hanne Gaby Odielle; international clothing designer, Tommy Hilfiger. Also included are Canadians like Marina Nemat, who defied certain execution in her teens at Evin prison in Tehran; McDonald's of Canada Chair, George Cohon, who persevered through 14 years to break into the Russian market; Rick Hansen, who pushed himself around the world in a wheelchair to raise awareness of people with disabilities; Katie Taylor who's broken the glass ceiling by becoming the first female Chair of a major Canadian Bank; Donald Ziraldo, who put Inniskillin Winery on the map by making Icewine into an immensely popular beverage worldwide; etc. As Jack Canfield, renowned co-author of the *Chicken Soup For The Soul®* series says in the book's Foreword, "Having the conviction to reach beyond your fears and take chances means you're ready to achieve lasting success." (https://castlecarringtonpublishing.ca/pushing-the-boundaries/)

Until I Smile at You (2020)
How one girl's heartbreak electrified Frank Sinatra's fame!
Peter Jennings with Tom Sandler

It's 1936. Take Ina Ray Hutton, the "Blonde Bombshell of Rhythm," add 22-year-old Ruth Lowe, who become Ina Ray's pianist. Ruth marries music publicist Harold Cohen, but he dies in the midst of debilitating surgery. Ruth is devastated, full of heartache, a grief-stricken widow far too early. Consumed by anguish, she pours her heartache into a lamenting anthem that becomes an internationally famous song—"I'll Never Smile Again"—destined to electrify the career of 25-year-old vocalist Francis Albert Sinatra. Ruth next composes what becomes Sinatra's theme song, "Put Your Dreams Away." And then, Act Two begins for Ruth Lowe: she withdraws from the limelight to become a caring wife, loving mother, society doyenne, and friend to many. Amazingly, this superstar has escaped the investigation and adoration that her life so richly deserves—until now. (https://castlecarringtonpublishing.ca/until-i-smile-at-you/)

Ruth's Wonderful Song: A Story for Kids (2021)
Peter Jennings

Ruth's Wonderful Song is a true story of a young woman who loved to play her bright yellow piano. She wrote a wonderful song that people are still listening to more than 80 years after she wrote it. Tom, Ruth's son, tells the story of how Ruth wrote her wonderful song and what happened next. (https://castlecarringtonpublishing.ca/ruths-wonderful-song/)

Coming in 2022/2023 from TransGender Publishing
Publishing Transgender Life Stories and Non-fiction
https://transgenderpublishing.ca/

PUBLICATION EXPECTED IN 2022
The Love Beneath: A Journey to Love and Womanhood
Diamond Stylz-Collier

They say hindsight is always 20/20. But even as an adult looking back on the many facets of love in my life, it's still a little blurry. When I got older, I realized how important love was to my survival and sanity, in my coming-of-age story. I started openly telling these stories on YouTube in 2008. These were vulnerable and honest stories about intimate relationships and how my burgeoning transness impacted the world around me. These entanglements were sometimes full of joy while some were poignant and hard to relive. So many people across identities related to the underlying themes of these videos, so I decided to write a book that combined those experiences, my reflections, and my audience reactions. This book is a reflection of moments of love throughout some of the darkest and happiest times in my youth. (https://transgenderpublishing.ca/the-love-beneath/)

PUBLICATION EXPECTED IN 2022
The Thunder Roars, The Lightning Illuminates
Jonathon Thunderword and Margot Wilson
(https://transgenderpublishing.ca/the-thunder-roars/)

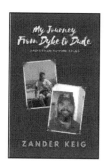

PUBLICATION EXPECTED IN 2023
My Journey from Dyke to Dude and Other Sordid Tales
Zander Keig

My Journey From Dyke to Dude chronicles the life of Zander Keig, a man who was presumed dead in the womb, assigned female at birth, paralyzed following vaccination at age six, joined a Mexican gang in middle school, was admitted to a mental hospital as a teen, dropped out of high school, enlisted in the military, became an undercover narcotics agent, graduated college and obtained three graduate degrees, became a social worker serving homeless veterans at the Department of Veterans Affairs and transgender servicemembers for the US Navy, and was awarded the National Social Worker of the Year by the National Association of Social Workers. Zander's story goes beyond telling people that it gets better and humorously explains how one person changed their life in almost every way possible and thrived amidst the chaos. (https://transgenderpublishing.ca/from-dyke-to-dude/)

PUBLICATION EXPECTED IN 2023
Out of the Cave: Emerging from My Darkest Moments into God's Eternal Light
Shi Menefee

I am a Black, transgender male who grew up in a fundamentally conservative Christian home. When I was 3 years old, my mother remarried. Her new husband was the pastor of the church we attended. This man was guilty of sexual and physical abuse of my mother's children and some of their children. Sadly, this is the experience of all too many children growing up in the Christian church in the Black community.

Members of the LGBTQ+ community have been and continue to be traumatized by individuals in the church, who guard the law but fail to live up to it themselves. I know because I lived it firsthand in my own home. Some LGBTQ+ people have survived conversion therapy and/or were subjected to electroconvulsive shock therapy in attempts to force them to change their sexuality or gender orientation. Others, like me, have been demonized, ostracized, shamed, condemned, damned, and judged by our Black churches, families, and communities.

Out of the Cave is the story of how I emerged from my early life to become a whole and resilient individual. Today, as a counselling professional, I am reminded on a daily basis of the importance of providing a space of hope and possibility every day. (https://transgenderpublishing.ca/out-of-the-cave/)

PUBLICATION EXPECTED IN 2022/23
Life Trips: Navigating LGBTQ+ Aging, Illness and End of Life Decisions
Edited by Jude Patton and Margot Wilson
Volume One: Generations of Hope
Volume Two: Generations of Change
Volume Three: Generations of Pride
Volume Four: Generations of Challenge

Studies indicate that LGBT+ people are still discriminated against in most health care settings and in long term care facilities despite advances made in the past few years in gaining more rights. Evaluating physical and mental health care needs, facilitating access to health care providers and advocating for clients' right as well as end of life decisions and planning for personal legacy options are important aspects of navigating LGBTQ+ aging. Having served as a health navigator for clients with chronic illness and offering end of life doula services to LGBTQ+ community members, Jude Patton collaborates with and advocates for his clients to successfully manage their health care needs. Jude is a proud, open and out, elder trans man, who has worked with under-served populations for most of his career, including LGBTQ+ folks, geriatric clients, developmentally disabled adults, homeless/chronically mentally ill and drug addicted clients. *Life Trips* is planned as a series of edited volumes that address the issues of LGBTQ+ aging, illness, and end of life decision-making and will be published by TransGender Publishing. Additional volumes include: Volume II: Generations of Change, Volume III: Generations of Pride and Volume IV: Generations of Challenge. (https://transgenderpublishing.ca/life-trips/)

PUBLICATION EXPECTED IN 2022
Taking Care of Angela
Angela Wensley and Margot Wilson

My name is Angela, and I am a transsexual woman. I have always believed myself to be female, even though I spent the first forty-two years of my life being socialized as a male. To be transsexual is no longer a new phenomenon, although many misconceptions still surround it. One thing has remained unchanged is the great pain and personal upheaval that necessarily accompanies the transition from one gender to another. Looking back now, many years after having had gender reassignment surgery, it seems impossible for me to have accomplished what I have. Changing from man to woman involved no less than a total restructuring of every single relationship in my life, with my spouse, family, friends, workplace, and my everyday interactions in society. For me, being transsexual is a beautiful gift, an honour, an evolutionary jump, as it were, to a higher state of being, one in which I am closer to God and to all humanity.

My personal journey can be likened to casting off in a boat without oars into a swiftly flowing river. Standing on the banks of that river, intrigued but not knowing where it would lead me, I had dipped my toes into the water, even waded out to where it was deeper, where I could feel the tug of the current. How I longed to be swept away by the river: however, my fears kept me from the test, and I always retreated to the security of the shore. Ultimately, spying a rowboat on the riverbank, I climbed in, pushed off into the stream, and waited as the small craft inevitably became caught up in the stronger current of mid-stream. Without oars, I could not return to where I had started and had little ability to control my course, though my direction downstream was certain. I was little prepared for the swiftness of the current, or the treacherous rapids and canyons that lay downstream out of sight. How easy it would have been to flounder in a back-eddy or to wreck on the many rocks that projected from the dark waters. Fortunately, with what little control I had over my course, I avoided destruction and travelled the long and lonely distance. Finally, one day, the current slowed, and I found myself past the mouth of the river, in the ocean that is woman.
(https://transgenderpublishing.ca/taking-care-of-angela/)

PUBLICATION EXPECTED IN 2023
Both Sides of the Great Divide
Nikita Carter

Nikita Carter tells her story about awakening. At 60 years of age, a series of shattering experiences led to her being broken open to the awareness that she was a trans woman, and she had to make the changes in her life to reflect that truth. Her life has comprised extraordinary experiences and people throughout, which includes being a musician, composer, educator, Artistic Director, producer, and trans woman.

(https://transgenderpublishing.ca/both-sides-of-the-great-divide/)

PUBLICATION EXPECTED IN 2022
Gender Odyssey: Journey of an Intrepid Androgyne
Ariadne (J. Ari) Kane and Margot Wilson

Ariadne (J. Ari) Kane is a gerontology specialist with Theseus Consulting & Coaching Service. (S)he has developed several workshops focusing on issues of gender, sexuality and health in the latter decades of the lifespan. Many are designed for the LGBT Community. (S)he has been a leading authority on gender diversity in postmodern America and has given presentations at many universities and institutes in the United States and Canada. (S)he is one of the creators of the Gender Attitude Reassessment Program, a workshop on gender for sexologists and healthcare professionals. (S)he co-authored *Crossing Sexual Boundaries* with Professor Vern Bullough. *Gender Odyssey: Journey of an Intrepid Androgyne* is the distillation of 40+ hours of recorded conversation that provide a decadal representation of an intrepid traveler who has forged an idiosyncratic path through gender exploration, variance and expression. (https://transgenderpublishing.ca/gender-odyssey-journey-of-an-intrepid-androgyne/)

PUBLICATION EXPECTED IN 2022
From Shame to Freedom: A Gender Variant Woman's Journey of Discovery
M. Gayle Roberts

Born in England during WW II, Gayle Roberts immigrated to Canada in 1951 and is an UVic alumnus with an MSc in Physics. She transitioned in 1996 as her high school's Science Department Head and science teacher. Gayle coauthored the guidebook Supporting Transgender and Transsexual Students in K-12 Schools and is author of *From Shame to Freedom: A Gender-Variant Woman's Journey of Discovery*. Gayle feels strongly that trans individuals should document their life experiences. She utilizes specific literary writing techniques (creative nonfiction) to create factually accurate narratives. *From Shame to Freedom* is one of those narratives.
(https://transgenderpublishing.ca/from-shame-to-freedom/)

PUBLICATION EXPECTED IN 2023
Young Kid, Old Goat: Transgender Journey to Understanding the Man Within
Jude Patton and Margot Wilson

Jude Patton is an elder transman and LGBTQ activist, advocate and educator since before his own transition in 1970. He founded Renaissance Gender Identity Services in the early 1970s and began publishing *Renaissance Newsletter* in the mid-1970s. Jude started one of the first informal support groups for FTM men and incorporated these into The John Augustus Foundation. Joined by Joanna Clark, these became known as J2CP Information Services, taking over Paul Walker's work with Erickson Educational Services. In *Young Kid, Old Goat*, Jude's personal life story and ongoing work is highlighted.
(https://transgenderpublishing.ca/young-kid-old-goat/)

PUBLICATION EXPECTED IN 2023
Unconditional Love: Stories of LGBTQ+ People and Our Emotional Bonds with Companion Animals
Edited by Jude Patton and Margot Wilson

Our experiences with marginalization often affect our feelings of self-worth. While many people in our lives are unable (or unwilling) to provide the emotional support we need before, during and post-coming out, or transition, our companion animals never fail to see us as we truly are and never fail to express their unconditional love for us. No wonder we love them and derive multiple benefits from our relationships with them. They are woven into the fabric of our lives. *Unconditional Love* is planned as an edited reader that tells the stories of how the unconditional love of (and for) our companion animals has supported, encouraged, confirmed, validated, endorsed and sanctioned our authentic selves. Our reading audience includes those in the LGBTQ+ community who have found sanctuary and validation in the love shared with our animal companions as well as those in the broader community who revel in the company of our non-human loved ones.
(https://transgenderpublishing.ca/unconditional-love/)

Coming in 2022/23 from Perceptions Press
Publishing innovative, avant-garde (and occasionally provocative) transgender fiction and non-fiction
https://perceptionspress.ca/

PUBLICATION EXPECTED IN 2022
Watching the Fire Catch
Carolyn Bell

Aurelia Kempe and her much younger employee, Jory Schneider, forge an unlikely friendship when Jory arrives on a small island off the coast of British Columbia, Canada. Surrounded and comforted by the beauty of their natural world, neither unaware of nor complacent toward the existing threat to their environment by uninformed and sometimes malevolent forces, we join Aurelia, Jory, and their circle of friends and neighbours as they live each day to the fullest. (https://perceptionspress.ca/watching-the-fire-catch/)

PUBLICATION EXPECTED IN 2023
Eman8
Will2Love Series Book 4
Paul Van Der Spiegel

Eman8 is Book 4 of the *Will2Love Series*.
(https://perceptionspress.ca/eman8/)

Coming in 2022/23 from All Genders Press
Publishing LGBTQ+ fiction and non-fiction
https://perceptionspress.ca/

PUBLICATION EXPECTED IN 2022
Secrets Echoed
House of Phoenix Chronicles Book 2
Wilhelm Ostir

Ten years after the events that changed the very fabric of the Arcane and Mundane communities and set a new era of peace in motion, the incredible journey of Rose, Ethan, and Oliver continues. The Noble House of Phoenix, the most ancient of all Arcane bloodlines, must now forge and navigate new allegiances while living among the Mundane.

As the darkness claims control, the three siblings are, once again, thrust into the heat of battle. When multiple disappearances rock the Arcane community, the three siblings put aside their careers, differences, the spaces that separate them, parenthood, and time to join forces, working together again to save their families, friends, and the world as they know it.

In this battle of good and evil, the Magical Three learn of the Curpendulums, a most advanced form of magic. Will the Curpendulums provide the answer to their struggles against the darkness? Or will they prove to be the very weapon that the darkness needs to destroy all Arcane bloodlines and enslave the world? Will magic be lost forever? Lines are drawn, sides are taken, and new secrets are revealed, leaving all to wonder if the echoes of a dark past will remain or be forever changed.
(https://allgenderspress.ca/secrets-echoed/)

PUBLICATION EXPECTED IN 2022
The Ignatius 7
House of Phoenix Chronicles **Book 3**
Wilhelm Ostir

When RJ, a Mundane archaeology graduate student, is mysteriously injured during a walk across campus, he makes a discovery that uncovers one of the greatest secrets of the Arcane and Mundane worlds and forever alters how he understands the battle between good and evil.

Learning the truth of Merlin's darks plans and discovering that magic can happen even for those born with no magical power, RJ now holds the key to stopping the destruction of the Mundane across the globe. As time continues to unravel and as missing relics of the past emerge, a bizarre, twisted fate in which the Knights of the Round Table are at the heart of Merlin's plan for total power is revealed.

RJ and his roommate, Dalton, set out to discover their college's history while meeting resistance every step of the way. RJ's journey quickly takes an interesting turn when he receives help from unexpected allies, including the Ignatius 7 and others.

Growing frustrated with the ongoing echoes of time, RJ must formulate a new approach to handling time's bizarre game by channelling the power of technology, mind, magic, and love to bring an end to the battle, save both the Arcane and Mundane, all the while listening to his heart, falling in love, balancing the complex life of a college student, and dealing with his estranged family.
(https://allgenderspress.ca/the-ignatius-7/)

PUBLICATION EXPECTED IN 2023
House of Phoenix Chronicles
Wilhelm Ostir
Things are Not What They Seem Book 4
(https://allgenderspress.ca/things-are-not-what-they-seem/)
The Curpendulums Book 5
(https://allgenderspress.ca/the-curpendulums/)

The **House of Phoenix Chronicles** *is planned as a series of books filled with wizards, witches, fairies, elves, dwarfs, centaurs, mermaids, and dragons in the fight of their lives to protect their ways of life, their families, and the earth. The Phoenix siblings,*

Roslynn and her older identical twin brothers, Oliver and Ethan, embark on a remarkable journey of friendship, romance, hatred, and mystery as truths are revealed, challenges faced, and battles with ancient darkness fought. Bending magic to their will, Roslynn, Ethan and Oliver, step in and out of time, breaking the rules at every stage of their remarkable journey. Along their way, they meet friends from the past, present, and future, and discover an ancient secret that could forever change the fabric of history, including our understanding of Medieval times and the Knights of the Round Table: a curse sent by darkness to unravel time as it is known. One minute, magic was at its height, the center of life and the community. In the next, cities and villages lay in ruins, a mere echo of a time that was. Can the three siblings channel their family's magic, one of the most powerful magical bloodlines ever to live, for good? Or will their efforts backfire, leading to the destruction of all magical beings? Will they be able to break the curse that affects their family? Can they save their bloodline and the ways of magic? Will they help bring magic back to earth, or will they become the continuation of the curse?

Made in the USA
Columbia, SC
21 May 2022

60514327R00148